CONTEMPORARY ISSUES IN

LAW ENFORCEMENT and POLICING

CONTEMPORARY ISSUES IN LAW ENFORCEMENT and POLICING

Edited by
Andrew Millie
Dilip K. Das

International Police Executive Symposium

CRC Press
Taylor & Francis Group
Boca Raton London New York

CRC Press is an imprint of the
Taylor & Francis Group, an **informa** business

CRC Press
Taylor & Francis Group
6000 Broken Sound Parkway NW, Suite 300
Boca Raton, FL 33487-2742

ISBN-13: 978-1-4200-7215-0 (hbk)

Library of Congress Cataloging-in-Publication Data

Contemporary issues in law enforcement and policing / editors, Andrew Millie and Dilip K. Das.
p. cm.
Includes bibliographical references and index.
ISBN 978-1-4200-7215-0 (alk. paper)
1. Police. 2. Law enforcement. 3. Terrorism. I. Millie, Andrew. II. Das, Dilip K., 1941- III. Title.

HV7921.C648 2008
363.2--dc22 2008011650

Visit the Taylor & Francis Web site at
http://www.taylorandfrancis.com

and the CRC Press Web site at
http://www.crcpress.com

Contents

List of Illustrations

List of Tables

Preface

Law enforcement and policing in the 21st century must be conducted against a backdrop of great scrutiny and myriad expectations. Practitioners face immense pressure to be tough and resolute in the face of post-9/11 terrorist threats, while at the same time they must meet demands for accountability and closer relationships with local communities. Other pressures arise from decreasing monopolies in law enforcement, organizational changes, and technological developments.

Such tensions and pressures are illustrated by a recent high-profile operation: policing for the Asia–Pacific Economic Cooperation (APEC) Conference held in Sydney, Australia, in September 2007. New South Wales Police had to maintain law and order, and allow 21 world leaders and their representatives to meet without distractions, threats of violent protests, and dangers of terrorism, while at the same time allowing legitimate and peaceful protests. The chosen solution was to segregate conference venues and routes by constructing a steel fence through the center of the city, and deploying massive numbers of police personnel.

The highly visible presence of the police on the streets of Sydney demonstrated the different priorities for contemporary law enforcement simply by what the officers wore. Most officers in New South Wales carry guns. On this occasion some were also equipped with full paramilitary regalia including shin and knee protectors, gloves, stab-proof vests, helmets with protective visors, and the option for riot shields. At the other extreme, a large number of officers wore short trousers and short-sleeved shirts and rode around the city on mountain bicycles, and a significant number of officers donned in-between uniforms of standard cargo-pants and boots, jackets, and baseball caps. Despite differences in appearances, all the officers were on hand to meet the same objective.

Perhaps Sir Robert Peel, the pioneer of modern policing, would not have recognized the needs for deadly weapons, battle dress, and overt displays of paramilitarism, as he famously declared, "the police are the people and the people are the police" (see Hurd, 2007). While the organizational structures and management philosophy of the "new" police were influenced by military tradition (see John Murray's Chapter 6), Peel did not want the officers to be soldiers. His vision was a quiet, efficient, *people's* police service whose members were charged with the "absence of crime and disorder" rather than demonstrations of preparedness for a "war against crime." However, as the Australian episode illustrates, operational and political realities mean today's law enforcement is not always a straightforward pursuit.

This volume brings together contributions about law enforcement and policing from respected international writers. It is not an exhaustive account of *all* issues facing the police, but a collection of essays covering current challenges and recent developments. The key themes are the day-to-day stresses of policing; ethics and corruption; terror; strategies and investigations; and restorative approaches.

Police issues are widely covered in the literature and some articles of great value demand wider readership. One of the editors of this volume, Dilip K. Das, is the founding editor-in-chief of Taylor & Francis' *Police Practice and Research: An International Journal* (PPR). Since its inception in 2000, this peer-reviewed journal has included many quality contributions of value to police practitioners and academics. This volume originated from a discussion about PPR articles that produced the greatest impacts or covered major issues applicable to today's police. Although PPR is widely available, we thought that a selection of top articles merited greater availability via collection into a single volume.

The themes were, in effect, chosen by PPR's global community of readers since we have included here the most popular articles based on online "hits." It is interesting to note that most of the chapters appeared in special issues of the PPR including papers presented at the annual meeting of the International Police Executive Symposium (www.ipes.info) with which PPR is affiliated. However, we did not want to make "old wine in a new bottle." Accordingly we considered in the Introduction to the book the key arguments covered by each chapter. The concluding chapter assesses the pragmatic aspects and challenges posed by the contributions.

Jane Oakley of the journal division of Taylor & Francis kindly agreed to make available ten articles for this collection and provided a list of the most frequent online "hits." This list was used to indicate an article's value in terms of readers' broad interest. We admit that this is a crude measure, but it provided a useful starting point and an indication of major topics and relevance to readers. To ensure balance to the volume—and prevent one subject such as police strategy and investigation from dominating—we sought other articles covering topics of importance for today's police. The result is a fascinating collection of essays covering some of the major contemporary issues for law enforcement and policing.

We are enormously grateful to Jane Oakley, Aimee Wood, and their colleagues in the journal division of Taylor & Francis and the editorial board of PPR for allowing the articles to be reproduced. We would like to thank the authors of all chapters and also Carolyn Spence, Marsha Pronin, and others at CRC Press/Taylor & Francis Group for their assistance in preparing the work for publication.

Andrew Millie and Dilip K. Das

Reference

Hurd, D. (2007) *Sir Robert Peel: A biography*, London: Weidenfeld & Nicolson.

Contributors

Gordon Bazemore is a professor in and chair of the Department of Criminology and Criminal Justice and director of the Community Justice Institute at Florida Atlantic University. His research has focused on juvenile justice and youth policy, restorative justice, crime victims, corrections, and community policing.

Jean-Paul Brodeur is the director of the International Center of Comparative Criminology and a professor in the Department of Criminology, Montreal University, Canada. He has written several works about the sociology of police forces.

Jharna Chatterjee has been a member of the Royal Canadian Mounted Police and the Canadian Department of Justice. She worked with Liz Elliott of Simon Fraser University in investigating restorative policing in Canada.

Dilip K. Das is a professor and heads the Criminal Justice Department at Grambling State University in Louisiana. He is president of the International Police Executive Symposium and editor-in-chief of *Police Practice and Research: An International Journal* and of the *World Police Encyclopedia*. He also serves as a human rights consultant to the United Nations.

Liz Elliott is a co-director of the Centre for Restorative Justice and an associate professor of the School of Criminology, Simon Fraser University, Burnaby, British Columbia. She is a former social worker and has extensive field experience in the areas of community and prison justice. Her research interests include transformative justice, abolitionism, prison justice, prison education and writing, sociology of punishment, criminal justice ethics, and violence in Canadian society.

Venessa Garcia is an assistant professor of criminal justice at Kean University in New Jersey. She earned an MA and PhD in sociology at the State University of New York at Buffalo. Her fields of research include the sociology of law, police studies, and women in criminal justice. She has published a number of academic articles and reports. Her family court research resulted in a co-authored book titled *Domestic Violence and Child Custody Disputes: A Resource Handbook for Judges and Court Managers* (1997).

Curt T. Griffiths is a professor and coordinator of the Police Studies Program of the School of Criminology at Simon Fraser University, Canada. Among his primary teaching and research interests are the organizational and operational dynamics of policing, comparative police studies, the effectiveness of police strategies and interventions, and issues in police performance.

Stéphane Leman-Langlois earned a PhD in criminology from the University of Toronto and is an associate professor of criminology at Montreal University's School of Criminology. He is a member of the International Centre for Comparative Criminology and has worked in the areas of crimes against humanity, policing, technologies, terrorism, and cybercrime.

Andrew Millie is a lecturer in criminology and social policy in the Department of Social Sciences of Loughborough University in the United Kingdom. He is also the director of the masters' programs in criminology and criminal justice. His research focuses on anti-social behavior, policing, crime and the city, crime prevention, and sentencing.

John Murray is a former chief police officer for the Australian Capital Territory and currently serves as a private consultant on justice-related matters, working from Adelaide, Australia.

Tim Prenzler teaches police studies and security management at the School of Criminology and Criminal Justice, Griffith University, Brisbane, Australia. He is also a member of the Australian Research Council Centre for Excellence in Policing and Security based at Griffith University.

Jerry H. Ratcliffe is a professor of criminal justice at Temple University, Philadelphia, Pennsylvania. He started his career as an officer with the Metropolitan Police in London and has worked in research and academia in Australia and the United States. He is a fellow of the Royal Geographical Society and has published books on criminal intelligence, crime mapping, and policing drug markets. He researches and lectures on environmental criminology, intelligence-led policing, and crime reduction.

Carol Ronken is a senior research and policy development officer at the Bravehearts child protection charity in Australia. From 1998 to 2003, she taught at the School of Criminology and Criminal Justice at Griffith University and was a member of the Ethics and Regulation of Public and Private Policing program of the Key Centre for Ethics Law, Justice, and Governance. She worked with Tim Prenzler on a number of research projects in the areas of police accountability and ethics.

Jerome H. Skolnick is the Claire Sanders Clements Dean's Chair Professor of Law Emeritus at the School of Law, University of California at Berkeley. He also taught at the University of California at San Diego, the University of Chicago, and Yale University; served as a visiting fellow at Oxford; and published extensively on the sociology of law, law enforcement, and policing.

Per Stangeland is a professor at Møre Research, University College Campus, Volda, Norway. He was the deputy director of the Institute of Criminology in Malaga, Spain. He has now returned to Norway and is working on a project involving crimes among methadone patients.

Jeanne B. Stinchcomb is a professor in the Department of Criminology and Criminal Justice at Florida Atlantic University. Her teaching and administrative experiences range from colleges and training academies to the Federal Bureau of Investigation and the Miami–Dade Department of Corrections. As a consultant, she has developed promotional examinations for police departments, provided in-service training, and conducted evaluation research. Her publications cover organizational culture, boot camps, leadership, and workforce issues. Her most recent textbook (2005) is *Corrections: Past, Present, and Future.*

Introduction: Expectations for 21st Century Law Enforcement and Policing

Law enforcement and policing across the world have been subject to fundamental changes since the start of the 21st century. Most notable are the immediate and long-term impacts of high-profile terrorist attacks on the United States, Bali in Indonesia, Spain, and the United Kingdom that produced political and operational pressures for strong, intelligence-driven, paramilitary policing. Conversely, many countries face growing pressures for greater local accountability with calls for "softer" neighborhood-based models of community policing. There are also ongoing difficulties maintaining order during and after conflicts as exemplified by Afghanistan and Iraq.

These are big challenges and police in many countries have had to adapt and change. Advances in technology, along with new strategies and investigative techniques, have also stretched the officer's traditional role. The new officer is under increasing pressure to be tough, yet compassionate and technologically adept. In 1981, John Avery, a former commissioner of New South Wales Police in Australia, noted that a decision had to be made between having a police force and a police service. Today's police are pulled in both directions. On the one hand, they are meant to be tough and resolute, particularly in the face of post-9/11 terrorist threats (Brodeur, 2007; Clarke and Newman, 2007), but they are also expected to be ethically driven (Kleinig, 1996; Neyroud and Beckley, 2001), adhere to rule of law principles (Mani, 1999; Millie and Das, 2008), and engage with the communities they serve (Skogan and Hartnett, 1997; Myhill, 2006).

This volume contains a collection of essays covering a range of contemporary law enforcement and policing issues. The essays appeared in *Police Practice and Research: An International Journal* (PPR) and include the most requested articles from the journal's website. While we are not certain why certain articles enjoyed greater demand, it is a fair assumption that two reasons were their importance and relevance. The articles come from the United States, Canada, Australia, and Norway (the author is a Norwegian; the locale for the contribution is Spain). Reflecting the nature of a journal that seeks contributions from both practitioners and researchers, contributors to this volume include innovators, respected police researchers, and academics.

Significance

The most requested articles focused on five key themes that gained prominence in the early years of the new century: the pressures of day-to-day policing; ethics and corruption; terror; police strategy and investigations; and restorative approaches. The book is divided into these five themes of two chapters each. This introduction presents the key arguments covered within each topic. The final "Conclusions" chapter considers the pragmatic aspects and challenges posed by the different contributions.

Part I: Day-to-Day Policing

Part I covers the daily activities and experiences of contemporary policing. In Chapter 1, "Searching for Stress in All the Wrong Places," Jeanne B. Stinchcomb considers stress in the law enforcement field in the United States. She notes that "the American way of dying is now predominately associated with…the 'wear-and-tear diseases' that are thought to be linked to stress." The police are not exceptions to this general trend. In other words, the problems of everyday policing in the United States are fundamentally U.S. problems and "stress is an occupational hazard of modern living." Having noted stress as a problem for contemporary living, Stinchcomb strives to understand what aspects of law enforcement may be promoting chronic stress and occupational burnout and states that:

> Contrary to popular opinion, it is not the danger of police work that is most stress-inducing. Substantial evidence indicates that stress is more likely to be produced by the routine, day-to-day features of work life that tend to be taken for granted. Like a chronic cough or an ongoing illness, chronic organizational stress is continually present in the everyday work environment. Unlike episodic stress, it is not the result of a one-time crisis. Instead, it is the product of a slow, continual process of erosion that occurs over time.

The daily hassles of the job rather than the rare traumatic incidents and life-and-death decision making are most likely to cause stress in police work. Stinchcomb lists factors that are responsible for everyday stress for police officers: (1) lack of consultation and communication; (2) inadequate guidance and support from administrators; (3) insufficient feedback; and (4) little or no input into department policy, along with authority that is not commensurate with responsibility—too little authority and too much responsibility.

In Chapter 2, "Constructing the *Other* within Police Culture," Venessa Garcia investigates police culture in terms of the "othering" of certain departments or occupations and the promotion of a we–they paradox that may be regarded as another occupational stressor. In particular, Garcia examines how police culture stigmatizes and sanctions or penalizes community-oriented policing (COP) officers. Her study reveals the key components of stigmatization as lack of agency support and officer ridicule. It seems that the day-to-day experiences are not only important in causing stress (as noted in Chapter 1), but also generate stigmatization. Garcia also discovered that most COP officers who participated in her study did not tend to perceive that their status as "real" officers was challenged. While this is encouraging, a sizable minority felt challenged. More work is required to determine how replicable these findings are.

Part II: Police Ethics and Corruption

Part II concerns ethics and corruption. In Chapter 3, Jerome H. Skolnick discusses "Corruption and the Blue Code of Silence." He provides evidence that such a code exists and examines case material to explain how the code is reinforced. Based on participant observation research in the New York County Prosecutor's Official Corruption Unit, Skolnick investigates how the code impedes police investigations and considers measures to address the code. Key to the development of a code of silence is the existence of a culture in which loyalty is the norm. Of course, loyalty is a good quality, but when misplaced it can also hinder investigations of corruption, brutality, and malpractice.

Some rather disturbing examples are discussed and Skolnick offers possible solutions, including the use of independent monitors. He concludes that we can have little confidence in the integrity of policing, without efforts to penetrate the "walls of silence" by using investigations of independent monitors if that proves necessary.

The theme of police ethics and corruption continues in Chapter 4. Tim Prenzler and Carol Ronken provide an Australian perspective in their chapter about innovations in the development and maintenance of ethical standards by Australian police departments. Over the past two decades, a number of high-profile investigations have covered police misconduct in Australia, notably the Fitzgerald inquiry (1989) in Queensland and the Wood Commission in New South Wales (1997; see Chan and Dixon, 2007 for a 10-year assessment). Prenzler and Ronken also investigate strategies to prevent misconduct and maximize ethical conduct and propose three models of integrity development. They conducted a survey of eight police departments and found some innovative and promising programs in operation, including drug and alcohol testing, targeted integrity testing, and complaint profiling. However, they found that none of the departments utilized what could be regarded as comprehensive or advanced programs of integrity development and maintenance.

Part III: Policing Terror

Police integrity is of paramount importance for the third theme of this volume, the policing of terrorism. In Chapter 5, "Terrorism Old and New: Counterterrorism in Canada," Stéphane Leman-Langlois and Jean-Paul Brodeur provide important perspectives surrounding current debates. They devise a typology of terrorism according to the scope of the stated objectives and the justifications given for the acts committed. Particular attention is given to "new" terrorism and the best strategies to prevent or repress it. In their view, although new terrorism has features in common with the old, it also has "features that call for an equally new counterterrorism" approach. Their analysis is based on four assumptions: (1) efficient counterterrorism necessitates knowledge of the kind of organization to be fought; (2) the knowledge needed must support action—it must efficiently match police responses to core features of terrorist organizations; (3) although the tactics of important terrorist organizations such as the Basque ETA have not evolved completely, the nature of terrorism in Canada and worldwide has undergone a momentous change; and (4) counterterrorism must adapt to changes in terrorism. Leman-Langlois and Brodeur also explore possible strategies to deal with the new terrorism in Canada.

In Chapter 6, "Policing Terrorism," John Murray explores the impact of an increased emphasis on policing terrorism on other priorities, notably community-oriented policing. Law enforcement and policing in the new century can be characterized by a tension between calls for tough and resolute policing (police "forces") and softer, locally accountable, neighborhood-based models (police "services") (cf. Avery, 1981). Murray notes that "the terrorist events of September 11, 2001 have changed the world forever. To some observers, so too has the public profile of policing. In many countries now there are signs of police reverting to…paramilitarism which is…at odds with community policing." He argues convincingly that turning away from community policing would, in fact, be counterproductive because the community is where trust and mutual respect can be built. Early warnings about terrorist acts are much more likely to be provided and "a hostile or fearful community, for example, will be disinclined to cooperate with police." Murray considers different models for policing and the development of cultures that help or hinder the policing of terrorism and community policing.

Part IV: Police Strategy and Investigations

Part IV considers recent developments in police strategy and investigations. The stereotypical view of criminal investigation shows police officers crowded around a map containing lots of pins that represent crimes, victims, or suspects. Nothing is wrong with the picture but crime mapping has, of course, become much more sophisticated with the development of computer tools and methodologies such as hotspotting. In Chapter 7, Jerry Ratcliffe develops the hotspotting approach into a matrix that serves as a framework for the spatio-temporal targeting of crime reduction. He adds a temporal component to the traditional spatial emphasis and notes that "the temporal component has received less research attention, but it is arguably of equal value to an operational police commander or crime prevention officer."

Examples from Australia illustrate the technique. Ratcliffe provides "a first attempt to describe a typology of crime hotspots in a spatio-temporal manner." The attempt is comprehensive and suggests appropriate crime prevention and detection methodologies.

Hotspotting also has a place in Per Stangeland's real-life case study cited in Chapter 8, "Catching a Serial Rapist," which discusses the criminal profiling of a serial rapist in Malaga, Spain. The main focus is the geographical profile, which is made more detailed by considering a possible awareness area, activity space, and buffer zone of a serial offender. The profile submitted to the police did not, however, identify the rapist. Stangeland analyzes the reasons for this failure by considering the hits and misses of the investigation.

The determination of the suspect's means of transport was inaccurate and affected the accuracy of the computer model. The rapist was eventually caught and further insights were provided from interviews with the rapist. The main focus of the chapter is the geographical profiles, and it explains methods of improving future investigations. The author recommends supplementation of geographical profiles by thorough on-site observations and improved police access to public and civil registers, especially if an offender has no prior criminal record.

Part V: Restorative Policing

The fifth and final part takes us in a different but related direction by considering developments in restorative policing. In Chapter 9, Jharna Chatterjee and Liz Elliott consider restorative policing from a Canadian perspective.

The main influences in the development of restorative policing were the Mennonite and aboriginal traditions in Canada and the influence of conferencing as introduced by the Royal Canadian Mounted Police in the mid-1990s. This was an approach imported and adapted from New Zealand and Australian experiences. The authors examine the role of the Royal Canadian Mounted Police in the development of restorative practice. The Youth Criminal Justice Act implemented in 2003 has affected police discretion and restorative approaches. Its impact in Canada is discussed.

Chatterjee and Elliott note that, "one issue of contention with the conferencing model is its focus on shame." Concerns related to the practice of shaming are highlighted, particularly linking shaming with violence. The authors also question the role of police officers in conferencing. They ask whether the police should act as facilitators in conferences or attend as interested parties or not participate at all. They believe the role of police in the conferencing process "marks a return to an original goal for police, to act as peace officers." They also suggest that facilitators must "clearly understand restorative justice, receive ample and ongoing training, and the capacity to help participants manage shame in helpful ways."

Issues of police involvement in restorative justice are taken forward in Chapter 10, "Police Reform, Restorative Justice, and Restorative Policing." Gordon Bazemore and Curt Griffiths take the view that the restorative justice model can assist the police in community engagement, forming meaningful partnerships, and building community capacity. The authors see restorative practice as a fundamental shift in intervention objectives, from punishment or treatment to an emphasis on repairing harm. Bazemore and Griffiths see such an approach as "best developed with maximum input from victim, offender, and their supporters through a non-adversarial process. This process, in turn, has value in its own right. For example, as a means of promoting stakeholder ownership of the problem created by the crime in question." Despite the successes, the authors see the need for a systematic vision of restorative policing: "Effective, principled implementation of restorative policing depends on a holistic, systemic vision that seeks to incorporate restorative justice principles in all aspects of the profession."

Summary

Whether restorative policing is the right route for contemporary law enforcement is another matter, but it shows one potential and promising pathway. It is only one challenge for policing during the early years of the century. As explored in this volume, other significant challenges to the role of the police officer include the day-to-day stresses, ethics and corruption, changes in priority caused by international terrorism, community policing imperatives, and developments in police strategies and investigative techniques. As this volume makes obvious, none of these expectations or issues stands alone. Concerns about police ethics and corruption have clear relevance to the policing of terrorism and to uses of new techniques and strategies; they also contribute to the stresses of day-to-day policing. Similarly, the "othering" of community-oriented policing can have repercussions for units attempting more innovative restorative approaches. The present emphasis on counter-terrorism diverts resources that should be dedicated to other community priorities. How these contemporary issues are addressed or prioritized will determine the future approaches of law enforcement and policing.

References

Avery, J. (1981) *Police: Force or Service?* Sydney: Butterworths.

Brodeur, J-P. (2007) High and low policing in post-9/11 times, *Policing: A Journal of Policy and Practice,* 1 (1): 25–37.

Chan, J. and Dixon, D. (2007) The politics of police reform: Ten years after the Royal Commission into the New South Wales Police Service, *Criminology and Criminal Justice*, 7 (4): 443–468.

Clarke, R. V. and Newman, G. R. (2007) Police and the prevention of terrorism, *Policing: A Journal of Policy and Practice*, 1 (1): 9–20.

Fitzgerald, G. (1989) *Report of a commission of inquiry pursuant to orders in council*, Brisbane: Goprint.

Kleinig, J. (1996) *The ethics of policing*, Cambridge: Cambridge University Press.

Mani, R. (1999) Contextualizing police reform: Security, the rule of law and post-conflict peacekeeping, *International Peacekeeping*, 6 (4): 9–27.

Millie, A. and Das, D. (2008) Police education and training in four countries: Getting rule of law messages across, in Aromaa, K. and Redo, S. (Eds.) *For the rule of law: Criminal justice training and teaching across the world*, Helsinki: HEUNI.

Myhill, A. (2006) *Community engagement in policing: Lessons from the literature*, London: Home Office.

Neyroud, P. and Beckley, A. (2001) *Policing, ethics and human rights*, Cullompton, U.K.: Willan.

Skogan, W. and Hartnett, S. M. (1997) *Community policing, Chicago style*, New York: Oxford University Press.

Wood, J. (1997) *Royal commission into the New South Wales police service: Final report*, Sydney: Government of the State of NSW.

Day-to-Day Policing

I

Searching for Stress in All the Wrong Places: Combating Chronic Organizational Stressors in Policing*

1

JEANNE B. STINCHCOMB

Contents

Stress is an occupational hazard of modern living. In today's fast-paced, high-tech society, the debilitating effects of stress are not limited to those engaged in police work. From college students to air traffic controllers, firefighters, and working mothers, stress has become as much a part of life in the 21st century as computers and cell phones. In fact, illnesses related to stress have now replaced infectious diseases as the leading cause of death. No longer do people die primarily as a result of the influenza, typhoid, cholera, and other epidemics that produced rampant mortality rates among our ancestors.

The American way of dying is now predominately associated with degenerative diseases that take their tolls slowly and unobtrusively over time—heart

* This chapter first appeared in Police Practice and Research, 2004, 5(3): 259–277.

disease and cancer (Hoyert et al., 2001)—the "wear-and-tear diseases" that are thought to be linked to stress (Selye, 1956: 275). Nor has law enforcement been any exception to this general trend. Mortality rates for police personnel have been found to be elevated for cardiovascular disorders (Guralnick, 1963; Krietner et al., 1985), various forms of cancers (Milham, 1983; Vena et al., 1986; Violanti, Vena and Petralia, 1998), and premature deaths (Richard and Fell, 1976). The success with which modern medicine has controlled and prevented most infectious diseases has not translated into equally successful efforts to combat degenerative diseases. At least in part, this is because stress-related afflictions are not exclusively physiological, but rather involve psychological and even sociological dimensions. As a result, they are not equally distributed among various occupational work groups.

In an effort to more effectively reduce the debilitating physical and psychological consequences of work-related stress in law enforcement, this chapter examines the literature on police-related stress. Particularly, it distinguishes between the episodic, street-level stressors visibly associated with police work and the chronic organizational stressors that lurk obscurely behind the scenes. Routine stressors in the bureaucratic work environment do not generate the media attention, public empathy, or responsive concern of high-profile traumatic incidents. Yet, as much of the literature reflects, those unobtrusive day-to-day stressors persisting quietly in the organizational background may well exert the most harmful effects. To the extent that the most significant sources of chronic police stress have traditionally been inaccurately identified, it is also likely that accompanying solutions have been inadequately pursued. Thus, the purpose here is to build upon empirical evidence pointing toward more proactive and productive directions for diagnosing and combating police-related stress.

Work-Related Stress

Everyone struggling to survive the demands of life in the 21st century is to some degree vulnerable to the devastating impact of stress. Those employed in the human services are especially vulnerable because of the stress-provoking conditions surrounding work in the helping professions—including responsibility for other people's lives (Cherniss, 1980), unpleasant encounters (Albrecht, 1979), and the gap between aspiration and achievement (Edelwich, 1980). The reasons that stress is more likely to be involved in the helping professions than in other lines of work encompass both the nature of such jobs and the nature of stress.

Looking first at the concept of stress, it is apparent that there is no uniform agreement on what, in fact, stress is. To some, stress is a stimulus in the environment that creates tension, threat, or anxiety—and, ultimately, a need to readjust. From this perspective, stress has often been viewed as exposure to catastrophic situations—wars, riots, natural disasters—or traumatic incidents—death, accidents, violence. It has even been recognized that the normal but noxious characteristics of everyday life such as noise, crowds, and traffic congestion can be stress-provoking. This is especially true if exposure to these more subtle sources of stress occurs chronically over long periods. But whether catastrophic or commonplace, such disruptions have now become identified as *stressors* rather than as stress itself. Stressors are disrupting conditions that create the need for a readjustment that can potentially produce stress (Selye, 1956).

Others have taken the position that stress is the manner in which the body responds physiologically and/or psychologically when trying to adjust to these stressful stimuli. Physiological reactions to stress can include anything from headaches, stomachaches, and backaches to more severe conditions such as ulcers, heart attacks, and strokes. Psychologically, stress-related indicators may range from simple irritability to more serious anxieties, depression, flashbacks, and panic attacks. But again, these physiological and psychological symptoms are precisely that—*symptoms* of response to stress, rather than the actual condition of stress. Neither stimulus nor response perspectives take into account the *interactive* nature of stress. Nor do they explain why some people are more negatively affected by stressors than others.

It is interesting to note that the notion of *stress* first emerged in the field of physics, where it refers to the distortion produced by an external force placing strain on an object. The amount of damage that results will depend on both the strength of the force and the ability of an object to withstand it. Translated into the social sciences, stress becomes the complex manner in which individuals interact with their environment (Cooper and Marshall, 1977; Cox, 1978). These interactions can then produce unhealthy physical and psychological outcomes. From an interactive perspective, stress has been defined as an *imbalance* between environmental demands and individual resources (modified from Cherniss, 1980: 22). Stress thus occurs when the demands placed on us exceed our capacity to deal with them. More specifically, this means that stress develops when we are not able to *avoid, alter,* or *control* those demands (Stinchcomb, 1986). Only those nerve-wracking situations that are outside of our sphere of control will become stressful.

Key Ingredient: Control

Earlier it was noted that stress is more likely to be involved in the helping professions because of both the nature of such work and the nature of stress itself. In terms of work, this means that the *less control* employees have over what they are expected to do and the outcome of their efforts, the *more stress* they are likely to experience. It is only what we are not capable of controlling that has the capacity to create stress for us. It may be a parent dealing with a rebellious teenager, a secretary suffering under a demanding supervisor, or a police officer confronting an unsupportive management system.

Whatever its source, stress is directly related to lack of control. The less control we have over a situation, the more stressful it will be. In fact, that is why many people are significantly more fearful of flying than driving, despite the reality that flying is inherently safer. In that regard, research indicates that jobs involving responsibility for people are more stressful than others, especially if they also provide little opportunity to see positive results (Pines and Aronson, 1981: 15). Obviously, police work scores high on both of these dimensions.

Job Stress and Burnout

Eventually, ongoing stressors drain energy and enthusiasm. The detrimental effects of this continuous wearing-down process accumulate slowly but steadily, like the relentless pounding of the surf eroding beaches along the shoreline. Similarly, this continuous grinding-away process eventually takes a toll on a worker's physical, mental, and/or emotional health—a toll that may eventually appear as the psychological disorder known as "burnout" (Veninga and Spradley, 1981).

When employees reach the stage of burnout, they are no longer concerned for their clients (Maslach, 1976). Eventually, they may lose all enthusiasm for their work, adopting a cynical, shoulder-shrugging, "who cares?" attitude. This psychological withdrawal reflects an effort on the part of burned-out employees to try to protect themselves from the stress of constantly irritating conditions in the workplace that they cannot control. The apathetic attitude that they project is, in all likelihood, masking a deep-felt concern for the inability to do a good job in the face of insurmountable obstacles.

Police personnel in particular are vulnerable to burnout (Kroes, 1976; Silbert, 1982) and its devastating physical and psychological effects—ranging from alcoholism and divorce to digestive disorders, coronary heart disease, and even suicide (Kroes, Margolis and Hurrell, 1974b; Robin and Anson, 1990; Terry, 1981; Violanti, 1996). What exactly is it about employment in law enforcement that may promote chronic stress and occupational burnout?

Episodic Stress in Law Enforcement

When the subject of work-related stress in policing is raised, attention inevitably focuses on traumatic incidents. Certainly, police officers are exposed to any number of code-three, lights-and-sirens emergencies—from shooting situations to high-speed pursuits. These are known as *episodic stressors.* They are the traumatic incidents that a police officer can encounter on any given day, but the fact of the matter is that most days such incidents are not encountered.

The reality is that police work is much more routine than its sensational cops-and-robbers image (Brown and Campbell, 1990). In the United States, most officers retire without ever firing their weapons, and increasingly stringent organizational policies restrict most activities, from the use of force to high-speed pursuits. Moreover, when these types of traumatic events do occur, they almost always begin and end quickly. That is not to deny that they often have long-term consequences in the form of post-traumatic stress disorder (Stephens, Long and Miller, 1997) or suggest that less than full agency support is devoted to helping officers deal with aftermaths of such events. But few officers are actually exposed to these low-frequency (but potentially high-impact) events (Brown, Fielding and Grover, 1999: 313).

Facing danger—and even death—is not unique to police work (Davidson and Veno, 1980). Any number of occupations including firefighters and coal miners potentially face life-threatening work conditions. In fact, some contend that there is little sound evidence indicating that police work is any more stressful than other types of people-oriented work (Anson and Bloom, 1988: 229; Hart, Wearing and Headey, 1995: 133).

Police Stress: An Occupational Status Symbol?

Research has not provided evidence of a causal link between stress and more common types of front-line duties, e.g., delivering death notices, dealing with domestic violence, responding to sudden death. In fact, such operational functions have been associated with relatively low levels of self-perceived stress (Brown and Campbell, 1994; Gudjonsson and Adlam, 1985).

In that regard, research points toward a possibly self-fulfilling prophecy: to the extent that police stress is glamorized and highly publicized as a significant problem, it may create a greater likelihood that officers will perceive their work as stressful (Terry, 1981)—even to the point of establishing stress as an "occupational status symbol" (Stinchcomb, 1987).

When episodic stressors occur, U.S. law enforcement agencies generally provide supportive resources to help officers deal with the effects. Many departments have mandatory policies that require psychological services for those involved in deadly incidents. This is in response to the tendency of officers to display the "John Wayne Syndrome" by seeking to preserve a macho ego image and avoid appearing weak by denying personal impacts of traumatic events (Reiner, 1985). As the term *episodic* implies, such incidents are short-term, infrequent occurrences. Despite their high-profile publicity, they are not the most prevalent sources of stress in policing.

Chronic Organizational Stress: Daily Hassles of Police Work

There is no doubt that confronting dangerous situations is a genuine risk of operational police work. The presence of such danger has promoted the general belief that policing is inherently stressful (Sigler and Wilson, 1988). However, this stereotype has been called into question by research showing that critical events do *not* represent the most significant stressors for police officers (Hart et al., 1995: 134). Contrary to popular opinion, it is not the danger of police work that is most stress-inducing. Substantial evidence indicates that stress is more likely to be produced by the routine, day-to-day features of work life that tend to be taken for granted.

Like a chronic cough or an ongoing illness, *chronic organizational stress* is continually present in the everyday work environment. Unlike episodic stress, it is not the result of a one-time crisis. Instead, it is the product of a slow, continual process of erosion that occurs over time. A body of emerging research points toward *organizational management practices* as prevalent and pervasive sources of stress for police officers (Alexander et al., 1991; Ayres and Flanagan, 1990; Biggam et al., 1997; Brown and Campbell, 1990; Crowe and Stradling, 1993). While its causes can range from rigid policies to reluctant decision-makers, evidence is mounting that chronic stress in law enforcement is more closely related to organizational concerns than operational crises (Band and Manuelle, 1987; Brown and Campbell, 1990; Greller, Parsons and Mitchell, 1992; Hart, Wearing and Headey, 1994).

In fact, it has even been suggested that the excitement generated by the occasional encounter with violence might mitigate organizational stressors (Crank and Caldero, 1991; Stotland, 1991). In terms of creating stress, it appears to be the organizational context in which people work that is more important than the work itself (Crank and Caldero, 1991; Hart et al., 1995:150; Kroes et al., 1974b; Spielberger, Grier and Greenfield, 1982; Storch and Panzarella, 1996).

In contrast to the fleeting nature of episodic stressors, organizational stressors are *routinely* encountered on a high-frequency basis. They are the constant annoyances encountered by police officers—the daily hassles and pressures of organizational life (Hart et al., 1994). From uncooperative co-workers to unsupportive administrators, these routine irritants can create a high-pressure, stress-charged work environment:

> On any given day, labor and management are at odds over working conditions and benefits. Male officers are angry at female officers, and vice versa. The black officers' association and the white officers' association are fighting. The detective bureau is unhappy with how patrol officers write reports, and patrol officers think the detectives hoard information.… The city manager is angry at the police union because negotiations are creating bad publicity. The chief is

> angry at being misquoted by the media, and everyone is angry with the chief. (Kirschman, 1998: 127)

The dilemma of organizationally induced stress is not unique to law enforcement. Studies indicate that in any number of occupational settings, the nature of the organization is the greatest stress provoker (Cooper, Davidson and Robinson, 1988; Davidson and Cooper, 1983). In both law enforcement and education, research suggests that tension between administrators and employees is the key stress-provoking factor (Sigler and Wilson, 1988; Sigler, Wilson and Allen, 1991). Similar findings have been reported in nursing (Hingley and Cooper, 1986). Overall, it appears to be the nature of the workplace rather than the nature of the work that is most troublesome.

Impact of Chronic Organizational Stress

It is one thing to confront violent offenders or dangerous situations. This is the type of work that every police applicant envisioned long before pinning on the badge. These are the types of stressors that, at least to a degree, are *expected* in policing. What applicants did not expect was to have to cope with chronic organizational irritants: the demanding supervisor; the difficult co-worker; the micro-managing administrator. Officers recognize that the "bad guys" are against them. But when they begin to feel that their own organization also plays an opposing role, "it is like being stabbed in the back by a member of the family" (Kirschman, 1998: 128). Such ongoing controversies and the feelings of betrayal generated take a significant toll on health and well-being.

Just as the push and pull of daily tides erode the beachfront over time, chronic stress wears down employees. Initially, like beach erosion, its impact is subtle and not easily detected. But eventually it becomes visible—and harmful. No one enters a police career in a burned-out state of mind. Like newlyweds embarking on their first marriage, most rookie officers start out energetic, enthusiastic, and contented—and perhaps somewhat idealistic. Just as years later some marriages are destined to end in divorce, some officers are likewise destined to succumb to job stress. It is a slow process down a long slope. If nothing is done to intervene along the way, the slope ends at the bottom in burnout.

First, job satisfaction begins to diminish. The work that once looked so appealing to the aspiring applicant somehow over the years becomes much less attractive to the stressed-out veteran. Then morale takes a downturn (Leitner, Posner and Lester, 1983; Lester et al., 1981). It becomes harder and harder to maintain an upbeat attitude or feel a sense of accomplishment. Too much seems to be out of control. Eventually, if the downward cycle continues, the veteran acquires a downtrodden, shoulder-shrugging "who cares?"

approach—a cynical attitude adopted as a reaction to and defense against dashed hopes (Graves, 1996). Physical, emotional, and personal problems may surface—from chronic fatigue, to overeating, loss of appetite, muscle tension, backache, irritability, hostility, anger, and the like. Ultimately, job-related stress can result in organizational alienation (Buck, 1972), increased sick-related absences, and premature retirement (Brown and Campbell, 1990: 305). Personally, the results can be even more devastating, taking their toll on family life as frustration and disillusionment with work affect an officer's relationships at home. Given the devastating impact of work-related stress, organizationally as well as individually, it is in everyone's best interests to identify how it can be prevented. In order to recognize how to prevent a problem, it is first necessary to determine precisely what causes it. Only then can intervention strategies be targeted toward specific dimensions of the problem. Proactively combating chronic organizational stress therefore requires pinpointing its explicit causes.

Sources of Chronic Organizational Stress

It is one thing to maintain that bothersome features of the work environment create more stress for police officers than adverse incidents in the field. But it is another thing to uncover exactly what it is about the organizational climate that is so stress-provoking. In that regard, research on leadership and organizational management in general, as well as organizationally induced stress in particular, provides some helpful clues. For example, it has been well documented that people have deep-seated needs to be involved in making decisions that affect them. This is one of the most consistent themes throughout the literature on management and leadership that relates to the importance of entrusting employees with sufficient power, authority, and discretion (Bennis and Nanus, 1997; Hersey, Blanchard and Johnson, 1996; Kouzes and Posner, 1995).

Regardless of whether it is identified as participatory management, decentralized decision-making, employee empowerment, or total quality management, this has been a widely accepted principle of modern organizational life. In fact, it is among the fundamental administrative concepts upon which current operational trends toward community-oriented policing and problem-solving are based (DeParis, 1997; Roberg and Kuykendall, 1997; Watson, Stone and DeLuca, 1998). In part, this fundamental need for involvement emerges from our basic desire for social acceptance (Maslow, 1954)—a need that is especially strong in the close-knit occupational culture of policing. But it also extends beyond group socialization to embrace higher values of individual development, self-determination, and self-worth. In that regard, a key function of work is to produce feelings of achievement, responsibility, personal growth, and recognition (all of which relate to self-control) in order to satisfy a worker's ego and self-actualization needs (Graves, 1996).

Earlier in the chapter it was noted that those features of the work environment over which we have the least control will be the most stressful. It therefore stands to reason that officers who have more organizational input, autonomy, and discretionary decision-making ability will feel more capable of controlling their work-related destiny. In fact, research indicates that more control over the work environment is related to less stress for officers (Brown, Cooper and Kirkcaldy, 1996). In essence, workers do not want to be treated like children. Once people reach adulthood, they expect to be relatively independent—to actively make more of their own decisions and control their lives in ways that were not permitted when they were younger. Moreover, being asked to provide input into the decision-making process is status-enhancing. Such involvement affirms that an employee is a trusted member of the organization and has valuable ideas to contribute. Perhaps as a result of that affirmation, more participatory styles of organizational leadership seem to produce greater satisfaction (Brooks and Piquero, 1998:601). But in many places, employees have been treated in the same passive, dependent manner as if they were children (Argyris, 1957).

For instance, in U.S. law enforcement, officers are issued guns and badges, but are still micro-managed by a centrally controlled bureaucracy. Few police agencies are organized in the type of decentralized manner that delegates decision making, empowers lower-level employees, and encourages input from all ranks (Ayres and Flanagan, 1990: 11–13). In that regard, the nature of the administrative structure may be a significant source of stress. Organized along military lines, the environments of most police departments are rigidly hierarchical and highly bureaucratic (Finn, 2000: 19), promoting an inflexible management style that does not accommodate lower-level involvement. In fact, the traditional top-down management of police organizations has been identified as a common source of stress (Kroes et al., 1974a; Reiser, 1974; Standfest, 1996) for a number of reasons:

> In an attempt to maintain control at the top and minimize independent thinking in a centralized organization, detailed regulations and procedures have been created. Under this philosophy of management, all the officer on the street has to do is follow the regulations to the letter. To make sure that these regulations are enforced, there are a multitude of levels of supervision that watch over and control the behavior of the officers on the street. This is enforced through disciplinary action against anyone who breaches the rules of conduct.... [But] officers do not leave their ability to think independently at home. Rather, they are intelligent individuals who have found ways to work within the system.... Walking the line laid down by the regulation-makers produces unneeded additional tension.... (Anderson, Swenson and Clay, 1995: 119)

The disciplinary process that emerges from this management philosophy has been cited for its tendency to both destroy personal initiative and produce organizational stress (Bouza, 1990; Brown, 1981; Sparrow, Moore and Kennedy, 1990). Perhaps this is one reason why officers from larger agencies—that have more formal communications, steeper organizational hierarchies, and fewer opportunities for decision-making participation—appear to experience more stress than officers from smaller agencies (Brooks and Piquero, 1998: 615). Because rigid organizational structures inhibit effective interpersonal communication, they have been cited as straining relationships among ranks, divisions, and individuals (Finn, 1999: 377). More specifically, police stress has been attributed to:

- Lack of consultation and communication (Brown and Campbell, 1994; Kirkcaldy, Cooper and Ruffalo, 1995)
- Inadequate guidance and support from administrators (Ayres and Flanagan, 1990; Brown and Campbell, 1990; Kirschman, 1998; Spielberger et al., 1982)
- Insufficient feedback (Brown et al., 1996)
- Little or no input into department policy, along with authority that is not commensurate with responsibility—that is, too little authority and too much responsibility (Standfest, 1996)

As officers mature over time in terms of knowledge and experience, they can be expected to generate stronger demands for participatory involvement and become more resentful of insensitive management styles that do not allow for such input (Hersey et al., 1996). Structural design and organizational processes are therefore stress-provoking because of their assault on an officer's image as a professional (Kroes et al., 1974a). True professionals are trusted to use their discretion and make independent decisions without constant organizational oversight. But police officers are not. As one observer noted, this creates the occupational dilemma of being "both powerful and powerless at the same time—powerful because their every action has potentially critical consequences, and powerless because they are constantly scrutinized, supervised, and reined in by their department" (Kirschman, 1998: 128).

Targeting Causes Rather than Effects

The stress-inducing role of the organizational environment, administrative structure, and management practices of police agencies has been well documented, but that information has not generally been used to guide stress prevention and intervention strategies. In recent years, law enforcement agencies have become increasingly aware of stress and its potentially debilitating effects, and many have taken steps to deal with it. In doing so, however, they have tended to view stress as an *individual disorder* rather than an *organizational dysfunction*. That means attacking stress as a problem of personal adjustment, and therefore placing accountability on individual employees.

Under the individual disorder approach, it is the employee's responsibility to take advantage of the resources provided by the organization to assist in more effectively dealing with job-related stress. From this perspective, remedies have largely focused on teaching employees how to cope more effectively with stress. However, at best, improving coping techniques only reduces the debilitating impact of stress. At worst, it completely overlooks the administrative sources of stress that created the problem in the first place.

As a result, traditional stress-related remedies have suffered from significant deficiencies. First, they have overlooked causes and accentuated effects. In other words, emphasis has been placed on developing individual coping strategies—to reduce the negative effects of stress—rather than addressing the organizational shortcomings that could potentially eliminate its causes. In the search for individual solutions to organizational problems, stress-reducing efforts in law enforcement are typically directed toward symptoms rather than causes. This means that traditional remedies for police stress have been *reactive responses*, as opposed to *proactive prevention* strategies.

Most police agencies deal with officer stress by referring employees to either counseling or training. As a service offered after an officer has been exposed to episodic stress, counseling is, by nature, reactive. But because training is provided to prevent officers from developing harmful physical, mental, and emotional reactions to stress, the approach is often considered proactive. However, a valid argument exists for viewing both systems as reactive.

Clinical Intervention Model

In the field of law enforcement, it is easy to become distracted by high-profile critical incidents that pump adrenaline, capture public attention, and merit distinguished service awards. High-profile events represent what police work is all about, but as noted in this chapter, they do not constitute the primary sources of police stress:

> Danger is not a daily occurrence for most cops, but organizational stress and office politics are. We teach cops how to deal with danger as though it happened every day, but rarely, if ever, do we teach them to anticipate and then manage the daily grind of a bureaucratic system. (Kirshman, 1998: 127)

In an attempt to prevent the onset of post-traumatic stress syndrome, most agencies assure that officers involved in traumatic incidents have access to psychological services. When departments first acknowledged their responsibility to assist officers in this capacity, clinical counseling was the model of service commonly provided. As a result, this *clinical intervention model* remains the standard response to officer stress, regardless of its source. Through employee assistance programs, clinical services are now widely available in most U.S. police departments. Because they are so accessible to officers struggling with all types of stress-related problems, it follows that agencies may well assume that they have fulfilled their obligations related to employee stress through the clinical model. But they have not.

The counseling-for-everyone approach is effective only insofar as it addresses the specific nature of an employee's stress. Certainly, it is helpful to talk with a trained therapist after coming close to death in a shooting incident, but will it be equally beneficial after months of teeth-gritting frustration with organizational bureaucracy? It has been suggested that it may be more appropriate for police departments to begin appointing organizational rather than clinical psychologists (Hart et al., 1995: 151). Psychological counseling cannot do anything do prevent recurrence of officer stress. Clinical psychologists cannot prevent organizational stress any more than medical doctors can prevent the common cold. After-the-fact treatment is better than nothing but it will not prevent the virus (or the stress) from spreading.

Individual Coping Model

In addition to the clinical intervention model, many contemporary agencies embrace the *individual coping model* by offering stress prevention training. In fact, the most common method for addressing stress in U.S. law enforcement today is to train officers to recognize its signs and then develop individual coping strategies for dealing with it (Finn, 2000: 22; Sewell, 1999: 364). Such coping techniques can include anything from physical exercise to dietary changes, biofeedback, hobbies, sports, and even transcendental meditation.

As with counseling, sending employees to stress-related training is not without benefit. Learning the importance of regular exercise, nutritional improvement, and relaxation techniques is likely to enhance physical health. Learning how to balance work and personal life by making time for family, hobbies, and sports is likely to enhance mental health. Both physical and emotional results can be rewarding for employees who incorporate the message of such training into their lifestyles. But like the clinical intervention model, the individual coping model cannot prevent stress. A major drawback of both models is that they are reactive rather than proactive. These approaches can prevent the onset of the debilitating physical or mental symptoms of stress, but that is not the same as preventing stress itself.

The individual coping model can keep the constant stomachache from turning into an ulcer, the muscle tension from escalating into a heart attack, the anxiety from becoming suicidal depression. However, it does nothing to remove the chronic stressors that created the stomachache, tension, or anxiety in the first place because the model seeks *individual solutions* to *organizational problems*. In other words, the problem has been totally misdiagnosed. Under the coping model, the individual is seen as sick—or potentially becoming sick—if nothing is done quickly to alleviate the debilitating effects of organizational stress. This perspective leads some to mistakenly conclude that stress prevention training is a proactive approach. In medicine, helping someone to feel better after exposure to a virus is not considered proactive prevention.

Stress Prevention Hierarchy: Primary, Secondary, and Tertiary Intervention

Translated organizationally, stress prevention can be addressed at any of three hierarchical levels:

1. **Primary prevention** — Eliminating or reducing sources of stress
2. **Secondary intervention** — Mitigating potential consequences of exposure
3. **Tertiary intervention** — Proving support for a stressed officer. (Brown and Campbell, 1994)

Thus far, this discussion and the strategies used by most police organizations have addressed only levels two and three of the stress prevention hierarchy. The clinical intervention model provides counseling support for stressed officers and seeks to reduce the potential psychological consequences of exposure to organizational stressors. The individual coping model similarly provides support by assuring officers that they are not unique in terms of exposure to occupational stress, and, through training, attempts to mitigate its negative physical, mental, and emotional results.

However, few (if any) agencies are targeting the primary prevention strategies that represent the top of the hierarchy. That would require properly diagnosing the problem, examining its causes, and developing strategies for preventing its occurrence. In the clinical intervention model, no attempt is made to diagnose the root of the problem and eliminate its source. Rather, emphasis is placed on helping an individual better adjust to the problem. In the individual coping model, an effort is made to determine what the problem is, but it is improperly diagnosed as individual disorder rather than organizational dysfunction. As a result, both approaches have been ineffective in terms of primary prevention. Both models "fail to address the underlying organizational problems that form the basis of much of the stress experienced by officers" (Finn, 1999: 375) because they target the symptoms and effects of police stress rather than its causes and sources:

> With very few exceptions, stress management programs attempt to teach the employee how to cope with the stressors present in the work environment. This is essentially an inoculation approach, which does not address the issue of changing the work environment to make it inherently less stressful.... Teaching employees to cope with stress treats the effect while ignoring the cause. (Beehr and O'Hara, 1986)

For these reasons, an organizational rather than individual approach has been recommended as more productive (Hart et al., 1995: 151). Nevertheless, it is a lot easier to place responsibility on "sick" employees to get well than for organizations to take responsibility for determining what ingredients in the work environment make employees unhealthy. If workers slowly became ill as a result of exposure to some noxious form of pesticide, lead paint, or asbestos-filled insulation, the Occupational Safety and Health Administration would enforce laws requiring the employer to clean up the worksite. But no enforcement equivalent protects those suffering from the debilitating effects of chronic organizational stress. The workplace is not potentially less harmful simply because the source of the contamination is organizational exasperation rather than biological infestation.

Primary Prevention: Commitment, Participation, Action

Despite concerns about their lack of success, clinical intervention and individual coping models continue to prevail. In fact, not only do they fail to address the sources of chronic organizational stress, but it has also been observed that "the help rendered may simply be a palliative that serves to patch people up and return them to the situation causing the problem in the first place" (Brown and Campbell, 1994). We have been treating individual victims of stress rather than trying to eliminate its organizational causes.

We may not yet be able to change the weather, prevent cancer, or cure the common cold, but we can take steps to change organizational stressors. To prevent the stress virus from infecting unsuspecting employees, police departments must place greater emphasis on improving organizational health (Cox, 1992). Developing a primary stress prevention strategy that targets chronic organizational stress requires administrative dedication, self reflection, and risk taking. More specifically, those requirements can be translated operationally into three key ingredients— **commitment, participation,** and **action** (Stinchcomb, 1995: 197).

Commitment — The first essential ingredient is for management and executive staff to recognize the organization's role, i.e., *their* role, in generating employee stress and make a firm commitment to do something about it. This means progressing beyond the misguided faith that stress can be addressed sufficiently through the coping techniques that employees learn in counseling sessions or training programs. It means identifying the true sources of chronic organizational stress. It also means proactive dedication to addressing the stress-provoking features of the work environment, even if some of the stressors are intimately associated with the administrators and their management styles. Recognition of these stressors is the first step in the transition from individual coping strategies to organizational prevention measures (Brown et al., 1996).

Participation — It may well be painful for administrators to embark on the self-reflective insights that will help to identify chronic organizational stressors, but it is not advisable for them to do so in isolation. Managers may not be aware of how they contribute to organizational stress, and they cannot expand that awareness by sealing themselves off from everyone below their rank. Once a commitment is made to tackle organizational stress issues, one of the best things that administrators can do is to get staff involved in the process through participatory management. By including all ranks in a search for chronic organizational stressors, a two-fold (substantive and symbolic) benefit occurs. First, on a substantive level, broader input goes into the problem identification process. This makes it more likely that the most prevalent stressors will actually be uncovered. Secondly, a symbolic message is sent that administrators are concerned about chronic organizational stressors and have confidence in the ability of employees to effectively assist in targeting them. Because lack of participation has been identified as one of the most consistent organizational stressors in the literature on police stress, involving all ranks in problem identification may also provide a subsidiary benefit by addressing this shortcoming.

Action — Sincere commitment and participatory feedback obviously must be followed by action. This means completely refocusing traditional stress-related organizational interventions. No longer is the emphasis on helping employees adjust to stress-provoking administrative practices. It shifts to alleviating the practices. The precise strategies to be undertaken will be determined by the nature of the stress-related problems identified. Keeping in mind the typical stressors uncovered in the literature on chronic organizational stress, some relevant responses might include:

- Proactively monitoring management decisions in terms of their anticipated stress-related impacts and searching for implementation methods

to minimize the impacts (Finn, 1999: 378), e.g., explaining the reasoning behind a decision rather than simply issuing an order.
- Training command staff in effective management techniques (Finn, 2000: 23), especially with regard to developing greater awareness of how their decisions, actions (or inactions), and general management style can be stress-provoking for others.
- Listening more actively to employees; this is known to reduce cynicism, build esteem, and promote self-worth (Graves, 1996).
- Decentralizing management authority, empowering employees, and involving them more intimately in the decision-making process (Sewell, 1999: 366–367).
- Concentrating on team-building, problem-solving, and resolving conflicts in an orderly manner (Finn, 1997).
- Improving communication and disciplinary practices, as well as providing greater clarity, feedback, and administrative support (Kirschman, 1998: 127).
- Changing the stress-inducing features of organizational policies and practices (Territo and Sewell, 1999: 359). This may mean taking a critical look at what has been taken for granted for many years. Several years ago, the Philadelphia Police Department created the first organizational stress manager position with responsibility for examining department policies and procedures and recommending ways to make them less stressful (Finn, 1999: 376).

These are but a few of the many alternative approaches that may be employed to address chronic organizational stress from the perspective of primary prevention. Considerable success has been reported in organizations that implemented such approaches. For example, a growing number of agencies found that even modest organizational modifications can lead to enhanced morale and productivity among line officers (Finn, 1997). The commitment–participation–action model places responsibilities for developing and maintaining a healthier, more productive workforce by eliminating organizational stressors from the work environment firmly with administrators.

That is a formidable challenge. It means taking personal responsibility for what has often been blamed on "the system" or "the nature of the job." The approach requires changing an organization in ways that many individuals may not support. It calls for replacing reactive responding with proactive prevention. The options are clear. Continue with responses that react to the effects of stress or activate preventive solutions that directly target the sources of stress. The choices for police leaders are equally apparent: remain part of the problem or become part of the solution.

Conclusions

Perhaps because stress is so endemic to modern life in general, and to police work in particular, it has for years become accepted as an inevitable by-product of coping with the 21st century. As part of the inherent price of living in modern times, we once likewise accepted exposure to everything from secondary smoke to city smog, but passive acceptance of police-related stress has begun to give way to conscious-raising concerns and subsequent interventions. That does not, however, mean that concerns have been strategically targeted or interventions are sufficiently effective.

Some see stresses as environmental stimuli that are more accurately described as stressors. Others envision stresses as the physiological and/or psychological responses of individuals that are more accurately viewed as symptoms. Incorporating both of these variables into an interactive perspective results in viewing stress as an imbalance between environmental demands and individual coping resources (Cherniss, 1980). Only the demands that we cannot avoid, alter, or control will become stressful. In police work, this means that control emerges as a key variable in the alleviation of stress. In traditional stress-related strategies employed by law enforcement agencies, however, the focus has been misguided. Certainly, police officers have little if any control over traumatic incidents encountered on the job. By limiting stress responses to the provision of counseling assistance following traumatic incidents, agencies concentrate on episodic stressors that are relatively uncommon for most police personnel. Additionally, this clinical intervention model also overlooks the substantially more prevalent sources of chronic organizational stress. The individual coping model is not an improvement inasmuch as it attempts to improve the responses to stress rather than removing its causes. Thus, the clinical model provides assistance for only a very limited aspect of police-related stress, and the coping model addresses symptoms rather than causes.

In the clinical model, the treatment is insufficient to combat the major sources of the problem. The coping model misdiagnoses the problem. In both cases, reactive responses take the place of proactive initiatives. Both approaches place the burden on individual employees—to "get well" through counseling or avoid "getting sick" (through training). Neither approach deals with gaining control over stressors or preventing stress. The first step in controlling stressors and thus preventing stress is identifying the frustrations that create chronic organizational stress. This requires bold leadership, along with organizational self-analysis, managerial insight, and a firm commitment to change.

These observations are hardly new. More than 20 years ago, Murphy (1984) noted that the potential value of stress management interventions in law enforcement was undermined because the interventions were "often designed to teach workers to cope better with stressors rather than to eliminate or reduce sources of stress," and the organizations may have felt that they "met their obligations by simply introducing stress management programs." Why has so little been done to reduce chronic organizational stress in policing? After all, how much would it cost to involve more employees in decision making, communicate with them more frequently, praise them more sincerely, and discipline them more objectively? These interventions come without a fiscal price, but they impose another price. They require the organizational administration to admit that it is at fault and take some responsibility for corrective action. For many, that may be too high a price to pay.

References

Albrecht, K. (1979) *Stress and the manager*, Englewood Cliffs, NJ: Prentice-Hall.

Alexander, D. A., Innes, G., Irving, B., Sinclair, S. D., and Walker, L. D. (1991) *Police stress at work*, London: The Police Foundation.

Anderson, W., Swenson, D., and Clay, D. (1995) *Stress management for law enforcement officers*, Upper Saddle River, NJ: Prentice-Hall.

Anson, R. H. and Bloom, M. E. (1988) Police stress in an occupational context, *Journal of Police Science and Administration*, 16(4): 229–239.

Argyris, C. (1957) *Personality and work*, New York: Harper and Row.

Ayres, R. M. and Flanagan, G. S. (1990) *Preventing law enforcement stress: The organization's role*, Washington, D.C.: U.S. Department of Justice.

Band, S. R. and Manuelle, C. A. (1987) Stress and police officers' performance: An examination of effective coping behavior, *Police Studies*, 10: 122–131.

Beehr, T. A. and O'Hara, K. (1986) Methodological designs for the evaluation of occupational stress intervention, in I. S. Kasl and C. Cooper (Eds.), *Stress and health: Issues in research methodology*, New York: John Wiley.

Bennis, W. and Nanus, B. (1997) *Leaders: Strategies for taking charge*, New York: Harper Business.

Biggam, F., Power, K. G., MacDonald, R., Carcary, W., and Moodie, E. (1997) Self-perceived occupational stress and distress in a Scottish police force, *Work and Stress*, 11: 118–133.

Bouza, A. (1990) *The police mystique: An insider's look at cops, crime, and the criminal justice system*, New York: Plenum Press.

Brooks, L. W. and Piquero, N. L. (1998) Police stress: Does department size matter? *Policing: An International Journal of Police Strategies and Management*, 21(4): 600–617.

Brown, J., Cooper, C., and Kirkcaldy, B. (1996) Occupational stress among senior police officers, *The British Journal of Psychology*, 87: 31–41.

Brown, J., Fielding, J., and Grover, J. (1999) Distinguishing traumatic, vicarious, and routine operational stressor exposure and attendant adverse consequences in a sample of police officers, *Work and Stress*, 13(4): 312–325.

Brown, J. M. and Campbell, E. A. (1990) Source of occupational stress in the police, *Work and Stress*, 4(4): 305–318.

Brown, J. M. and Campbell, E. A. (1994) *Stress and policing: Sources and strategies*, New York: John Wiley.

Brown, M. K. (1981). *Working the street: Police discretion and the dilemmas of reform*, New York: Russell Sage Foundation.

Buck, V. E. (1972) *Working under pressure*, New York: Crane, Russak.

Cherniss, C. (1980) *Staff burnout: Job stress in the human services*, Beverly Hills: Sage.

Cooper, C. L., Davidson, M. A., and Robinson, P. (1988) Stress in the police service, *Journal of Occupational Medicine*, 24: 30–36.

Cooper, C. L. and Marshall, J. J. (1977) *Understanding executive stress*, New York: PBI Books.

Cox, T. (1978) *Stress*, Baltimore: University Park Press.

Cox, T. (1992) Occupational health: Past, present, and future, *Work and Stress*, 6: 99–102.

Crank, J. P. and Caldero, M. (1991) The production of occupational stress in medium-sized police agencies: A survey of line officers in eight municipal departments, *Journal of Criminal Justice*, 19: 339–349.

Crowe, G. and Stradling, S. (1993) Dimensions of perceived stress in a British police force, *Policing and Society*, 3: 137–150.

Davidson, M. and Cooper, C. L. (1983) *Stress and the woman manager*, Oxford: Blackwell.

Davidson, M. J. and Veno, A. (1980) *Stress and the woman manager*, Oxford: Blackwell.

DeParis, R. J. (1997) Situational leadership: Problem-solving leadership for problem-solving policing, *The Police Chief*, October, 74–86.

Edelwich, J. (1980) *Burnout: Stages of disillusionment in the helping professions*, New York: Human Sciences Press.

Finn, P. (1997) Reducing stress: An organization-centered approach, *FBI Law Enforcement Bulletin*, August. [http://www.fbi.gov/publications/leb/1997/aug975.htm] Accessed August 2007.

Finn, P. (1999) Reducing stress: An organization-centered approach, in L. Territo and J. D. Sewell (Eds.), *Stress management in law enforcement* (pp. 373–382), Durham, NC: Carolina Academic Press.

Finn, P. (2000) On-the-job stress in policing—reducing it, preventing it, *National Institute of Justice Journal*, January, 18–24.

Graves, W. (1996) Police cynicism: Causes and cures, *FBI Law Enforcement Bulletin*, 65: 16–20.

Greller, M. M., Parsons, C. K., and Mitchell, D. R. D. (1992) Additive effects and beyond: Occupational stressors and social buffers in a police organization, in J. D. Quick, L. R. Murphy, and J. J. Hurrell, Jr. (Eds.), *Stress and well-being at work: Assessments and interventions for occupational mental health* (pp. 33–47), Washington, D.C.: American Psychological Association.

Gudjonsson, G. H. and Adlam, R. (1985) Occupational stressors among British police officers, *Police Journal*, 58: 73–85.

Guralnick, L. (1963) Mortality by occupation and cause of death among men 20–64 years of age: 1950, in *Vital statistics special reports*, Bethesda, MD: U.S. Department of Health, Education, and Welfare.

Hart, P. M., Wearing, A. J., and Headey, B. (1994) Perceived quality of life, personality and work experiences: Construct validation of the police daily hassles and uplifts scales, *Criminal Justice and Behavior*, 21: 283–311.

Hart, P. M., Wearing, A. J., and Headey, B. (1995) Police stress and well-being: Integrating personality, coping, and daily work experiences, *Journal of Occupational and Organizational Psychology*, 68(2): 133-156.

Hersey, P., Blanchard, K. H. and Johnson, D. E. (1996) *Management of organizational behavior: Utilizing human resources*, Englewood Cliffs, NJ: Prentice-Hall.

Hingley, P. and Cooper, C. L. (1986) *Stress and the nurse manager*, Chichester: John Wiley.

Hoyert, D. L., Arias, E., Smith, B. L., Murphy, S. L., and Kochanek, K. D. (2001) Deaths: Final data for 1999, in *National vital statistics report*, Atlanta, GA: Centers for Disease Control.

Kirkcaldy, B., Cooper, C. L. and Ruffalo, P. (1995) Work stress and health in a sample of U.S. police, *Psychological Reports*, 76: 700–702.

Kirschman, E. (1998) Organizational stress, *Police Chief*, October, 127–134.

Kouzes, J. M. and Posner, B. Z. (1995) *The leadership challenge: How to keep getting extraordinary things done in organizations*, San Francisco: Jossey-Bass.

Krietner, R., Sova, M., Wood, S., Friedman, G., and Reif, W. (1985) A search for the U-shaped relationship between occupational stressors and the risk of coronary (heart) disease, *Journal of Police Science and Administration*, June, 123.

Kroes, W. H. (1976) *Society's victim: The policeman*, Springfield, IL: Charles C. Thomas.

Kroes, W. H., Hurrell, J. J., and Margolis, B. L. (1974a) Job stress in police administration, *Journal of Police Science and Administration*, December, 2(4): 381–387.

Kroes, W. H., Margolis, B. L., and Hurrell, J. J. (1974b) Job stress in policemen, *Journal of Police Science and Administration*, 2(2): 145–155.

Leitner, L. A., Posner, I., and Lester, D. (1983) Stress, mood and job satisfaction in police chiefs, *The Police Chief*, January, 54–55.

Lester, D., Benkovich, J. B., Dietrick, M., and Solis, A. (1981) Stress and job satisfaction in police officers, *Police Studies*, 4(1): 6–9.

Maslach, C. (1976) Burned-out, *Human Behavior*, 5: 16–22.

Maslow, A. H. (1954) *Motivation and personality*, New York: Harper and Row.

Milham, S. (1983) *Occupational mortality in Washington State* (Publication 83-116). Washington, D.C.: U.S. Government Printing Office.

Murphy, L. R. (1984) Occupational stress management: A review and appraisal, *Journal of Occupational Psychology*, 57: 1–15.

Pines, A. M. and Aronson, E. (1981) *Burnout*, New York: The Free Press.

Reiner, R. (1985) *The politics of the police*, New York: Harvester Wheatsheaf.

Reiser, M. (1974) Some organizational stresses on policemen, *Journal of Police Science and Administration*, 2(2): 156–159.

Richard, W. and Fell, R. (1976) Health factors in police job stress, in W. H. Kroes and J. J. Hurrell (Eds.), *Job stress and the police officer: Identifying stress reduction techniques* (pp. 73–84), Washington, D.C.: U.S. Department of Health, Education, and Welfare.

Roberg, R. R. and Kuykendall, J. (1997) *Police management, Second Edition*, Los Angeles: Roxbury.

Robin, G. and Anson, R. H. (1990) *Introduction to the criminal justice system*, New York: Harper and Row.

Selye, H. (1956) *The stress of life*, New York: McGraw-Hill.

Sewell, J. D. (1999) Administrative concerns in law enforcement stress management, in L. Territo and J. D. Sewell (Eds.), *Stress management in law enforcement* (pp. 361–369), Durham, NC: Carolina Academic Press.

Sigler, R. T. and Wilson, C. N. (1988) Stress in the workplace: Comparing police stress with teacher stress, *Journal of Police Science and Administration*, 16: 151–162.

Sigler, R. T., Wilson, C. N., and Allen, Z. (1991) Police stress and teacher stress at work and at home, *Journal of Criminal Justice*, 19: 361–370.

Silbert, M. H. (1982) Job stress and burnout of new police officers, *The Police Chief*, June, 46–48.

Sparrow, M., Moore, M. H., and Kennedy, D. M. (1990) *Beyond 911: A new era for policing*, New York: Basic Books.

Spielberger, C. D., Grier, K. S., and Greenfield, G. (1982).Major dimensions of stress in law enforcement, *FOP Journal*, Spring, 10/11: 80–82.

Standfest, S.R. (1996) The police supervisor and stress, *FBI Law Enforcement Bulletin*, 65: 7-10.

Stephens, C., Long, N., and Miller, N. (1997) The impact of trauma and social support on post-traumatic stress disorder, *Journal of Criminal Justice*, 25: 303–314.

Stinchcomb, J. B. (1986) Correctional officer stress: Is training missing the target? *Correctional Monograph: Issues in Correctional Training and Casework*, 19–23.

Stinchcomb, J. B. (1987) *Redesigning stress reduction training: Has stress become a status symbol*? Paper presented at International Conference on Corrections and Law Enforcement Training, Miami, FL.

Stinchcomb, J. B. (1995) *Managing stress: Performing under pressure* (Vol. 2). Lanham, MD: American Correctional Association.

Storch, J. E. and Panzarella, R. (1996) Police stress: State-trait anxiety in relation to occupational and personal stressors, *Journal of Criminal Justice*, 24(2): 99–107.

Stotland, E. (1991) The effects of police work and professional relationships on health, *Journal of Criminal Justice*, 19: 371–379.

Territo, L. and Sewell, J. D. (Eds.) (1999) *Stress management in law enforcement*, Durham, NC: Carolina Academic Press.

Terry, W. C. (1981) Police stress: The empirical evidence, *Journal of Police Science and Administration*, 9(1): 61–65.

Vena, J. E., Violanti, J. M., Marshall, J. R., and Fiedler, R. (1986) Mortality of a municipal worker cohort: Police officers, *American Journal of Industrial Medicine*, 10: 383–397.

Veninga, R. L. and Spradley, J. P. (1981) *The work/stress connection*, Boston: Little, Brown.

Violanti, J. M. (1996) Violence turned inward: Police suicide in the workplace, in G. R. Vanden Bos and E.Q. Bulatao, E. Q. (Eds.) *Violence on the job: Identifying risks and developing solutions* (pp. 229– 249), Washington, D.C.: American Psychological Association.

Violanti, J. M., Vena, J. E., and Petralia, S. (1998) Mortality of a police cohort: 1950–1990, *American Journal of Industrial Medicine*, 33: 366–373.

Watson, E. M., Stone, A. R., and DeLuca, S. M. (1998) *Strategies for community policing*, Upper Saddle River, NJ: Prentice-Hall.

Constructing the *Other* within Police Culture: Analysis of a Deviant Unit within a Police Organization*

2

VENESSA GARCIA

Contents

Police organizations have historically established special units to deal with certain crimes and special groups of people. Special investigative units have been established to deal with homicide, vice, organized crime, and gang activity; membership within these crime-fighting units is prestigious (Cole and Smith, 1999). However, those units do not carry equal value within the police organization in part because they are not consistent with the police values of what crime fighting is or they require too drastic a change in the current approaches to crime prevention and control (Crank and Langworthy, 1999; Lurigio and Skogan, 2000; Rosenbaum, 2000; Walker and Katz, 2002).

For example, police organizations have also established domestic violence units, community policing programs, and juvenile crime investigative units. These units, inconsistent with the traditional crime-fighting values within police organizations, have been stigmatized (Balkin, 1988; Grennan, 2000; Heidensohn, 1992; Miller, 1999; Williams, 1998) and indeed have been viewed as deviant. The difference between special investigative units dealing with homicide, vice, organized crime, and gang activity, and those dealing

* An earlier version of this chapter appeared in *Police Practice and Research*, 2005, 6(1): 65–80.

with domestic violence, juvenile crime, and community policing is found in their relationship to the perceived functions of police.

While police functions include crime fighting, order maintenance, and social services (Cole and Smith, 1999), police officers tend to place the highest value on the crime-fighting function (associated with masculinity); the least value is imposed on the social service function (associated with femininity) (Bell, 1982; Crank and Caldero, 2000; Drummond, 1976; Heidensohn, 1992; Miller, 1999; Perez, 1997). Thus, crime fighting has been identified as the norm for police activity and social service has been designated the *other*. While we can study any number of special police units or programs (domestic violence units, juvenile crime units, etc.) to examine the effects of placement of the *other* within a police department, this chapter focuses on only one: community-oriented policing (COP) programs.

COP programs started springing up in the United States in the 1980s. Depending on the size of the police department, they ranged from complex all-inclusive programs to the simple establishment of a COP officer position. Although COP programs were established as mechanisms to reduce crime, their service-oriented nature tended to create a boomerang effect (Crank and Caldero, 2000) that held to the ideal of police officials as crime fighters and not social workers. The result was the rejection of community policing. COP activities were not accepted as "real" police work. Negative sanctions were placed on some of these units and the officers assigned to them. As a result, COP officers may have experienced less job satisfaction and sought to return—like boomerangs— to more traditional police activities.

The purpose of this chapter is to examine the stigmatization and the resulting effects on police officers assigned to COP programs or positions. In order to properly assess implementation and success, program acceptance within the criminal justice organization must be examined. This chapter will discuss the inclusion of the *other* within the police organization and how this construction is defined and experienced by those possessing the COP officer label. Knowledge of the stigmatization of COP programs is important because it helps us improve their implementation. If, in fact, stigmatization comes from rank-and file employees or from the agency as a whole, it may impact the effectiveness of the entire program.

The following section summarizes the history and functions of the COP model and leads to a discussion of the social construction of community policing as the *other* and its stigmatization and rejection. The first part of the analysis attempts to determine whether COP officers feel they carry the *other* label. Second, if officers feel they are labeled this way, I will attempt to determine whether this rejection results from a lack of agency support, use of the program to penalize officers, years on the force, officer resistance, assignment as a COP officer (as opposed to volunteering), or the social service function of community policing. Third, I will attempt to determine the destructive effects of the label, that is, whether stigmatized COP officers (1) are subjected to agency penalties, (2) prefer not to engage in community policing, or (3) experience job dissatisfaction.

History and Functions of Community Policing

Community policing as it is known today was conceived as a result of increased police–citizen conflict and intense research during the 1970s. Civil unrest in the 1950s, 1960s, and 1970s resulted in a loss of police legitimacy (Barlow and Barlow, 2000). Police reformers began to re-evaluate the effectiveness of the professional model. This led to numerous police studies that revealed that traditional policing did not decrease crime or the fear of crime to the extent claimed (Cole and Smith, 1999). Responding to these findings, reformers including government officials turned to community policing (see Chapters 6 and 10 of this volume).

Community policing is a philosophy that encourages police officers to find ways of dealing with situations without necessarily making arrests (Mastrofski, Worden, and Snipes, 1995). These alternative methods are means by which officers engage in cooperative relations with communities under their jurisdictions in order to prevent crime. The philosophy behind the concept is that increased and improved communications can achieve a negotiated order of crime prevention that would simultaneously improve police–citizen relations (Crank and Caldero, 2000), and focusing on the needs and satisfaction of communities became a new focus that worked to reclaim police legitimacy (Williams, 1998).

Under the auspices of community policing in the United States, neighborhood residents are encouraged to develop neighborhood watch and youth programs such as midnight basketball, Safe Kids–Smart Kids, and youth courts. Such programs work to empower neighborhood residents to fix "broken windows" (Wilson and Kelling, 1982) and work with the police in dealing with crime and prevention. Under the direct control of police departments, community policing in the U.S. has implemented youth programs such as SRO (School Resource Officer), DARE (Drug Abuse Resistance Education), GREAT (Gang Resistance Education and Training), and PAL (Police Athletic League) youth recreation. Police departments reinstituted foot patrols; implemented bike patrols; started making door-to-door contacts; conducted citizen surveys; attended community meetings; provided crime prevention counsel to citizens; and worked with city agencies, local businesses, community leaders, and community crime programs (Langston and Richardson, 1995).

Adopting the community policing philosophy, police administrators intended to change the philosophy of traditional policing from reactive crime fighters to preventive service providers that help solve community problems. However, the needed communication skills to negotiate order, work in close contact with community groups and leaders, make successful individual contacts, and gain the trust and respect of community residents are not the types of traditional skills most respected in good officers (Miller, 1999; Schulz, 1995). Furthermore, encouraging the use of alternatives to arrest is contrary to police culture. As a result, community policing experienced a boomerang effect reflected in police resistance (Miller, 1999; Williams, 1998). This resistance to community policing led to stigmatization of the programs and the officers assigned to them. To understand why many police officers reject community policing, we must first understand the process of stigmatization.

Social Construction of Community Policing as *Other*

The social construction of reality is shared with others through culture (Berger and Luckmann, 1966). In order to understand the larger society, we learn to categorize, typify, and generalize or overgeneralize our experiences and the experiences to which we are exposed through friends, families, and the media (Bohm, 2002). These typifications and generalizations are then given meanings, values or devalues, names, and ultimately assigned to individuals or groups (Rosenblum and Travis, 1996).

In the course of socially constructing the *other*, we tend to dichotomize individuals and social groups into "we" and "they" categories based on the concept that every thesis has an antithesis. In short, society tends to separate social groups into the *normal* ("we") and the *other* ("they"). Most people fit neatly into one category or the other and thus reject anything outside those categories. Furthermore, we assume that members of these categories are different from each other. When we engage in this process of dichotomization, we assume that people fit into social groups due to factors independent of our perceptions, and we act on those perceptions.

Within police organizations and all other institutions in society, we find institutional definitions of *normal* and *other* (Acker, 1992; Crank and Caldero, 2000; Martin and Jurik, 1996; Reuss-Ianni, 1983). The normal or good cop engages in acceptable police functions or at least attempts to engage in such functions. "Real" police work is defined as crime fighting (Drummond, 1976; Miller, 1999). An officer is expected to seek out situations that allow crimes to be detected and criminals apprehended. Accordingly, a good officer holds to the noble cause of fighting crime and helping victims (Crank and Caldero, 2000) and to the image of being adventurous and brave (Herbert, 2001).

A good officer, at least in the U.S., must carry a gun and handcuffs and "charge the tower" at the site of a crime. However, in the process of becoming a good officer and internalizing police culture, he or she also becomes cynical and distrusting of the citizens policed (Crank and Caldero, 2000). Perez (1997) identified this cynicism as a "we–they" paradox detrimental to good policing. It is part of police culture, and officers who do not recognize and practice the unspoken rules may somehow find themselves placed in the *other* category.

How is an officer designated an *other*? Simply put, he or she engages in activities contrary to those accepted as "real" police work. COP fits this perception. A good officer is so focused on achieving a "good pinch" associated with crime fighting, he or she loses focus of the good means required to achieve this noble cause (Crank and Caldero, 2000). Community policing is an attempt to achieve the noble cause by focusing on the means, but the means are not the valued masculine, aggressive, traditional techniques of crime fighting. Instead, the means are more closely associated with the social work roles of early policewomen who were employed to work specifically with issues involving women and children (Miller, 1999). It is important to note, however, that this does not imply that another, separate police culture may be detected (see Herbert, 1998). It means that the existing police culture devalues deviations from the "real" police work norm.

Miller (1999) presented an excellent comparison of the role of early policewomen and community policing. She uncovered the role of early policewomen as intelligence gatherers working to befriend residents in the communities they patrolled, thus gaining their trust; such is the task of the present-day COP officer. Furthermore, Miller compared the decentralized nature of community policing with the jobs of early policewomen in the establishment of annexes or police substations, historically established to protect women and children. Early policewomen had high levels of discretion to accomplish their tasks.

Historically and presently, women have been criticized for not possessing the necessary "good cop" masculine traits of rationality, aggressiveness, bravery, objectivity, suspicion, and brutality required to fight crime and apprehend enemies (Charles, 1981; Miller, 1999). These cultural lacks led to claims that women were inherently not competent to perform police functions and were then extended to police jobs performed by both women and men that deal with stigmatized crimes, criminals, and police functions (Bell, 1982; Buzawa and Buzawa, 1990; Drummond, 1976; Garcia, 1995, 2003; Grennan, 2000; Heidensohn, 1992; Heidensohn and Brown, 2000).

One question that must be asked is whether police studies assumed a male norm or whether traits of masculinity are embedded in police organizations in the absence of empirical evidence. The answer requires reference to the history of police organizations and the formal and informal practices of recruitment, promotion, and access to resources (Chakravarty, 1998). For example, the physical agility tests used to recruit police in the U.S. continue to stress the importance of upper body strength although police research concluded that it is not required in about 75% of routine police work (Greene and Klockars, 1991), and most police department policies prohibit extreme risks in testing applicant physical agility.

U.S. police recruitment also continues to allow preferential treatment to military veteran applicants (Belknap, 2001). These practices continue to emphasize male activities and masculinity. While masculinity is often taken for granted in police research, the multiplicity of police cultures identified in the research (Herbert, 1998) is rooted in masculinity.

Working outside of police culture has led to resistance and stigmatization. Having been so stigmatized, police organizations have reacted through obvious forms of rejection, for example, developing separate annex police stations where policewomen can interact with communities (Miller, 1999), hiring civilians to operate domestic violence police units, and locating juvenile detective bureaus apart from mainstream detective bureaus (Garcia, 1995). The existence of these units and the allocation of resources to them do not mean that they are fully accepted by their organizations. It has long been argued that police agencies and other organizations implement programs to give the image of appearing legitimate. However, if an organization fails to make the necessary structural changes to ensure success of the program, then it only reflects image management (Barlow and Barlow, 2000; Crank and Langworthy, 1999).

Building on the findings of previous studies and measuring the *other* label, this chapter explores whether COP officers perceive their status as real police officers to be challenged and will examine the following hypotheses:

1. COP officers who report a lack of agency support for the COP program are more likely to report status challenges.
2. COP officers who report the drawbacks of COP work including consternation of fellow officers, harassment, teasing about not doing "real" police work, and accusations of not pulling their weight are more likely to report status challenges.
3. COP officers who have been on the police force fewer than five years are more likely to report status challenges.
4. COP officers who perceive that rank-and-file officers resist changes necessary to accomplish community policing are more likely to report status challenges.
5. COP officers assigned to their positions (and did not volunteer) are more likely to report status challenges.
6. COP officers who engage in high levels of social service activities with youths will be more likely to view their status as "real" officers challenged.
7. COP officers experiencing this stigma will experience high levels of agency penalties in resistance to the COP program.

8. COP officers will experience job dissatisfaction.
9. COP officers will choose to engage solely in patrol work rather than work in community policing.

Methodology

The study used secondary data originally collected in September 1995 by Langston and Richardson (2000), for the U.S. National Institute of Justice and distributed by the Inter-University Consortium for Political and Social Research. The investigators conducted telephone interviews of 88 rank-and-file COP officers from municipal, city, and county law enforcement agencies throughout the U.S. The interviews were 40 to 60 minutes in length and sought to explore officers' perceptions of the value and effectiveness of community policing. To develop a reliable and valid survey instrument, the investigators (1) engaged in an extensive literature review and extracted questions dealing with community policing used in prior surveys, (2) conducted site visits of COP programs, and (3) performed a pilot test of the instrument.

Langston and Richardson (1995) selected a sample of 30 agencies from a national survey sponsored by the National Institute of Justice in which 974 agencies claimed to use some form of community policing. The 30 agencies fulfilled certain criteria: (1) they were city, municipal, or county agencies employing 50 to 200 sworn officers and (2) they engaged in at least 6 of 16 community policing activities, including co-production with citizens and community groups, participation in citizen surveys, use of citizen input to improve department operations, public and private inter-agency involvement, specific community policing programs, decentralization and localization of investigations, and crime analysis.

To ensure diversity, eight agencies each from the Midwest, South, and West, and six agencies from the Northeast were randomly selected. Three COP officers from each agency were sampled for the study. The investigators obtained a 98% response rate for a sample of 88 officers. Survey questions focused on officer, agency, and community demographics; COP program descriptions; traditional police duties; agency and supervisor support of community policing; interactions of COP and non-COP officers; job satisfaction; training; and perceived effectiveness. The unit of analysis was the individual officer. I first explored whether the COP officers perceived themselves as labeled *other*. One survey question asked whether the officer perceived that his or her status as a "real" officer was challenged.* I then attempted to determine whether departmental factors caused the respondent to perceive his or her status as a "real"

* DV = status challenged; 0 = no and 1 = yes.

Table 2.1 Frequencies of Independent Variables

Variable		Frequency	Percent[a]
Lack of agency support	No	28	32
	Yes	60	68
Officer ridicule	No	54	71
	Yes	22	29
Years on force	<5	17	20
	5 or more	70	81
Rank/file resistance to change	No	34	43
	Yes	46	58
Assignment to COP	No	50	57
	Yes	38	43
Level of COP activity w/youth	Low	53	61
	High	34	39

[a] Percentage may not equal 100 due to rounding.

officer to be challenged.* Third, I examined the possible negative effects of the perception that status as a "real" officer was challenged.†

Findings

I found that 58 respondents (or 66%) reported that their status as "real" officers was not challenged, while 30 (or 34%) of reported that their "real" officer status was challenged. Table 2.1 shows the frequencies of the independent variables. Sixty-eight percent of the officers reported a lack of agency support for the COP program while 32% reported agency support. Fifty-four respondents (71%) did not feel that drawbacks of COP work included officer ridi-

* I examined the lack of agency support for the COP program (0 = no; 1 = yes), whether a drawback to the COP job included consternation of fellow officers, harassment, teasing for not doing "real" police work, and accusations of not pulling one's weight (0 = no; 1 = yes); how long the COP officer was on the force (0 = <5 years; 1 = >5 years or more); whether rank-and-file officers resisted changes necessary for community policing (0 = no; 1 = yes); whether the officer was assigned to COP (0 = no; 1 = yes); and whether the officer engaged in a high level of social service activities dealing with youth (0 = low level; 1 = high level).

† This examination focused on status challenge as the independent variable. Dependent variables included choice to do patrol work (0 = COP only or mix; 1 = patrol only), job satisfaction (0 = dissatisfied; 1 = satisfied), and level of agency penalty in resistance to COP programs (0 = low penalty; 1 = high penalty). Officers were asked whether their agencies were supportive in eight categories: human resources, equipment, material resources, attitude, scheduling, promotions, interdepartment interactions, and lack of understanding of community policing. Scores ranged from 0 to 8 (0–4 = low; 5–8 = high). Bivariate analyses included examination of cross-tabulations and Pearson chi squares (χ^2).

cule, while 22 (29%) reported that the job included officer ridicule. Twenty percent (17) of the respondents served fewer than five years on the police force at the time of the survey and 81% served five or more years.

Respondents who reported that rank-and-file employees resisted changes necessary to accomplish community policing represented 58% of the total; 43% did not report resistance from rank-and-file employees. Forty-three percent of the respondents reported that they were assigned as COP officers and 57% reported that they volunteered. Finally, 61% reported low community policing activity with youth and 39% reported high activity.

Determinants of Status Challenge

The bivariate analyses presented in Table 2.2 revealed that, while most of the respondents did not perceive their status to be challenged by other officers, a significant relationship existed between status challenged and lack of agency support.* Of the 60 officers who felt that the COP program lacked agency support, 25 (42%) felt that their "real" officer status was challenged. Of the 28 officers who believed they had agency support for the COP program, 5 (18%) reported status challenge. These figures indicate that officers who perceived that their agencies did not support the COP program were more likely to report status challenge than officers who reported agency support.

A significant relationship† was found between status challenge and officer ridicule (Table 2.2). Of the 22 officers who reported ridicule, 14 (64%) felt that their status as "real" officers was challenged, while 17% (9 of 54) who *did not* report officer ridicule believed their status was challenged. Officers who did not experience ridicule (83%) were more likely to see their status as not challenged than those who experienced ridicule (36%).

Officers who served fewer than five years on the force (47%) were more likely to report status challenge than officers who served five years or more (30%; see Table 2.2). The analysis revealed that that relationship was not significant.‡ However, a significant relationship existed between a lack of status challenge and rank-and-file resistance to necessary change.§ Interestingly, officers who reported resistance were less likely to view their status as challenged than officers who did not report such resistance, 20% and 53%, respectively (Table 2.2). In the same way, officers who reported that rank-and-file officers were resistant to necessary changes were more likely to report no challenge to their status than officers who reported no resistance to necessary change.

* χ^2 (1, N = 88) = 4.817, p = 0.028.
† χ^2 (1, N = 76) = 16.340, p = 0.001.
‡ χ^2 (1, N = 87) = 1.791, p = 0.181.
§ χ^2 (1, N = 80) = 9.051, p = 0.003.

Table 2.2 Dependent Variables: Status Challenged by Independent Variables

	Lack of Agency Support		Officer Ridicule		Years on Force		Rank/File Resistance to Change		Assignment to COP		Level of COP Activity w/Youth	
	No	Yes	No	Yes	5 or more	>5	No	Yes	No	Yes	Low	High
No status challenge	23	35	45	8	9	49	16	37	29	29	32	26
	82%	58%	83%	36%	53%	70%	47%	80%	58%	76%	60%	77%
Status challenge	5	25	9	14	8	21	18	9	21	9	21	8
	18%	42%	17%	64%	47%	30%	53%	20%	42%	24%	40%	24%
Total	28	60	54	22	17	70	34	46	50	38	53	34
	100%	100%	100%	100%	100%	100%	100%	100%	100%	100%	100%	100%
N	88		76		87		80		88		87	
$\chi 2$	4.817*		16.340*		1.791		9.051*		3.224		2.414	

* $p < 0.05$.

Table 2.3 Level of Agency Support by Status Challenged

	Challenge to Status as "Real" Officer		
	No	Yes	Total
Low agency penalty	23	4	27
	40%	13%	31%
High agency penalty	35	26	61
	60%	87%	69%
Total	58	30	88
	100%	100%	100%

Note: $\chi 2 = 6.441$, df = 1, $p = 0.011$ (significant $p < 0.05$).

Officers assigned to COP appeared less likely to report status challenge than officers who volunteered for the position, 24 and 42% respectively (Table 2.2); however, this relationship was not significant.* Finally, in terms of officers reporting low or high community policing activity with youth, no significant relationship with status challenge was noted.†

Effects of Status Challenge

Bivariate analyses to determine the effects of the stigmatization of serving as a COP officer focused on status challenge as the independent variable. The analysis revealed a significant relationship between level of agency penalty and status challenge.‡ Cross-tabulations revealed that 61 respondents (69%) reported receiving high levels of agency penalties (see Table 2.3). Officers who reported status challenges (87%) were more likely to report high levels of agency penalties than officers who reported no status challenges (60%). Conversely, officers who reported no status challenges were more likely to report low levels of agency penalties (40%) than officers who reported status challenges (13%).

Seventy-two (84%) of the respondents reported that they would *not* choose to engage in traditional patrol work as their only task if they had the choice. Fourteen (16%) reported that they would choose patrol work only (see Table 2.4). However, no significant relationship§ was noted between status challenge and wanting to engage in community policing as an officer's sole task.

* χ^2 (1, $N = 88$) = 3.224, $p = 0.073$
† χ^2 (1, $N = 87$) = 2.414, $p = 0.120$.
‡ χ^2 (1, $N = 88$) = 6.441, $p = 0.011$.
§ χ^2 (1, $N = 86$) = 1.983, $p = 0.159$.

Table 2.4 Choice by Status Challenged

	Challenge to Status as "Real" Officer		
	No	Yes	Total
CP only/mix	50	22	72
	88%	76%	84%
Patrol only	7	7	14
	12%	24%	16%
Total	57	29	86
	100%	100%	100%

Note: $\chi 2 = 1.983$, df = 1, $p = 0.159$ (not significant $p > 0.05$).

Forty-three percent of the officers reported job dissatisfaction, while 58% reported job satisfaction (see Table 2.5). However, no significant difference was seen between officers who reported status challenges (47% reporting job satisfaction) and officers who reported no status challenges (63% satisfied).*

Discussion

The main finding was that most community-oriented policing (COP) officers *did not* tend to perceive their status as "real" officers to be challenged. While past research focused on the stigmatization of women in the work force and on stigmatized duties and positions such as community policing, this finding may point to the possibility that COP programs and COP officers are not as stigmatized as had been thought.

One explanation for this finding may be that different departments may use different methods to engage in community policing. For example, some police departments may focus their community policing efforts on such community-oriented programs as DARE, School Resource Officers, and Neighborhood Watch. Others may be more involved in programs that have more traditional flavors such as problem-oriented policing and SARA (scanning, analysis, response, and assessment). These latter programs involve communities but they serve more traditional roles in fighting crime and apprehending offenders. These forms of community policing may not be very different from traditional policing and would therefore create little conflict between COP and non-COP officers. It is also possible that while COP programs may

* χ^2 (2, $N = 87$) = 5.394, $p = 0.067$.

Table 2.5 Job Satisfaction by Status Challenged

	Challenge to Status as "Real" Officer		
	No	Yes	Total
Satisfied	36	14	50
	63%	47%	58%
Unsatisfied	21	16	37
	37%	53%	43%
Total	57	30	87
	100%	100%	100%

Note: $\chi 2 = 2.187$, df = 1, p = 0.139 (not significant p >0.05).

be stigmatized, this stigmatization may not extend to COP officers. Conversely, the findings may point to problems in the methodology. For example, the survey may have yielded a different result if the choices had been scaled instead of appearing in a "yes" or "no" format. Furthermore, the survey might have included a greater number of respondents and perhaps more probing questions about the issue of stigma.

Nevertheless, one cannot lose sight of the important fact that as many as a third of the respondents felt stigmatized as COP officers. This large proportion warrants further investigation. Examining the determinants of status challenge I found, as expected, that a lack of agency support for COP programs made COP officers feel that their status as "real" officers was challenged (as shown in Table 2.3). This finding supports the literature indicating that police organizations tend to devalue social service type functions (Bell, 1982; Cole and Smith, 1999; Crank and Caldero, 2000; Drummond, 1976; Miller, 1999; Perez, 1997).

I found support for the hypothesis that officer ridicule of COP officers was more likely to result in feelings of status challenge (Table 2.2). As reported in the literature, officers who engage in stigmatized work tend to be ostracized (Charles, 1981; Miller, 1999). The data did not, however, support the hypothesis that officers on the police force for shorter periods were more likely than more seasoned officers to feel status challenges. While the relationship followed the predicted direction, it was not significant. This finding points to the need for further analyses. For example, it is possible that time on the force interacts with other variables such as whether an officer volunteered for the position, how long until retirement, how burned out an officer is, and how effectively committed he or she is to the organization, i.e., emotionally and via self-identity (McElroy, Morrow, and Wardlow, 1999).

Interestingly, I found a significant relationship between rank-and-file resistance to changes necessary to accomplish community policing, but not in the predicted direction (Table 2.2). The analyses showed that officers who reported rank-and-file resistance to the changes necessary to accomplish community policing were less likely to feel status challenges. Again, this may point to the possibility that respect for fellow officers is not diminished simply because the function is devalued.

Additionally, further analyses should be conducted to control for gender based on the literature about the stigmatization of women in policing (Bell, 1982; Buzawa and Buzawa, 1990; Drummond, 1976; Garcia, 1995, 2003; Grennan, 2000; Heidensohn, 1992; Heidensohn and Brown, 2000; Martin and Jurik, 1996). It may reveal that officers may not internalize this resistance (as labeling theorists would argue). McElroy et al. (1999) found that effective organizational commitment influenced officers' decisions to stay with the job. This commitment also related to the ages of the officers. Based on these findings, officers on the job longer may be more committed to the organization, identifying with the organization more than younger officers and, thus not internalizing the stigma.

The analyses showed no significant relationship between assignment to or volunteering as COP officers and status challenge. However, as with years on the job, I suspect an interaction of the variables may become apparent if a larger survey is undertaken. It is possible that younger officers who just graduated from the academy and are eager to engage in "real" police work tend to be assigned, whereas older police officers who are burned out and in need of inaction may be more likely to volunteer and, thus, are affected differently by feelings of status challenge.

Finally, the analyses failed to support the hypothesis that higher levels of COP activity dealing with youth produced feelings of status challenge. A possible explanation is that police department subcultures that devalue working with youth may not have COP programs designed to engage in this activity at a significant level. Officers in departments that place greater value on working with youth would probably be less inclined to feel stigmatized when assigned to work with this population.

Focusing on the effects of status challenge, the study supported the hypothesis that status challenge would lead to high levels of agency penalty. The analysis revealed that officers who reported status challenges were more likely to experience higher levels of agency penalties in the form of lack of human resources and equipment, attitude, and isolation than officers who did not report status challenges. This finding supports the literature on stigmatization and dichotomization (Acker, 1992; Rosenblum and Travis, 1996). The *other* label appears to be accompanied by certain sanctions.

Conclusions

The main study finding was that most community-oriented policing officers *did not* tend to perceive their status as "real" officers to be challenged. However, a sizable minority were challenged and the study findings have real implications for successful implementation of COP programs. Therefore, I make the following recommendations:

1. Train administrative and rank-and-file police personnel on the importance of community policing.
2. Provide agency incentives and needed resources for COP programs and officers.

If administrative personnel do not support a COP program, an agency cannot expect the rank-and-file officers to support it. Training officers about positive police–citizen relations, increased legitimacy, and long-term crime prevention can increase the acceptance and successful implementation of community policing. Agencies should find ways to increase their available human and material resources, improve their attitudes and employee understanding about community policing, increase interdepartment interactions, and improve scheduling of promotions for COP officers to put them on equal footing with non-COP officers. If rank-and-file officers see that the administration takes community policing seriously, they will also treat it seriously (Crank and Langworthy, 1999; Maguire, 1997).

References

Acker, J. (1992) Gender institutions: From sex roles to gendered institutions, *Contemporary Sociology*, 21: 565–568.

Balkin, J. (1988) Why policemen don't like policewomen, *Journal of Police Science and Administration*, 16: 29–38.

Barlow, D. E. and Barlow, M. H. (2000) *Police in a multicultural society: An American story*, Prospect Heights, IL: Waveland Press.

Belknap, J. (2001) *The invisible woman: Gender, crime and justice* (2nd ed.), Belmont, CA: Wadsworth.

Bell, D. J. (1982) Policewomen: Myths and realities, *Journal of Police Science and Administration*, 10: 112–120.

Berger, P. L. and Luckmann, T. (1966) *The social construction of reality: A treatise in the sociology of knowledge*, New York: Anchor Books.

Bohm, R. (2002) Myths of crime, criminals, and crime control policy, in Braswell, M. C., McCarthy, B. R., and McCarthy, B. J. (Eds.) *Justice, crime and ethics* (4th ed., pp. 287–306), Cincinnati: Anderson.

Buzawa, E. S. and Buzawa, G. C. (1990) *Domestic violence: The criminal justice response*, Westwood, CT: Auburn House.

Chakravarty, S. (1998) Mainstreaming gender in the police: The Maharashtra experience, *Development in Practice*, 8: 430–438.

Charles, M. T. (1981) The performance and socialization of female recruits in the Michigan State Police Training Academy, *Journal of Police Science and Administration*, 9: 209–223.

Cole, G. F. and Smith, C. E. (1999) *Criminal justice in America* (2nd ed.), Belmont, CA: Wadsworth.

Crank, J. P. and Caldero, M. A. (2000) *Police ethics: The corruption of noble cause*, Cincinnati: Anderson.

Crank, J. P. and Langworthy, R. (1999) An institutional perspective of policing, in Gaines, L. K. and Cordner, G. W. (Eds.) *Policing perspectives: An anthology* (pp. 380–396), Los Angeles: Roxbury.

Drummond, D. S. (1976) *Police culture*, Thousand Oaks, CA: Sage.

Garcia, V. (1995) *The D.I.R.T. squad and the diaper dicks: Deviance within the police department*, Presented at Annual Meeting of American Sociological Association, Washington, D.C.

Garcia, V. (2003) Difference in the police department: Women, policing and doing gender, *Journal of Contemporary Criminal Justice*, 19: 330–344.

Greene, J. R. and Klockars, C. B. (1991) What police do, in Klockars, C.B. and Mastrofski, S. D. (Eds.), *Thinking about police* (2nd ed., p. 279), New York: McGraw-Hill.

Grennan, S. A. (2000) The past, present, and future of women in policing, in Muraskin, R. (Ed.), *Its a crime: Women and justice* (pp. 383–398), Upper Saddle River, NJ: Prentice-Hall.

Heidensohn, F. (1992) *Women in control? The role of women in law enforcement*, New York: Oxford University Press.

Heidensohn, F. and Brown, J. (2000) *Gender and policing: Comparative perspectives*, New York: St Martins Press.

Herbert, S. (1998) Police subculture reconsidered, *Criminology*, 36: 343–369.

Herbert, S. (2001) 'Hard charger' or 'station queen'? Policing and the masculinist state, *Gender, Place and Culture*, 8: 55–71.

Langston, E. and Richardson, D. (1995) *Community police officer survey: A street level view, Executive Summary and Methodology*, Washington, D.C.: U.S. Department of Justice.

Langston, E. and Richardson, D. (2000). *Street-level view of community policing in the United States* [computer file]. ICPSR version. Washington, D.C.: Center for Criminal Justice Studies.

Lurigio, A. J. and Skogan, W. G. (2000) Winning the hearts and minds of police officers: An assessment of staff perceptions of community policing in Chicago, in Glenor, R. W., Correia, M. E., and Peak, K. J. (Eds.), *Policing communities: Understanding crime and solving problems* (pp. 246–256), Los Angeles: Roxbury.

Maguire, E. R. (1997) Structural change in large municipal police organizations during the community policing era, *Justice Quarterly*, 14: 547–576.

Martin, S. E. and Jurik, N. C. (1996) *Doing justice, doing gender*, Thousand Oaks, CA: Sage.

Mastrofski, S. D., Worden, R. E., and Snipes, J. B. (1995) Law enforcement in a time of community policing, *Criminology*, 33: 539–564.

McElroy, J. C., Morrow, P. C., and Wardlow, T. R. (1999) A career stage analysis of police officer work commitment, *Journal of Criminal Justice*, 27: 507–517.
Miller, S. L. (1999) *Gender and community policing: Walking the talk*, Boston: Northeastern University Press.
Perez, D. W. (1997) *The paradoxes of police work: Walking the thin blue line*, Incline Village, NV: Copperhouse.
Reuss-Ianni, E. (1983) *Two cultures of policing*, New Brunswick, NJ: Transaction Books.
Rosenbaum, D. P. (2000) The changing role of the police: Assessing the current transition to community policing, in Glenor, R. W., Correia, M. E., and Peak, K. J. (Eds.), *Policing communities: Understanding crime and solving problems* (pp. 46–63), Los Angeles: Roxbury.
Rosenblum, K. E. and Travis, T. M. C. (1996) *The meaning of difference: American constructions of race, sex and gender, social class, and sexual orientation*, New York: McGraw-Hill.
Schulz, D. M. (1995) *From social worker to crimefighter: Women in United States Municipal Policing*, Westport, CT: Praeger.
Walker, S. and Katz, C. M. (2002) *The police in America: An introduction* (4th ed.), New York: McGraw-Hill.
Williams, B. N. (1998) *Citizen perspectives on community policing: A case study in Athens Georgia*, Albany: State University of New York Press.
Wilson, J. Q. and Kelling, G. L. (1982) The police and neighborhood safety: Broken windows, *Atlantic Monthly*, 249: 29–38.

Police Ethics and Corruption

II

Corruption and the Blue Code of Silence*

3

JEROME H. SKOLNICK

Contents

Like criminal law itself, the "blue code of silence" is a normative injunction but unwritten. Sometimes called a blue wall, curtain, or cocoon of silence, it is embedded in police subculture. At its best, the feelings of loyalty and brotherhood that sustain the code may facilitate policing and protect officers against genuine threats to safety and wellbeing (Kleinig, 2000: 7). However, the same code of loyalty and brotherhood can, as a code of silence, sustain an oppositional criminal subculture protecting the interests of police who violate the criminal law.

Such an unrecorded code has been noted as a feature of policing across continents, wherever scholars or commissions of inquiry have studied police corruption. For example, major investigations into police corruption in the United States—the Knapp (1973) and Mollen (1994) Commissions in New York and the Christopher Commission in Los Angeles (1991)—all cited the code as an obstruction to their inquiries into police corruption or excessive force.

Such a code was observed in Australia by the Fitzgerald inquiry in Queensland (1989) and by the Wood Royal Commission in New South Wales (1997; see also Chapter 4). It was discussed by Maurice Punch in his studies of scandals in New York, London, and Amsterdam (1985: 3–5). Since the code was uncovered by investigations of police corruption across three continents, I shall assume that it is a feature embedded in police culture generally and shall address questions relating to it:

What is the etiology of the code?
How is the code reinforced?

* This chapter first appeared in *Police Practice and Research*, 2002, 3(1): 7–19.

How does the code impede investigations?
Are there measures of accountability that can address the code and reduce corruption and brutality?

When considering the etiology of the code, it is logical to consider the prior issue of "causes" of police corruption. This constitutes a major research question. Nevertheless, both corruption and the code, I shall argue, are entwined in certain characteristics of police culture and organization that facilitate and sustain it. These features cannot, strictly speaking, be considered the "causes" of police corruption, partly because the concept of police corruption encompasses a number of crimes ranging from petty larceny to extortion to armed robbery and homicide, and partly because understanding why any crime occurs, whether committed by police or ordinary perpetrators, is a complex undertaking. With that caveat, I shall try to develop a theoretical argument, linking (1) the narrow world of values, understandings, and conceptions of loyalty in the culture of policing to (2) the code, as (3) a key facilitator of police corruption and violence.

What Is the Etiology of the Code?

To fulfill its mandate, police work is done in unpredictable and sometimes violent environments. Based on the potential danger of their workplaces coupled with their authority to use force to overcome resistance, police develop a close-knit subculture that has its own demands and expectations. Loyalty to fellow officers is a key feature of the culture of policing, regardless of whether criminality is involved. Kleinig (2000: 8), in his "ethical analysis" of the code, compares the culture of policing to norms found in ideals of friendship and family.

The notion of loyalty to fellow officers is first encountered by police officers at their academies. This sense of loyalty tends to be reinforced throughout their careers. This is not surprising. Norms of loyalty and mutual support are found in many occupational groups including doctors, lawyers, and office workers. However, the unique demands placed on police officers—for example, threats of danger and public scrutiny—generate a tightly woven environment conducive to the development of feelings of loyalty.

The refusal to report misconduct to proper authorities or falsely claim no knowledge of misconduct is a common manifestation of these sentiments. Another is providing false testimony—falsification—to cover up or support the misdeeds of fellow police officers (Mollen, 1994: 36–43). Since the code threatens the integrity of the justice system, it has been recognized as a serious problem in police departments across the United States. Officers who feel bound by it too easily lose sight of the damage the code can inflict on innocent third parties and on the overall integrity of the justice system.

Investigations into police corruption, lying, and brutality have uncovered striking examples of the code. Absent inquiry, the powerful mandate of silence usually lies dormant, almost like an incubating disease. In such situations, the code manifests itself as a refusal to offer information that might incriminate or embarrass a fellow officer. It may also be evident when police understand that they can count on police witnesses to misconduct to back up any story they tell irrespective of the truth of the story.

It would be impossible to summarize the large body of evidence and documentary support for such a code. Nevertheless, I can point to a number of representative instances of official investigations and scholarly reports that have commented on the blue code.

Commissions

New York City's Mayor David Dinkins established the Mollen Commission in 1992 to investigate the nature and extent of corruption in the New York City Police Department (NYPD), evaluate the department's procedures for preventing and detecting corruption, and recommend changes to improve the procedures. The commission described the loyalty code as "the unwritten rule that an officer never incriminates a fellow officer" (Mollen, 1994: 51).

Mollen argued that the code facilitated corruption, first "by setting a standard that nothing is more important than the unswerving loyalty of officers to one another," thus emboldening "corrupt cops and those susceptible to corruption"; and second, by thwarting "efforts to control corruption…by lead[ing] officers to protect or cover up for others' crimes—even crimes of which they heartily disapprove" (Mollen, 1994: 51, 52).

Two decades earlier, New York City's Knapp Commission was informed that "the tradition of the policeman's code of silence was so strong…that it was futile to expect…testimony [concerning corrupt activities] from any police officer, even if he himself were caught in a corrupt act and were offered immunity in exchange for his testimony" (Knapp, 1973: 47).

Los Angeles' Christopher Commission, formed after the incident involving the beating of Rodney King and headed by Warren Christopher (later Secretary of State in the Clinton administration), found the code of loyalty and silence to be a virtually impenetrable obstruction:

> Perhaps the greatest single barrier to the effective investigation and adjudication of complaints is the officers' unwritten "code of silence." While loyalty and support are salutary and even necessary qualities, they cannot justify the violation of an officer's public responsibility to ensure compliance with the law, including LAPD regulations. The code of silence influences the behavior of many officers in a variety of ways, but it consists of one simple rule: an officer does not provide adverse information against a fellow officer. (Christopher, 1991: 168)

> Under the code it is impermissible to criticize other police. Such criticism is viewed as particularly reprehensible if it is made to outsiders. Any criticism which does occur is kept under the control of those who have authority and influence within the Force. Any dissidents are able to be dealt with for a breach of the code, with the approval of other police. (Christopher, 1991: 202)

The blue code is not restricted to law enforcement in the United States; its existence has been documented in police departments in other westernized countries. For example, from the 1989 Fitzgerald inquiry in Queensland Australia:

> The unwritten police code is an integral element of police culture and has been a critical factor in the deterioration of the Police Force. It has allowed two main types of misconduct to flourish. A practical effect of the code is to reduce, if not eliminate, concern at possible apprehension and punishment as a deterrent to police misconduct. (Fitzgerald, 1989: 202)

Scholarly writings in law and social science have also identified a loyalty code that usually results in silence about police misconduct, but can also influence testimony. For example:

- The blue wall [or code] of loyalty and silence is "an unwritten code in many departments which prohibits disclosing perjury or other misconduct by fellow officers, or even testifying truthfully if the fact would implicate the conduct of a fellow officer" (Chin and Wells, 1998: 237).
- "The tacit norm is to never do something which might embarrass another officer. To draw critical attention to a colleague is strictly taboo in the police world" (van Maanen, 1978:126).
- "Police officers follow a strictly enforced custom of refusing to offer testimony that would adversely affect another officer" (Colbert, 1993: 550).
- William Smith describes a code of mutual protectiveness and intense loyalty as "the unwritten rule of police behavior that constrains an officer from informing on or testifying against another officer…animated by intense loyalty to the group, and mutual protectiveness against outsiders" (1973: 21).

CNN broadcast the beating of Rodney King by Los Angeles police around the world. CNN asked me to interpret the beating and the *Los Angeles Times* requested me to write a guest editorial. For both media, I pointed out that while most viewers were focused on and appalled by the beating—as I was—I was at least as attuned to the dozen Los Angeles police officers who could be seen watching the beating and doing nothing to end it. I thought that this televised event so well illustrated the power of ties of loyalty among the police:

> Street incidents generate and sustain the norms that police live by….The literature on the world of policing deals with the "Blue Code of Silence"—cops

> are not supposed to tell outsiders or investigators the truth about police corruption or brutality. Because so many other officers stood by and watched the beating of King, those who participated must have believed that they could count on their colleagues to lie in case of an investigation. This time, the police witnesses, knowing about the videotape, will probably not compound their offense by lying about what really happened. But can we believe that they would have told the truth without the tape? (Skolnick, 1991: 7)

Most recently, the code was implicated in a Los Angeles Police Department scandal that an investigator, Professor Erwin Chemerinsky of Southern California Law School, calls a story of evil and malevolence, not simply corruption and mediocrity. Chemerinsky's study (2000) concluded that the police department's deepest problem is an internal culture that not only gave rise to the scandal, but also tolerated it. A code about extraordinary police brutality and corruption was invoked for years. It came to light only when a convicted ex-officer, Rafael Perez, revealed that he and a former partner shot and paralyzed a gang member named Javier Francisco Ovando. They then framed him, sending him to prison on charges of attacking the police (Glover and Lait, 2000: A1). Ovando was released after serving 3 years of a 23-year sentence.

Perez admitted to having committed a number of crimes with other officers, including armed robberies and the theft of cocaine. He admitted to checking out six pounds of cocaine for a court appearance and not returning it to the evidence locker. Perez was part of an elite, almost self-governing anti-gang unit designated Community Resources Against Street Hoodlums (CRASH) that had a history of police brutality (Skolnick and Fyfe, 1993: 4–6). It was only after prosecutors threatened to indict his wife that Perez broke the code.

Perez reviewed over 1500 cases with investigators, who noted that 70 to 80% of his revelations were corroborated (Glover and Lait, 2000: A1). As of September 9, 2000, Perez' confessions led to the vacating of approximately 100 criminal convictions* (Shuster, 2000: A17). Five officers faced criminal charges

* For articles about police criminality, see Tina Daunt, "Council OKs Settlement in Rampart Case," *Los Angeles Times*, August 9, 2000, p. B1 (conviction for gun possession overturned because gun was allegedly planted by police); Scott Glover and Matt Lait, "Murder Case Derailed by Rampart Link," *Los Angeles Times*, August 10, 2000, p. A1 (key witness recants, saying Ramparts officers forced him to falsely identify murder suspect); Matt Lait and Scott Glover, "Case Overturned as Fired Officer's Role is Revealed," *Los Angeles Times*, August 9, 2000, p. A1 (drug sales conviction overturned); Edward Boyer, "Two More Convictions Overturned as Result of Rampart Fallout," Los Angeles Times, June 2, 2000, p. B3 (gun possession convictions achieved through police perjury); Hugo Martin, "Inmate Freed in Rampart Scandal Files Lawsuit," *Los Angeles Times*, June 7, 2000, p. B3 (framed with gun and cocaine for drug dealing).

and 70 others faced departmental discipline. Still more retired. At the time of writing, the investigations were ongoing, and these numbers were climbing.

How Is the Code Reinforced?

Those who read the book or saw the movie about Frank Serpico (the New York City officer who "blew the first whistle" leading to the Knapp Commission investigation of the NYPD) will recall that Serpico, an idealistic young cop, found an envelope in his locker. When he asked why, he was told that it was his share of collections from illegal gamblers. Serpico recognized that the purpose of the envelope was to implicate him in a corrupt practice, thus ensuring that he could be counted on to protect the corruption that flourished all around him. Serpico refused the envelope and was shunned by his fellow officers as a potential "rat."

The most recent disturbing illustration of the code occurred when officers of NYPD's 70th precinct did not protest when they saw a Haitian immigrant, Abner Louima, being marched around the station house with his pants around his ankles. Officer Justin Volpe proudly showed off the results of a sadistic anal assault. He waved a broken broomstick stained with blood and feces around for all his fellow officers to see, even bragging to Sergeant Kenneth Wernick that "I took a man down tonight." No officer came forward that night to report Volpe. Why should Volpe have believed that he could count on fellow officers to abandon their obligations to report crimes and apprehend perpetrators? A key reason was fear of retribution, as explained by Officer Bernard Cawley in his testimony before the 1994 Mollen Commission:

> Question: Were you ever afraid that one of your fellow officers would turn you in?
>
> Answer: Never
>
> Question: Why not?
>
> Answer: Because it was the Blue Wall of Silence. Cops don't tell on cops. And if they did tell on them, just say if a cop decided to tell on me, his career's ruined. He's going to be labelled as a rat. So if he's got fifteen more years to go on the job, he's going to be miserable because it follows you wherever you go. And he could be in a precinct he's going to have nobody to work with. And chances are if it comes down to it, they're going to let him get hurt. (Mollen, 1994: 53–54)

If loyalty is one reason for sustaining the code, and fear of retaliation a second, a third is that police, more than most workers, usually know about other officers' misconduct such as visiting a "beat wife" or prostitute, or "cooping" (sleeping on duty) in a movie theatre seat.

> As a rookie, Serpico was also introduced to the fine art of "cooping," a time-honored police practice that in other cities goes under such names as "huddling" and "going down." (Maas, 1973: 79)

No one wants to open a Pandora's box of snitching and counter-snitching. Some of the officers who saw Louima with his pants down may have administered "tune ups" to teach lessons of compliance. Volpe and three other officers assaulted Louima who, they believed wrongly, punched Officer Volpe in a fracas that erupted outside a Brooklyn nightclub, so at least three other officers were already complicitous with Volpe.

Another issue is what might be called the bad cop–good cop dilemma. Police are caught between the imperatives of the blue wall of silence and department rules compelling an officer who knows of police misconduct to notify internal affairs investigators immediately. If the officer promptly reports an incident, he is labeled a "rat" or a "cheese eater." If he fails to report misconduct, he may later have a hard time explaining why he failed to report promptly. Because of these pressures, police usually lapse into silence and talk about the misconduct of other cops only when pressured by internal affairs investigators or when threatened with prosecution.

How Does the Code Impede Investigations?

Let me offer another case from New York. I have been studying, through participant observation, the Official Corruption Unit (OCU) of Manhattan District Attorney Robert Morgenthau, an office that prosecutes police who are alleged to be corrupt* (Skolnick, 2000: 53). The OCU is one of several police overseers in Manhattan. The others are the Civilian Complaint Review Board (CCRB) and the U.S. Department of Justice (DOJ). The CCRB deals mostly with complaints about low-level excessive force (pushing, shoving), abuse of authority (orders to move on), and insults and racial slurs. The DOJ prosecutes high-profile civil rights cases.

The OCU is authorized to investigate the corruption of any public official, but concentrates mainly on police cases. It maintains a regular but sometimes rocky relationship with the Internal Affairs Bureau of the NYPD. William Burmeister, the head of the OCU until recently and a prosecutor for 10 years, sometimes felt that the Internal Affairs Bureau (IAB) moved too quickly to expose the names of officers under investigation and this put other cops on their guard.

* Some of this analysis originally appeared in my article "Code Blue" in *The American Prospect*, March, 2000.

However honest and diligent IAB investigators may be, their organizational imperatives differ from the OCU's. The NYPD wants to dispose of scandals and their related publicity as quickly as possible. The district attorney usually wants to see how far the corruption has spread, by turning crooked police into undercover investigators who wear "wires" to collect evidence that will hold up in a courtroom prosecution.

This situation creates a long run–short run dilemma. If prosecutors favor the long run, they allow the misconduct to continue in order to catch all the perpetrators, but the public will continue to be subjected to the crimes of crooked police. If prosecutors favor the short run by arresting and charging quickly, they may alert other crooked police to the investigation. To say that there are no easy answers merely reaffirms the nature of the dilemma.

Burmeister admits that when he took the job of heading the OCU in 1990 he did not fully comprehend how pervasive corruption, brutality, perjury, and the code were in the NYPD. His eyes were opened by the practices he found investigating Manhattan's 30th precinct, located in Washington Heights, a heavy drug-dealing neighborhood. Burmeister says that the investigation—which is featured in the Mollen Commission report—was started through a conversation with a defense attorney who acknowledged that his client was guilty. The attorney told Burmeister that his client actually had three kilos of cocaine in his possession, not two, as the police charged, and claimed the police stole one of the kilos. After investigation, the prosecutor found that they had stolen the kilo.

OCU investigations are often secret and employ tactics such as stings, wires, and wiretaps familiar to organized crime investigations. Burmeister showed me a sting videotape in which a sergeant and an officer stopped a Spanish-speaking driver in Washington Heights. The driver was actually an undercover agent working for the OCU, not the NYPD (New York cops are told what the predominant dress color of the day is for NYPD undercover agents, so that police can identify them). The videotape shows a brown paper bag containing several thousand dollars in marked money on the front seat. One of the officers discovers it. He is seen on videotape stuffing some of the money into his pants. This officer was apprehended and agreed to wear a listening device while investigating other officers suspected of corruption. This is dangerous work, but it is critical in New York, where the testimony of an accomplice is not admissible as evidence in a court trial without corroboration.

Most victims of police corruption and brutality are criminals, usually drug dealers, prostitutes, or gang members like Ovando in Los Angeles. It is difficult to convict police who are accused of assaulting persons of low social character or status. Police rarely take the witness stand to testify because no defendant can be required to testify against himself under the U.S. Constitution and thus cannot be cross examined.

It is especially difficult to convict police who are not corrupt but are overzealous in using force. In the Rodney King case, the officers accused of criminal assault were acquitted after persuading a suburban, nearly all white, Simi Valley, California jury that despite the evidence of the videotape, 57 powerful strokes were necessary to apprehend King. The police were convicted of violating Rodney King's civil rights only after they were retried in a federal court in Los Angeles and Rodney King was permitted to testify. In the Louima case, two of the officers charged with beating Louima in a patrol car were acquitted by a jury in a federal court in Brooklyn. Judges and juries are reluctant to send otherwise unblemished police to prison for inflicting punishment on seeming "low lifes."

Whatever the specific charges in police brutality cases—aggravated assault, violation of civil rights—they are usually based on a clear legal line that police are never permitted to cross. No matter how heinous a crime, once police have subdued a suspected criminal and have him safely in custody, they are not allowed to use retributive force. The classic defense to accusations of police brutality is, of course, that the suspect resisted arrest. Indeed, police executives sometimes view resisting-arrest cases as the inclinations of officers to administer vigilante justice.

I followed such a case the OCU prosecuted against officers of the Manhattan North Drug Initiative, a highly touted NYPD effort to rid northern Manhattan of drug trafficking. The raid occurred less than a month after officers from Brooklyn's 70th precinct were arrested and charged with beating, sodomizing, and torturing Abner Louima. The case received little attention in the press, possibly because the assault was not sadistic and the victims had been in the course of committing a crime. The facts are as follows.

Jose Polanco, a drug dealer, sold illegal drugs from an apartment on West 172nd Street. Five officers, two of whom were supervisors, obtained a warrant to search the apartment. One of the officers, a sergeant, testified that it took several minutes to gain entry into the barricaded apartment. Polanco, who was given immunity to testify, said he flushed all his drugs down the toilet when he heard the police pounding on the door. By doing so, he undercut criminal cases that might be made against him or the buyer. Neither he nor the buyer had drugs in their possession and the police did not witness a sale. After searching the well-vacuumed apartment, the only drug the police could find was a minute amount of cocaine residue on the tip of a screwdriver. (Professional drug sellers are scrupulous in maintaining control of drugs they possess for sale.)

The dealer testified that he and the buyer, a middle-aged Dominican man named Norman Batista who moved to New York 19 years earlier and worked for 16 years as a busboy, were ordered to their knees and searched. The dealer then testified that the police began to beat them, told them to shut up and take the beatings, and told them not to scream. Polanco, a sturdy-looking, experienced drug seller, testified that he complied. He also testified that he could hear loud cries of pain as Batista was further beaten. Polanco and Batista adopted fetal positions to protect themselves so they were unable to state which officers administered the blows and kicks.

After being taken into custody, Batista experienced severe pain for several hours and the police offered to release him from custody. Since he was in severe pain, he refused their offer and eventually was transported to an emergency room at New York Metropolitan Hospital—not to the nearer Columbia–Presbyterian Hospital. An emergency room physician found that Batista sustained seven broken ribs (four on one side and three on the other) from powerful kicks administered while he was lying on the floor. Batista suffered additional injuries to his chest, cheek, testicles, and knees and spent six days in the hospital.

The doctor was shocked by Batista's condition and disbelieved the police claim that Batista resisted arrest. No charges were filed. The doctor alerted an assistant district attorney in the Manhattan office. The case was assigned to Burmeister's OCU because of the unit's experience in prosecuting police. It was tried by Diane Kiesel, later appointed a trial judge in New York City. Two officers, Detective Olga Vazquez and Officer Richard Thompson, who had been on the force for seven and five years, respectively, were charged with first-degree assault (that carries a potential sentence of 25 years).

Vasquez and Thompson were tried together and waived a jury trial (as defendants are permitted to do in New York State, but not in a federal court without the consent of the prosecutor). Police often waive jury trials in New York City where jurors are likely to be people of color and where judges are thought to be sympathetic to police officers. Moreover, their attorneys argued, it makes no sense to send good police officers to prison when one alleged victim is a person who buys drugs. Since no police came forward to testify, Kiesel argued to the judge that Batista had, without doubt, been criminally assaulted by police. Even if the prosecution could not prove that the defendants administered the beating, they had a duty as police to prevent the crime. Since they did not do so, the prosecution argued, they were accessories.

Judge Ronald Zweibel acquitted the police defendants, even though one or more of the officers must have inflicted the injuries and one or more of them must have seen the beating take place. On the day of the acquittal, approximately 75 off-duty police officers jammed the courtroom. They applauded loudly, and embraced each other with evident joy when the acquittal was announced.

How should we think about the police brutality in the Batista case? In the Louima case, Mayor Giuliani, who usually supported the police, called Officer Volpe's anal assault on Abner Louima "sick" and "perverse." The force used on Batista, not so overtly sadistic, allowed for the possibility of different moral interpretations. Indeed, what emerged was something like a culture war with the police and the judge on one side and the emergency room doctor and the prosecutors on the other. The police who went to court to hear the verdict clearly supported their fellow officers. In their view, a drug dealer and a buyer frustrated the good cops by disposing of the drugs. Since the drug seller and buyer could not be punished legally, the police administered well-deserved beatings. In this case, the officers clearly used excessive force but were not corrupt. Unlike the unusual case of Rodney King, whose beating was videotaped by a civilian onlooker, the beating of Jose Polanco could not be proven. The only witnesses were police, and they held fast to the code, and like the officers who attended the trial, a New York judge was disinclined to imprison so-called good cops for the offense. By contrast, the emergency room physician was appalled by the brutality of the beating and referred the case to prosecutors. In the minds of these experienced prosecutors, the beating crossed way over the line of acceptable policing. The beatings constituted criminal assaults even if a victim was buying drugs.

The Batista case shows how difficult it can be to prosecute police when they administer street justice without personal gain—traditional corruption—and invoke the code. The Policeman's Benevolent Association (PBA) union provides legal counsel for officers who routinely invoke a rule (gained through negotiations with the powerful union) allowing police to make no statements to Internal Affairs investigators for 48 hours. (In the Louima case, the accused officers' legal strategies were formed by PBA lawyers who usually invoke their constitutional rights to remain silent. "Prosecuting police with their stable of PBA lawyers is like prosecuting the Mafia with their lawyers," Burmeister told me.)

Teaching a lesson of compliance with a "tune up" is most likely to occur in specialized units like the Manhattan North Drug Enforcement Initiative. These so-called elite units, like the Los Angeles CRASH unit, often compete to determine which is the toughest or the most productive in crime reduction. They are reminiscent of the elite detectives memorialized in the book and film titled *Prince of the City* and glorified in *The French Connection*, and saw themselves as hunters to whom the ordinary rules of policing did not apply.

Like them, the drug enforcers accused in the Batista case counted on the code to frustrate the efforts of even the best prosecutors. However, unlike the accusations against the *Prince of the City* police, and the "Dirty Thirty" of the Mollen Commission report, these accusations were about a vicious, deliberate beating of a drug buyer, not about corruption. Such enforcement can be rationalized as morally acceptable zealousness—as viewed by the police who applauded the verdict in the courtroom and the judge who announced it.

Are There Measures of Accountability That Can Address the Code and Reduce Corruption and Brutality?

Police brutality and corruption may be reined in by positive police leadership, especially in relation to the code. During the 1990s Chief Richard Pennington* took over the New Orleans Police Department, that then had the unfortunate reputation as being the most brutal and corrupt in the United States and turned it into a respectable department (Skolnick and Fyfe, 1993: 33–35, 214–215). The situation was so bad, he told me in a conversation (May, 1999), that his Internal Affairs investigators had not made a case in five years. He fired them all and replaced them with investigators he felt he could trust. He brought in outside consultants—including the late Jack Maple, who was instrumental in shaping the computerized statistical review of crime data (Compstat) in New York City and helped to reduce crime significantly in New Orleans (Perlstein, 2001: 1).

Police corruption does not take place in a vacuum. Whatever the mandates of police culture, they are undermined or reinforced by police managers and supervisors who will not tolerate corruption and have not previously been associated with it. Bringing in a new chief may be a necessary measure to eliminate corruption and the code that facilitates, it but that measure may be insufficient.

Several widely publicized cases in New York City, especially the sadistic anal assault of Abner Louima, and also the shootings of Amadou Diallo and Patrick Dorismond and the protest demonstrations and civil rights lawsuits that followed, have all led to a reconsideration of NYPD practices, culture, and policies. The Louima case was especially significant. Even the most reflexively pro-police supporters could not countenance the vicious violation, nor could anyone defend the actions of the 70th Precinct officers who, in classic code conformity, hung together, saw nothing, and heard nothing. Eventually, prosecutors in the U.S. Attorney's office in a series of three trials convicted the four officers who beat Louima. Justin Volpe was sentenced to 30 years in a federal prison; Charles Schwarz, 15 years; and Thomas Weise and Thomas Bruder, 5 years each.

One of the more unusual features of the case was a civil rights suit filed by Louima's lawyers (Peter Nuefeld, Barry Scheck, Johnnie Cochran, and Sanford Rubenstein) against the City of New York and the Policeman's Benevolent Association labor union. The lawsuit charged that union delegates were aware that incriminating statements were made by the police accused of beating and sodomizing Louima, but failed to report them to investigators. Louima's lawyers targeted a provision of the contract between the city and the union prohibiting investigators from questioning police suspected of serious misconduct or committing crimes for 48 hours.

Under the terms of the settlement (on July 12, 2001) the city agreed to the largest amount ever paid to settle a police brutality case, $7.125 million. The PBA agreed to pay Louima an additional $1.625 million, to my knowledge the

* Now chief of the Atlanta Police Department.

first time a police union anywhere in the United States paid a brutality claim. Even more significantly, Louima and his lawyers insisted upon policy and practice changes in how NYPD addresses police brutality. The city agreed to have a civilian panel instead of the department prosecute police brutality cases and also agreed to revise and strengthen police training on the use of force.

Among the changes, perhaps the most significant was the city's agreement to phase out the so-called 48-hour rule when union contracts expire. Under the rule, an officer who shot a robber leaving a bank could not be required by his supervisors to answer questions about what led to the shooting. The officer was first to speak with a union representative and a lawyer employed by the union. Not until 48 hours had expired could a police official discuss the events with a supervisor.

Certain high-ranking police officials did not approve of the 48-hour rule, especially when administrative sanctions were contemplated. "It was an affront that no one could talk to a city employee like that," former NYPD Commissioner Raymond Kelly told *The New York Times* reporters, Alan Feuer and Jim Dwyer (2001: 1). Louima's lawyers believed that the 48-hour rule permitted the PBA to conspire with officers to cover up the truth in cases of police brutality. This became clear in the second trial when Michael Immit, a union trustee, testified that he attended roll calls at the 70th Precinct station house and, in effect, reminded the officers of the code, by saying, "Sit tight. Don't talk about it. Don't talk to anyone unless something official comes down" (Feuer and Dwyer, 2001: 1).

It is worth recalling that the public and police officials focused on the anal attack in the bathroom in the Louima case. In fact, the four officers who arrested Louima drove him to a deserted lot and beat him—a practice known as a "tune up" in police jargon. Had the tune up been the only punishment Louima suffered, the loyalty code would almost certainly have sustained the officers when they filed charges of resisting arrest.

Louima's lawyers saw such instances as a pattern in which the PBA conspired with officers to cover up the truth. Even more broadly, they saw the rule as sustaining an environment in which officers could count on their fellows to remain silent and actively defend them even when they deliberately committed acts of brutality. Feuer and Dwyer (2001: 1) stated that, "Louima's success in suing the police union opens up a new legal front for holding police officers accountable."

In Los Angeles, a special anti-gang unit is at the center of a scandal that targeted the Ramparts section that includes some of the city's most violent and impoverished neighborhoods (Helfand et al., 2000: A1). The gang focus of the unit and the area where it operated meant that many of police victims were young, male, and non-white. Many of the victims sued the city. A *Los Angeles Times* article reported that the city council approved spending more than $1.2 million to settle four cases stemming from the scandal, and estimated that the city's liability could exceed $125 million. So many federal civil rights suits were filed that the logistics became unmanageable; the attorneys had to report to different judges almost simultaneously. As a result, all pretrial motions were assigned to the same judge (Rosenzweig, 2000: 3).

In one suit, a federal judge ruled that the LAPD could be sued under the Racketeering Influenced Corrupt Organization (RICO) statute enacted to prosecute organized crime (Weinstein, 2000: A1). At the time, the RICO ruling was controversial and may not have withstood appeal; nonetheless, allowing a federal judge to rule—for the first time—that a major police department might be considered a criminal gang is an astonishing development. At the time of writing, the U.S. Department of Justice placed the department under federal supervision, something that even the Rodney King incident, although broadcast around the world, could not accomplish. The beating of Rodney King led to the passage of a federal civil rights statute that gives the Department of Justice the authority to monitor police departments when it proves and a court finds a "pattern and practice" of civil rights violations.

In response, city and federal officials, in concert with a federal judge, selected a monitor, Michael Cherkasky, after a national search (Daunt, 2001: 1). Cherkasky is a former New York City prosecutor who established a reputation as a tenacious and successful organized crime fighter. He heads Kroll Associates, a firm of investigators best known for searching for assets hidden by such figures as former Haitian dictator Jean-Claude Duvalier, Ferdinand and Imelda Marcos, and Saddam Hussein. Cherkasky and his associates, one of whom, William Bratton, was a former New York City police commissioner, were charged with overseeing the implementation of the LAPD consent decree over a period of five years.

There are no easy solutions to combating patterns of police corruption and brutality in departments that seem resistant to positive change. "Police corruption is the single most difficult investigative thing I've done," Cherkasky told Los Angeles Times writer Tina Daunt. "You are dealing with people who know the system—and how to get around it" (Daunt, 2001: 1). Citing the code of police silence as an especially powerful barrier to ferreting out truth, Cherskasky concluded, "While the world of organized crime can be difficult to penetrate, the walls of silence can be even harder to penetrate in police departments" (Daunt, 2001: 1). Nevertheless, as citizens, city managers, courts, and police executives are increasingly coming to understand, they can have little confidence in the integrity of policing without efforts to penetrate the walls of silence and without investigations by independent monitors if that proves necessary.

References

Chemerinsky, E. (2000) *An independent analysis of the Los Angeles Police Department's Board of Inquiry report on the Rampart scandal*, September 11. (Revised edition available at http://llr.lls.edu/volumes/v34-issue2/chemerinsky.pdf)

Chin, G. J. and Wells, S. C. (1998) The blue wall of silence as evidence of bias and motive to lie: A new approach to police perjury, *University of Pittsburgh Law Review*, 59(2): 237.

Christopher, W. (1991) *Report of the Independent Commission on the Los Angeles Police Department*, City of Los Angeles.

Colbert, D. L. (1993) Bifurcation of civil rights defendants: Undermining *Monell* in police brutality cases, *Hastings Law Journal*, 44: 499.

Daunt, T. (2001) N.Y. mob prosecutor to take on the LAPD, *Los Angeles Times*, July 24.

Feuer, A. and Dwyer, J. (2001) City settles suit in Louima torture, *The New York Times*, Section A, July 13.

Fitzgerald, G. (1989) *Report of a Commission of Inquiry Pursuant to Orders in Council*, Government Printer: Queensland, Australia.

Flynn, K. (2001) Louima case one factor in changes for the police, *The New York Times*, Section B, Metro, 1, July 14.

Glover, S. and Lait, M. (2000) Rampart officer is arrested at gunpoint, *Los Angeles Times*, A1, July 29.

Glover, S. and Lait, M. (2000) D.A. set to charge officer in shooting, *Los Angeles Times*, A1, July 24.

Glover, S. and Lait, M. (2000) Most of Perez allegations are confirmed, panel told, *Los Angeles Times*, A1, June 20.

Helfand, D., Hall, C., and Riccardi, N. (2000) Campaign 2000: LAPD, activists choreograph a confrontation, *Los Angeles Times*, A1, August 17.

Kleinig, J. (2000) *The blue wall of silence: An ethical analysis*, New York: Center for Research in Crime and Justice, New York University School of Law.

Knapp, W. (1973) *Report of the Commission to Investigate Allegations of Police Corruption and the city's anti-corruption procedures*, New York: George Braziller.

Maas, P. (1973) *Serpico*, New York: Harper Paperbacks.

Mollen, M. (1994) *Report of the Commission to Investigate Allegations of Police Corruption and the anti-corruption procedures of the police department*, New York: City of New York.

Perlstein, M. (2001) Obituary: Jack Maple, advisor in New Orleans crime fight, *The Times-Picayune*, New Orleans, M1, August 7.

Punch, M. (1985) *Conduct unbecoming: The social construction of police deviance and control*, London: Tavistock Publications.

Rosenzweig, D. (2000) Court reassigns pretrial proceedings in Rampart cases to one judge, *Los Angeles Times*, B5, September 7.

Rosenzweig, D. (2000) City agrees to settle another Rampart case, *Los Angeles Times*, B4, September 7.

Rosenzweig, D. (2000) L.A. seeks to appeal racketeering ruling, *Los Angeles Times*, H3, August 31.

Shuster, B. (2000) LAPD culture is prime reform barrier, study says, *Los Angeles Times*, A17, September 9.

Skolnick, J. H. (2000) Code blue, *The American Prospect*, 11(10): 49.

Skolnick, J. H. (1991) It's not just a few rotten apples, *Los Angeles Times*, B7, March 7.

Skolnick, J. H. and Fyfe, J. J. (1993) *Above the law: Police and the excessive use of force*, New York: Free Press.

Smith, W. H. T. (1973) Deceit in uniform, *Police Chief*, XL: 9.

van Maanen, J. (1978) Kinsmen in response: Occupational perspectives of patrolmen, in Manning, P. K. and van Maanen, J. (Eds.) *Policing: A view from the street*, Santa Monica, CA: Goodyear.

Weinstein, H. (2000) Judge OKs use of racketeering law in Rampart suits, *Los Angeles Times*, A1, August 29.

Wood Royal Commission (1997) *Report of the Royal Commission into the New South Wales Police Service*, Sydney: State of New South Wales, pp. 32–33.

Yagman, S. (2000) RICO will probe who's the real gang, *Los Angeles Times*, B9, August 30.

Survey of Innovations in Development and Maintenance of Ethical Standards by Australian Police Departments*

4

TIM PRENZLER
CAROL RONKEN

Contents

In Australia, interest in anti-corruption measures has been driven by the same problems of police malpractice faced by many other countries. The seriousness of recent exposés and allegations of corruption, most notably in Queensland (Fitzgerald, 1989; CJC, 1999), New South Wales (Wood, 1997), Victoria (Ombudsman of Victoria, 1998), and Western Australia (McDonnell, 2000), has forced police departments and governments out of their traditionally passive approaches to police integrity. Corruption problems in Australian policing have attracted international attention, with the reform agendas providing valuable lessons (Newburn, 1997).

A key development has been the creation of watchdog agencies that engage primarily in audits of police investigations of complaints (Lewis and Prenzler, 1999). Hence, self-regulation remains the preferred approach. Despite the scale of the reform agenda in Australian policing, no comprehensive study has investigated the initiatives introduced over the past decade. The aim of this chapter is to provide a national review and assessment of police integrity strategies within the framework of a set of models.

* This chapter first appeared in *Police Practice and Research*, 2003, 4(2): 149–161.

Models of Internal Police Integrity Development

This section briefly reviews three models of police integrity development: minimalist, intermediate, and advanced. As indicated, the objects of study are initiatives in self-regulation by police departments (Marx, 1992: 152). This interest should not be taken as a rejection of external forms of control of police conduct. Civilian oversight has been an area of recent major innovation, and one where relations between oversight bodies and police internal affairs take different forms in different jurisdictions (Prenzler, 2000).

The presence of an external body—at the very least designed to review complaints, investigations, and disciplinary actions—appears essential in any modern democratic accountability system (Goldsmith, 1991). At the same time, while highly controlling forms of external oversight are conceivable, the universal policy preference is for police management to assume prime responsibility for ethical conduct as a corollary of its responsibility for operational matters (Bayley, 1995).

The models of internal integrity development described below are designed to function in the usual way that scientific models do; that is, they are abstractions from the data to assist in analysis and policy development. However, the models are not mutually exclusive. A police department at any given time may display elements of all three. Nonetheless, departments may find the models useful in evaluating their initiatives evaluated within the general frameworks discussed below.

Minimalist Model

For most of their existence, modern police agencies have operated under a simple minimalist model of accountability. The model developed separately with various permutations in Europe, the United States, and emergent colonial nations such as Australia in the late 18th and early 19th centuries. It is most widely associated with the introduction of the "New Police" in London in 1829. Concerns about political interference meant that the idea of the separation of powers, previously focused on the courts, was extended to police operational management. In terms of constabulary independence, the principle of separation of powers enshrined the necessity for police to operate at arm's length from elected officials. It was encapsulated by Lord Denning, an English judge (1968), who said that police "are answerable to the law and to the law alone."* This is generally considered an exaggeration, but in practice police commissioners and chiefs have enjoyed far more autonomy than other governmental department heads (Bryett et al., 1997).

* *R v. Commissioner of Police of the Metropolis,* ex parte Blackburn [1968] 2 Queen's Bench 118.

In terms of control of conduct, this traditional system gave primary responsibility to police disciplinary command. Interventions were conducted at varying levels in the hierarchy, depending on the gravity of allegations. Commissioners held wide discretion on final decisions. Inspectorates responsible for general audit functions often had disciplinary responsibilities. Elected officials provided some external scrutiny and democratic accountability through various means such as questions in Parliament. The elected representative assigned the police portfolio could lose his position in the event of a serious corruption scandal. Politicians could also resort to the establishment of independent commissions of inquiry if they were dissatisfied with the treatment of allegations against police. However, the main source of standing external control was provided by the courts via occasional civil or criminal cases against police, but more routinely through the examination of police evidence in criminal prosecutions and the application of the "exclusionary rule" when police evidence was obtained illegally (Sarre, 1989). The main elements of this model are

1. Line management control for complaints investigations and discipline
2. Judicial scrutiny of police conduct in the courts and use of the exclusionary rule
3. Detached political oversight with resort to independent inquiries as a last resort

It is now apparent that this minimalist model is entirely inadequate to detect and prevent police misconduct in any systematic and reliable fashion. The result of this inadequate accountability is a long history of scandal and mistrust of police in many countries. The system was not without a "hit rate" of sorts. For example, historical research in Australia has shown fairly high levels of dismissals of police through internal processes. At the same time, however, such actions have not uncovered the true levels of both opportunistic and organized police corruption (Finnane, 1999).

As demonstrated by Jerome H. Skolnick in Chapter 3, police officers display common group behavior in protecting their own and covering misconduct (Scarman, 1986; Fitzgerald, 1989). Additionally, the fact that only a small amount of police activity leads to trials means that the bulk of police work falls outside routine scrutiny in the courtroom (Sarre, 1989). Police can also become skilled in deceiving judges and juries, whether in disguising the fabrication of evidence in cases they are prosecuting or when they are prosecuted. Police solidarity can prevent disclosure even during probing judicial inquiries such as inquests and conventional types of corruption inquiries (Freckelton, 2000). The majority of judicial inquiries, until recent times, were severely constrained and tended merely to perpetuate suspicions about police behavior (Sherman, 1978; Wood, 1997). Similarly, victims of police abuses seeking redress in the civil courts are easily frustrated and deterred by evidentiary standards and legal technicalities (Freckelton, 2000). Although conventional judicial processes have at times assisted in exposing misconduct, they have failed to address the less blatant forms of individual malfeasance or penetrate the more organized and secretive forms (Goode, 1991; Goldsmith, 2000).

Intermediate Model

Most major inquiries into police in the past three decades emphasized both the weakness of traditional internally based approaches to corruption prevention and the problem of the structural exposure of policing to misconduct (Prenzler, 2000). The law enforcement and order maintenance functions of police place them under pressures to accept bribes for ignoring illegal behavior and also expose them to provocations and temptations to dispense summary retribution or obtain compliance through verbal and physical abuse (Newburn, 1997). Consequently, stakeholders and police administrators must accept that anti-corruption measures must be much more aggressive than in the past. A key element of this progressive approach has been the creation of internal affairs departments solely dedicated to the investigation of complaints and other intelligence about corruption. The advantage of a specialist unit is that it cannot be distracted by other tasks. It allows for the development of specialized skills and knowledge about corruption, and for the selection of committed investigators (Knapp, 1972).

The intermediate model also places considerable stress on stricter recruitment processes. Where the minimalist model relied on criminal history checks and personal references, more developed recruitment practices have drawn on personality tests and enhanced background checks. Training procedures increasingly emphasize ethics and instruction on more comprehensive codes of conduct (Kleinig, 1996). Training curricula were enlarged to include the social sciences in attempting to develop more culturally sensitive police with greater senses of the democratic context of their functions. Increasingly, this more sophisticated approach included the creation of independent civilian review bodies that typically audit police investigations and disciplinary decisions, with varying scope to direct further inquiries and appeal decisions (Goldsmith, 1991). The main elements of this model (inclusive of the minimalist model) are

1. A dedicated internal affairs department
2. An integrity focus in recruitment and training
3. Enlarged codes of conduct to guide discretionary decision making
4. External review (not part of focus of current study)

The intermediate model marks a decisive step forward in accepting the view that a strong institutional commitment was needed to detect and deter misconduct. Nonetheless, the approach remains primarily passive. It relies on traditional investigative techniques and on information from police and citizen informants. Not only is it difficult to collect objective evidence to verify complainants' allegations, but a good deal of corruption is consensual and it is unlikely that citizen participants will come forward unless coerced or induced. The model also retains a high element of trust in the capacity of the recruitment unit to weed out undesirables and relies on officer compliance with rules and codes of conduct on the job with limited supervision (Shapiro, 1987). Civilian overview is frequently considered weak. Agencies frequently lack investigative powers and the resources and authority to direct police (Kappeler, Sluder and Alpert, 1994).

Advanced Model

Policy makers and police managers are becoming increasingly aware of the limitations of the intermediate model. While it serves as a partial deterrent against misconduct and is useful for identifying and removing the more blatant and organized forms of abuse, it lacks a vital proactive capacity to prevent opportunistic corruption and penetrate secretive forms of corruption (CJC, 1999). An important aspect of this perspective is the view that police misconduct can take highly diverse and discrete forms. For example, one area of a police department may be free of problems with drugs or alcohol abuse but have a problem with abuse of strip searching. Another section may be free of graft and have a major problem with sexual harassment against police employees or the public. Victims of these abuses are unlikely to come forward in sufficient numbers to make an impact. Consequently, systems are required to identify and preempt the development of particular problems.

One of the consequences of this consciousness about corruption hazards is the enlargement of the powers of watchdog bodies to circumvent police solidarity through independent investigation and adjudication, often without the requirement of an initial complaint. The Police Complaints Authority in England and Wales (now the Independent Police Complaints Commission), and the New South Wales Police Integrity Commission, are examples of these more powerful bodies. However, these watchdogs do not abrogate police management responsibility. The basic principle remains that police are expected to take prime responsibility for misconduct prevention. The outcomes can then be tested by the oversight body (Bayley, 1995).

Many advanced corruption prevention strategies can be initiated by police, the watchdog body, or both, independently or through cooperative arrangements. These measures also do not serve to replace those in the minimalist and intermediate stages, but are inclusive of them. Many of the measures are only new in certain jurisdictions, having been considered or tried at different times since the early 1970s. Additionally, the evidence does not clearly indicate that all these measures work (Newburn, 1997). Nonetheless, some strategies such as integrated ethics training are essential elements of *pro forma* accountability mechanisms of communication and formal reinforcement of organizational standards. Some strategies—random integrity testing, spying, and psychological testing—are highly controversial, are not endorsed here, and are included for consideration only. However, the expectation must be that most strategies are put in place to create and maintain ethical police departments. In summary, the advanced model consists of the following broad approaches:

1. Proactive steps to misconduct detection and prevention
2. A diverse range of integrated strategies to layer and cross-reference prevention and detection of different types of misconduct
3. Use of advanced technology and covert methods of investigation
4. Monitoring of attitudes and behavior
5. Systematic attention to ethics and personal conduct in recruitment, training, deployment, and promotion
6. External review with significant independence for investigations and adjudication (not part of focus of current study)

The following briefly sets out the main strategies, drawn from a wide range of sources, that may be employed in an advanced model:

Overt use of recording devices can be used in areas at risk for misconduct such as suspect interviews and in detention facilities (CJC, 1997). Police use of small recording devices during routine police–citizen encounters can also assist to protect police from false complaints.

Covert high technology surveillance can overcome problems of lack of witnesses or lack of supervision capacity by secretly recording conversations and actions that may involve misconduct (Marx, 1992).

Integrity testing entails simulated corruption opportunities to monitor officers' compliance with the law and codes of conduct. Targeted testing is directed at individual officers or groups in cases where investigations fail to allay suspicions. Random integrity testing is highly controversial and designed to provide more comprehensive and objective sources of detection and prevention through the random assignment of monitored misconduct opportunities (Henry, 1990; KPMG, 1996).

Drug and alcohol testing was introduced in response to inquiry findings about police use of illicit drugs and drinking on duty (e.g., in New South Wales, Australia; see Wood, 1997).

Internal informants report behavior and information considered privy within informal police networks. Advertising the presence of these "spies" can aid deterrence (Henry, 1990).

Complaints profiling of individual officers and organizational units allows for interventions such as retraining, counseling, and management changes (Ede et al., 2002).

Supervisor accountability involves reviews of line managers' performance that include assessments of the levels of behavior problems occurring under their commands, with results clearly linked to promotion or continuation of command (Knapp, 1972; Mollen, 1994).

Integrity reviews can be used for all progression decisions. Recruitment processes may include psychological and ethics tests as well as independent referee reports. As personnel move through training and are deployed and promoted, the diversity of integrity assessments can be expanded to include integrity test results and complaint profiles (Newburn, 1997).

Mandatory reporting of observed, suspected, or rumored misconduct is designed to challenge the code of silence and is enforceable if unreported misconduct comes to light (Fitzgerald, 1989).

Witness protection includes provision of safe havens along with penalties for persecuting informants (Fitzgerald, 1998).

Compulsory rotation in corruption-prone sections is designed to prevent officers from exploiting corruption opportunities (by developing bonds with organized crime figures or establishing corruption networks) over the long term (Sherman, 1978).

Asset and financial reviews, targeted or random, may provide evidence of officers who live beyond their means or are at risk of succumbing to corruption opportunities (Palmer, 1992).

Surveys of police can be used to anonymously gauge officers' perceptions of levels and types of misconduct. Ethics surveys can identify predisposing attitudes toward misconduct (CJC, 1997).

Public surveys reveal perceptions of police conduct. Surveys and interviews with subgroups having direct contact with police, such as arrestees, can also assess specific indicators of police behavior (CJC, 1997).

Personnel diversification is aimed at breaking down the culture of solidarity through civilianization and recruitment of people from diverse ethnic backgrounds and older, more educated, people (Fitzgerald, 1989). Recruitment of women is especially conducive to breaking down the macho culture and reducing police–citizen conflict.

Compulsory integrated ethics training reinforces messages about organizational commitment to integrity throughout an officer's career and through the various areas of specialization. Ethics training should also help clarify expectations and assist in managing ethical dilemmas (such as how to reject gratuities without causing offence) (Kleinig, 1996).

Inquisitorial methods and a civil standard of proof have been adopted in police disciplinary hearings, judicial inquiries, and external tribunal hearings in response to failed prosecutions of police in criminal courts in which a higher standard of proof applies. The emphasis should be on fact finding and removal of incorrigible officers rather than criminal convictions and penalties. A fair appeals system is needed to balance the surrender of the right to silence (Prenzler, 2000).

Complaint resolution includes forms of mediation and communication or apology with complainants (CJC, 1997). Resolution is designed to balance the need to avoid covering up misconduct with the need to respond efficiently to the large numbers of complaints that hold little hard evidence of misbehavior. Complaint resolution can function diagnostically as a misconduct strategy when integrated with complaints profiling.

Monitoring and regulation of police procedures in areas such as informant relations and securing of drug exhibits can clarify processes and reduce opportunities for corruption (Wood, 1997; Dixon, 1999).

Decriminalizing vice is not strictly an internal initiative but police should lobby to reduce their involvement in areas of traditional market-driven corruption such as prostitution and illicit drugs (Sherman, 1978).

Risk analysis involves the use of complaints and other intelligence data to identify areas that represent corruption hazards and may be amenable to interventions such as tightened regulations, rotation, or overt surveillance (Knapp, 1972; Sherman, 1978).

The following section examines the use of these measures in Australian police departments.

Innovations in Integrity

Research Method

Reportage of anti-corruption strategies and integrity development initiatives in Australia are scattered across a variety of media such as police annual reports and internal reviews, oversight agency reports, conference proceedings, and newspaper reports. No publicly available reports have compared and assessed developments across the country, despite the emphasis on police reform over the past decade. The research project was devised to obtain a systematic national picture of integrity measures by surveying the commissioners of the main police departments of seven states/territories [New South Wales (NSW), Victoria (Vic.), Tasmania (Tas.), South Australia (SA), Western Australia (WA), Northern Territory (NT), Queensland (Qld.)] and the Australian Federal Police (AFP). Letters were sent in October 1999 explaining the background of the project and requesting data:

> We are seeking assistance with a research project examining current developments undertaken within police departments to monitor and, if necessary,

> improve the ethical conduct of police officers. We are primarily interested in documenting relatively new "proactive" strategies—for example, complaint profiling, integrity testing, and the use of high technology surveillance—but we are also interested in developments in more established areas—such as recruitment, training and auditing. …We are asking for any information on any initiatives that your department can supply, including any evaluation studies, discussion papers or policy statements.

This direct approach gave each agency maximum scope to explain and promote its strategies in what was clearly identified as a national comparative study. The method also served as a test of the capacity and willingness of police management to identify its integrity development measures in detail and expose them to scrutiny. In a few cases, follow-up requests were made for clarification of information. Police annual reports were also examined.

Findings

By February 2000, all departments had responded to the survey. Some provided a great deal of information including extracts from annual reports and policy and research documents. Others gave the requests cursory treatment, referring the researchers to other sources such as annual reports. It was decided to supplement information supplied directly with reviews of the latest annual reports of all departments These reports are usually very detailed and contain separate sections on integrity issues. Table 4.1 summarizes the combined findings in terms of the categories used in the description of the advanced model of integrity development. Responses were scored according to the apparent degree of application of the strategies.

The overall outcome is that none of the eight police departments, by their own accounts, had profiles consistent with an advanced model of integrity development (although, of course, developments have occurred since 2000). At the time of the study, most evidenced some elements of the advanced and intermediate models, either in practice or planned for implementation. Many, however, appear not to have moved far past a minimalist model. Table 4.1 covers only information supplied directly or included in annual reports.

As noted, the survey was intended as an assessment of the capacities of departments to articulate their integrity development strategies. However, it appears that a degree of under-reporting occurred, primarily in the cases of New South Wales and Victoria. NSW policing has undergone fundamental reform since the Wood Royal Commission (1994–1997) and various sources suggest greater use of covert surveillance, integrated ethics training, regulating procedures, and risk analysis than is apparent from this survey (Dixon, 1999).

Table 4.1 Scored Reported Misconduct Prevention Strategies of Australian Police Departments

Strategy	AFP	NSW	Vic.	Tas.	SA	WA	NT	Qld.
Overt recording								
Covert surveillance					1			1
Integrity testing (targeted)[a]		2	1		p	p		
Drug and alcohol testing	1	2	p			p		
Internal informants								
Complaints profiling	2		1	1	p			
Supervisor accountability				1	p		1	1
Integrity reviews	1			1	p			
Mandatory reporting								
Witness protection	1							2
Rotation								
Financial reviews								
Surveys of police								
Public surveys					1	1		1
Personnel diversification								
Integrated ethics training	1			1	p	1	1	1
Inquisitorial methods	1				1			
Complaint resolution	2			1	p	1		
Decriminalizing vice								
Regulating procedures	1						1[b]	
Risk analysis	1			1	p			

Notes: 1 = Some reference in material supplied but form of implementation not clear or not clearly consistent with advanced model description or no concrete examples given. No score means no information reported or found in material cited. 2 = Substantive strategy clearly reported in material supplied or cited. p = Reported as planned for implementation.

[a] Based on controversy about random testing, it was decided to confine scoring to targeted testing.

[b] Custody procedures.

The Victoria police similarly have a reputation for maintaining one of the toughest and most proactive ethical standards departments in Australia, but reported very little information. This may result from confidentiality considerations, time pressures on respondents, or a general unwillingness to devote time to unofficial requests for information.

What is perhaps particularly surprising is the fact that so many respondents did not identify a number of well-known advanced (but orthodox) corruption prevention measures such as utilizing recording devices in police interviews and in watch houses, the capacity to use covert surveillance, mandatory reporting, whistleblower protection, rotation of staff through high-risk areas, decriminalization of vice, regulating procedures, and the use of risk analysis. None of these is particularly resource-intensive, with the possible exception of whistleblower protection. Most are not even controversial. Workforce diversification was also ignored. In fact, diversification is policy in all departments, but this would seem to be a response to equity legislation rather than an integrity development strategy.

Table 4.1 shows that a number of strategies were scored 1 out of 2, usually because of incomplete information. For example, the Queensland Police Service annual report referred to "formal inspections and an internal audit program designed to examine the performance of commands, districts, and establishments," although this was clearly not linked to complaint profiles, risk assessments, or supervisor accountability and revealed no details about the audit process (QPS, 1999a: 13). Similarly, reference was made to a "multi-faceted, proactive approach to increasing ethics awareness. The cornerstone of this approach is the delivery of effective education and training programs." No information was provided about how effectiveness was evaluated (QPS, 1999a: 13).

The Queensland strategic plan also reported use of an Australian Bureau of Statistics survey of public perceptions of police professionalism and image (QPS, 1999b), but questions and responses were not reported. In other cases, 1 ratings were given in cases of partial implementation of strategies. For example, South Australian material showed the department had coercive powers for investigations but remained the only department that retained a criminal standard of proof for disciplinary matters. A recommendation was under consideration for lowering the standard for disciplinary matters only (SAPOL, 1998: 31ff.).

Two highly significant areas of reported innovation were integrity testing and drug and alcohol testing. New South Wales and Victoria have engaged in targeted integrity testing for several years and, at the time of writing, plans to introduce such testing were underway in Western Australia and South Australia. New South Wales has a comprehensive drug and alcohol testing program. The federal force has a more limited program focused on drug testing of recruit applicants. Victoria and Western Australia have plans to introduce drug and alcohol testing.

A large amount of material was supplied on these topics, particularly by New South Wales, and was used in a separate paper exploring the complex legal, ethical, and practical issues associated with integrity testing (Prenzler and Ronken, 2001). All the departments surveyed rejected random testing in response to police union resistance and ethical and practical concerns. New South Wales and Victoria are strongly committed to targeted testing, largely because it has been successful in exposing suspect officers who were able to evade discovery by other means (although Victoria did not supply data on the outcomes of tests). The NSW Police Service reported that of 90 tests finalized at the time of reporting, 37% were failed, 27% were passed, 12% were forwarded for further investigation, and 24% were inconclusive or were discontinued. A total of 51 criminal charges followed from the failed tests. Of these, 54% were against police, 23% against staff, and 23% against civilians.

At the time of the survey, alcohol tests in the NSW Police Service were conducted on a random basis, with targets selected by computer. Of 5473 tests conducted in 1998 and 1999, 13 officers returned positive tests. Testing for illicit drugs was conducted on a targeted basis in response to intelligence. The results for all drug tests up to the end of October 1999, as reported in data supplied to the researchers, showed that of 44 tests, 9 resulted in positive findings and other cases presented grounds for suspicion. In 1998, the department introduced an additional program of compulsory drug and alcohol tests following all incidents involving deaths or serious injuries. By the end of the 1998–1999 period, 125 officers had been tested in relation to 42 incidents. Two officers returned positive tests for illicit drugs, with no positive results for alcohol (NSWPS, 1999: 34). Positive tests drew a range of sanctions, with rehabilitation offered in some cases.

Targeted integrity testing appears to have been accepted as an essential anti-corruption tool in New South Wales and Victoria. Official support from senior management of the force and the unions was based on the same rationale accepted by the NSW Royal Commission when it supported a police submission in favor of introducing testing (Wood, 1997). In this view, testing serves multiple purposes of exposing and deterring corruption and also confirming ethical behavior, as summarized in the following statement from the NSW Police Service in response to the research questions:

> It is dangerous to assume that complaints alone can identify all instances of corruption. The investigation of corruption must be primarily proactive and supported by strategic analysis of intelligence.…Integrity testing becomes an important option in all investigations into corrupt behavior and achieves a number of goals. It tests for both corrupt and ethical behaviors and the appropriateness of organizational systems and procedures and serves as a deterrent to officers who may be exposed to corruption opportunities.

In their responses to the survey, some departments cited strategies not falling within the categories cited in Table 4.1. For example, the AFP (1999) referred to the use of contract employment as a way of facilitating removal of unsatisfactory members. Such termination provisions are highly controversial. In New South Wales, police union protests over the almost complete discretion contained in the "Commissioner's Confidence" provisions forced the introduction of an appeals system. A modified version of Commissioner's Confidence was under review in Western Australia. The WA police also introduced portfolio officers who "play a key role in educating local level managers with regular visits to metropolitan and country stations to raise awareness of ethics and integrity issues" (WAPS, 1998: 53). Victoria instituted a similar program involving ethics and professional standards officers (Victoria Police, 1999). Victoria also introduced a customer assistance unit that gave the public direct access to the ethical standards department.

An additional finding of the survey was that most departments had undergone major restructurings of their internal affairs departments in recent years. This was consistent with the intermediate model and an essential element of the advanced model. Restructuring largely involved centralization of complaint investigation and responsibility for integrity across the department, with specific innovations in areas such as complaint profiling and drug testing. Restructuring often resulted as part of a larger performance-oriented reform agenda and was influenced by the findings of corruption inquiries within the jurisdiction or in neighboring jurisdictions. Both the Fitzgerald inquiry in Queensland (1987–1989) and the Wood inquiry in New South Wales (1994–1997) identified problems in related police agencies such as the AFP. In some cases, the currency of restructuring meant that some of the strategies belonging to the advanced model were in the process of implementation at the time of the research. The South Australian response typifies this situation:

> In June 1997 Focus 21 was established as a major reform program to lead, manage and implement key elements of South Australia Police Future Directions Strategy....The program is addressing issues such as best practice, customer service, leadership, human resource management and practice, ethics and integrity and information systems and technology....In August 1998 the review of Internal Investigations Branch, Office of Disciplinary Review and Anti-Corruption Branch was completed....In October 1999 implementation of the recommendations commenced. The program has included a complete restructure of the Internal Investigation Section. This has resulted in an expansion of functions and responsibilities of the branch. To reflect this change the branch has been renamed to the "Ethical and Professional Standards Service"....Due to the restructure there are no current policies or procedures in place relating to those issues covered in your letter.

Discussion

The results of this survey were disappointing from the perspective of an advanced model of internal integrity development. Misconduct prevention was clearly on the agenda for Australian police departments, but in many cases the rhetoric of commitment to integrity did not appear to be matched by reported practice. This commitment was exemplified in the following response to the survey:

> The Queensland Police Service has gone to considerable efforts in the area in which you are interested. The establishment of the Ethical Standards Command is but one of numerous initiatives to date. The Queensland Police Service sees ethical behavior as central to the role of policing and as such ethical standards are a consideration in all programs delivered. Information is readily available on the Queensland Police Service web site and through annual reports.

Little information consistent with the advanced model was provided. Across Australia, strategies for monitoring and preventing misconduct appeared limited and rather haphazard; many strategies considered essential in the anti-corruption literature were not cited at all. This suggests a degree of dangerous complacency and, while highly organized corruption is of little concern now, diverse and hidden forms of misconduct may occur under such conditions.

Of additional interest was the lack of references to benchmarking via comparisons with other police departments or through the research literature on police corruption. External influences on changes to anti-corruption procedures seemed to come largely from major events such as the formation of Queensland and New South Wales commissions of inquiry. No agency reported routine research processes to keep abreast of trends in other jurisdictions or design anti-corruption measures within a framework of international knowledge and experimentation, although some partial exceptions were reported. The Queensland Police Service initiated the first National Ethics in Policing Conference in 1999, and most of the restructured internal affairs units appear to have research and policy subunits. Nonetheless, this pessimistic conclusion is consistent with broader reviews of police management practices in Australia that largely found reform to be externally driven, involving the adoption of a rhetoric of innovation and performance management but with limited substance (Chan, 1997; Fleming and Lafferty, 2000).

It should be kept in mind that all the police departments surveyed were subject to civilian oversight that provided an additional layer of misconduct monitoring and prevention. This was largely confined to review of police investigations of public complaints, but the trend was in the direction of greater intervention (Lewis and Prenzler, 1999). In some cases, most notably in New South Wales and Queensland, some of the innovations listed in the advanced model were handled by external bodies. For example, the Queensland Criminal Justice Commission conducted regular surveys of the public and police, and also engaged in integrity reviews and inquisitorial investigations. It also initiated covert surveillance and integrity testing, usually involving seconded police in operational roles under commission supervision (CJC, 1999).

Conclusion

Survey results showed that no Australian police department reported anti-misconduct strategies consistent with an advanced model of best practice. Most departments identified some elements of an advanced model, but all appeared to remain largely within the constraints of an intermediate model. Although the concept of proactive prevention is clearly on the agenda, a wide gap appeared between rhetoric and practice. Little evidence indicated an evaluative approach to integrity development or integration of corruption prevention initiatives through advanced research capacity. It is therefore incumbent on politicians, oversight agencies, and concerned citizen groups to push for implementation of a wider range of internal integrity development strategies. At the same time, it is apparent that advances had occurred and that a degree of learning and innovation was achieved in the mission to maximize ethical conduct since this survey was conducted.

References

AFP. (1999) *Annual report 1998–99*, Canberra: Australian Federal Police.

Bayley, D. (1995) Getting serious about police brutality, in Stenning, P. (Ed.), *Accountability for criminal justice: Selected essays* (pp. 93–109), Toronto: University of Toronto Press.

Bryett, K., Harrison, A., and Shaw, J. (1997) *The role and functions of police in Australia*, Sydney: Butterworths.

Chan, J. (1997) *Changing police culture*, Cambridge: Cambridge University Press.

CJC. (1997) *Integrity in the Queensland Police Service*, Brisbane: Criminal Justice Commission.

CJC. (1999) *Police and drugs: A follow-up report*, Brisbane: Criminal Justice Commission.

Dixon, D. (Ed.). (1999) *A culture of corruption*, Sydney: Hawkins Press.

Ede, A., Homel, R., and Prenzler, T. (2002) Reducing complaints against police and preventing misconduct: A diagnostic case study using hot spot analysis, *Australian and New Zealand Journal of Criminology*, 35: 27–42.

Finnane, M. (1999) From police force to police service? Aspects of the recent history of the New South Wales police, in Dixon, D. (Ed.), *A culture of corruption* (pp. 6–35), Sydney: Hawkins Press.

Fitzgerald, G. (1989) *Report of a commission of inquiry pursuant to orders in council*, Brisbane: Goprint.

Fleming, J. and Lafferty, G. (2000) New management techniques and restructuring for accountability in Australian police organisations, *Policing: An International Journal of Police Strategies and Management*, 23(2): 154–168.

Freckelton, I. (2000) Legal regulation of the police culture of violence: Rhetoric, remedies and redress, in Coady, T., James, S., Miller, S., and O'Keefe, M. (Eds.), *Violence and police culture* (pp. 140–181), Melbourne: Melbourne University Press.

Goldsmith, A. (ed.) (1991) *Complaints against the police: The trend to external review*, Oxford: Clarendon Press.
Goldsmith, A. (2000) An impotent conceit: Law, culture and the regulation of police violence, in Coady, T., James, S., Miller, S., and O'Keefe, M. (Eds.), *Violence and police culture* (pp. 109–139), Melbourne: Melbourne University Press.
Goode, M. (1991) Complaints against the police in Australia: Where we are now, and what we might learn about the process of law reform, with some comments about the process of legal change, in Goldsmith, A. (Ed.), *Complaints against the police: The trend to external review*, Oxford: Clarendon Press.
Henry, V. (1990) Lifting the blue curtain: Some controversial strategies to control police corruption, *National Police Research Unit Review*, 6: 48–55.
Kappeler, V., Sluder, R., and Alpert, G. (1994) *Forces of deviance: Understanding the dark side of policing*, Prospect Heights, IL: Waveland.
Kleinig, J. (1996) *The ethics of policing*, New York: Cambridge University Press.
Knapp, W. (1972) *The Knapp Commission Report on police corruption*, New York: George Braziller.
KPMG. (1996) *The New York City Police Department Random Integrity Testing Program*, New York: Commission to Combat Police Corruption.
Lewis, C. and Prenzler, T. (1999) Civilian oversight of police in Australia, *Trends and Issues in Crime and Criminal Justice*, 141: 1–6.
Marx, G. (1992) When the guards guard themselves: Undercover tactics turned inward, *Policing and Society*, 2(3): 151–172.
McDonnell, S. (2000) The one that got away, *Four Corners*, August 7, Sydney: ABC TV.
Mollen, M. (1994) *Commission to investigate allegations of police corruption and the anti-corruption procedures of the police department: Commission report*, City of New York.
Newburn, T. (1997) *Understanding and preventing police corruption: Lessons from the literature*, Police Research Series Paper 110, London: Home Office.
NSWPS. (1999) *Annual report 1998/99*, Sydney: New South Wales Police Service.
Ombudsman of Victoria (1998) *Operation BART: Investigation of allegations against police in relation to the shutter allocation system, final report*, Melbourne: Victorian Government Printer.
Palmer, M. (1992) Controlling corruption, in Moir, P., and Eijkman, H. (Eds.), *Policing Australia: Old issues, new perspectives* (pp. 102–131), Melbourne: Macmillan.
Prenzler, T. (2000) Civilian oversight of police: A test of capture theory, *British Journal of Criminology*, 40(4): 659–674.
Prenzler, T. and Ronken, C. (2001) Police integrity testing in Australia, *Criminal Justice*, 1(3): 319–342.
QPS. (1999a) *Annual report 1998–1999*, Brisbane: Queensland Police Service.
QPS. (1999b) *Strategic plan 1999–2001*, Brisbane: Queensland Police Service.
SAPOL. (1998) *Focus 21, providing direction: Final report*, Adelaide: South Australia Police.
Sarre, R. (1989) Towards the notion of policing "by consent" and its implications for accountability, in Chappell, D. and Wilson, P. (Eds.), *Australian policing: Contemporary issues*, Sydney: Butterworths.
Scarman, Lord. (1986) *Scarman report*, Harmondsworth: Penguin.
Shapiro, S. (1987) Policing trust, in Shearing, C. and Stenning, P. (Eds.), *Private policing* (pp. 194–220), Newbury Park, CA: Sage.

Sherman, L. W. (1978) *Scandal and reform: Controlling police corruption*, Los Angeles: University of California Press.
Victoria Police (1999) *Annual report 1998–1999*, Melbourne: Victoria Police Force.
WAPS. (1998) *Annual report, 1998*, Perth: Western Australian Police Service.
Wood, J. (1997) *Royal commission into the New South Wales police service: Final report*, Sydney: Government of State of New South Wales.

Policing Terror

III

Terrorism Old and New: Counterterrorism in Canada*

5

STÉPHANE LEMAN-LANGLOIS
JEAN-PAUL BRODEUR

Contents

When the Honorable Paul Martin succeeded Jean Chrétien as Canada's new Prime Minister in December 2003,† his most conspicuous move was to appoint a cabinet that included a new Ministry of Public Safety and Emergency Preparedness (MPSEP), clearly patterned on the United States Department of Homeland Security—although the Martin government was reluctant to admit it. The minister responsible for public safety was the Honorable Anne McLennan, also appointed Vice Prime Minister, an indication of the importance of the new ministry.

* This chapter first appeared in *Police Practice and Research*, 2005, 6(2): 121-140. The authors thank the Canadian Social Sciences and Humanities Research Council for financial assistance (Grant 410-2003-1259).

† Paul Martin succeeded Jean Chrétien through the Canadian constitutional process, Chrétien having resigned as Prime Minister. Martin was elected head of a minority government in 2004.

The creation of the MPSEP was not a response to a specific attack. Canada, although explicitly mentioned by an Al-Qaeda spokesman as one of seven targeted countries, has not been the object of recent terrorist attacks.* The MPSEP's creation is consistent with the conception of terrorism as a global problem whereby countries are accountable to fellow countries in countering the threat. It also bears witness to the new worldwide defensive stance that followed the tragedy of September 2001 that exemplifies a perceptible evolution toward what has been called *new* terrorism (Hoffman, 1997; Laqueur, 1997, 1999, 2003; Pape, 2003).

In our view, new terrorism has features that call for an equally new counterterrorism. Our analysis rests on four assumptions: (1) efficient counterterrorism necessitates knowledge of the kind of organization to be fought; (2) the knowledge must support action—that is, it must efficiently match core features of terrorist organizations with police responses (to the extent that new terrorism is in fact a police problem; see below); (3) although the tactics of important terrorist organizations such as the Basque ETA have not really evolved, changes in the nature of terrorism worldwide and specifically in Canada are momentous; and (4) counterterrorism must therefore adapt to changes in terrorism.

In line with these assumptions, this chapter is divided into four parts followed by a brief conclusion. First, we propose a broad typology of terrorism based on our current research. Second, we present typical examples of conventional and new terrorism in Canada and compare the features of both kinds. Third, we review the most threatening kind of terrorism that plagued Canada in the 1970s in order to highlight one of the most important factors of a successful police response: parallelism between police and terrorist strategies. Finally, we explore possible strategies to deal with the (harder-to-define) features of new terrorism in Canada.

Terrorism in Canada, 1973–2003: Operational Typology

Attempting to produce a typology of events that are rare and extremely diverse in nature can be a perilous undertaking. At worst, it can distort the events by imposing forms dictated by the researcher's needs rather than the particular characteristics of the events under consideration. In an attempt to avoid this, the typology we offer in this section is at once minimal in its

* Its safety is sometimes believed to result from serving as a refuge for terrorists. According to a view widely held in the United States, terrorists sheltered in Canada routinely cross the border to commit their nefarious acts. Only one high-profile incident supports this belief: the 1999 Millennium Bomber incident implicating Ahmed Ressam, who was caught with a trunkload of home-made explosives when he tried to enter the United States from Vancouver.

determining variables and maximal in its scope. It is meant to answer the specific question of how much influence the global new terrorist trend has had in Canada. We started our analysis in 1973 to exclude the large number of terrorist attacks committed between 1963 and 1973 by members of the *Front de libération du Québec* (FLQ) that represent paradigms of conventional terrorism. We discuss these instances of terrorism in the next part of this chapter.

We built a *qualitative* database of the large number of incidents that took place in Canada between 1973 and 2003, using a number of existing sources. One major source was Kellett et al. (1991), who produced a monumental reference on terrorism and political violence up to 1989 based in part on work by Ross (1988). We then completed the chronology through the 1990s and 2000s in part with the help of Mickolus (1980, 1993); Mickolus, Sandler, and Murdock (1989); Mickolus and Simmons (1997); and Vareilles (2001). We also added contextual information about the incidents and increased the amount of cross-incident linking in an effort to escape the conventional database approach that has proven to be somewhat sterile. We would like to move instead toward a narrative type of database in which incidents are considered together rather than extracted as discrete events.

We do not think it particularly promising to construct a classification of separated *incidents*. Incidents are deceptive both in their apparent internal unity (often constructed by the media) and in their artificially enhanced discreteness. The stories of terrorism we chose are complex, intermeshing, and vary greatly in the degree in which they resulted from planned actions. We would like to avoid some of the problems that Kellet et al. (1991) encountered with classification, especially when filing *incidents* and ignoring relationships between them, even the most obvious, such as the identities of the perpetrators. This approach led to their categorizing one attack by the Direct Action/Squamish Five members, the Litton Industries bomb of 1982, as "left wing" while the firebombing of the Red Hot Video premises a few months later was categorized as "single issue" terrorism. Opposition to pornography is apparently not considered a left wing activity. Even if the left wing and right wing categories were helpful—this incident-based classification clearly does not fit the reality it is meant to describe.

We also decided, at least for the present, to adopt a very wide interpretation of "terrorism in Canada" with respect to both the terrorism element (including hoaxes, threats, individual attacks, support activities such as fundraising, and failed or foiled plots) and also the Canadian content of the situations considered. Any link to Canada is interesting, even if it is only the refueling in Gander of an airplane hijacked in the United States and en route to a third country. Our project includes the study of all kinds of responses to terrorism, which in this case would simply be the refueling of the craft. Any plotting, preparation, and fundraising activities in Canada, even if the actual attacks are targeted elsewhere, are of course included.

For the more quantitatively inclined we can produce an approximate count of terrorist events in Canada drawn from 400 entries from 1973 to 2003: 6 hijackings; 2 airplane bombings; 73 disruptive hoaxes; 9 hostage takings or kidnappings; 4 letter bombs; 170 bombs, firebombs, and arson incidents; 59 threats; 35 attacks on individuals; 45 acts of vandalism; 14 plots and foiled attacks; and 32 instances of support. This list is partial and, at the time of writing, we are still gathering information. For instance, we are trying to take into account all cars, weapons, explosives, and other equipment stolen in order to conduct terrorist attacks.

For the purposes of this chapter, it is not necessary to devise a universal and definitive typology—one that effectively differentiates between the broad variants of Canadian terrorism and those of the new extremist terrorism should be sufficient. Toward that goal we study *situations*, rather than events or actors, meaning that events that are linked through their perpetrators or through practical consequences (for instance, murder following a kidnapping) are considered a unit. These situations are then arranged in four interrelated sets according to two qualitative variables. The first variable is the scope of the desired impact (however unrealistic from the observers' points of view). That scope can be very narrow, such as putting an end to the release of sour gas around a perpetrator's ranch, or extremely wide if it involves a fundamental change in society such as abandoning the capitalist–liberal system.

The second variable is the timeframe of the element that is held to have justified the act. When terrorist acts are responses to perceived (real or otherwise) slights or injustices that occurred in the past, we consider them "backward-looking." Conversely, if an act is meant to achieve a goal at a later time (e.g., to force an entity to fulfill a demand), we categorized it as "forward-looking." This provides four broad categories based on the underlying rationales of the perpetrators, as presented in Table 5.1.

Note that this rationale-based typology can also be applied to what is often called "state terrorism" in both its international state-sponsored and its domestic or repressive guises. We do not consider Canada to be engaged in state terrorism, but it has been known to give refuge to individuals who engaged in such terrorism in their own countries. Private enterprises whose actions support repressive regimes may also be considered as at least partially responsible (sociologically if not legally) for state terrorism.

Demand-Based Terror

Demand-based terror has always been the most common type of terrorism in Canada. Typically, it involves small groups, often *ad hoc* formations, focused

Table 5.1 Fundamental Rationales of Terrorists

	Scope of Desired[a] Impact	
Justification of Action[b]	Narrow	Wide
Forward looking	Demand-based terror	Revolutionary terror
Backward looking	Private justice terror	Restoration terror

[a] Likelihood of success or reasonableness of expectations and desires is not considered.

[b] Internal moral justification; no attempt is made to determine whether others would consider activity legitimate.

on a specific object that is perceived as a problem. It is forward-looking in the sense that the action taken is aimed at correcting a problem. Despite the frequent conviction that the authorities who might or should have been responsible are incompetent, corrupt, or constitute the source of the problem, the main goal is not to *punish* them but to ameliorate a situation. It is interesting to note that these demands are often not addressed to the state, as has traditionally been understood to be the case with conventional terrorism. In many cases, the acts amount to violent intimidation of private persons, groups, or enterprises. It should also be noted that the category does not quite fit the conventional "single issue" type described in the literature; that category spans both backward- and forward-looking categories.

In Canada, demand-based terror consists mainly of acts of vandalism by animal rights and ecology groups. Their targets include mink farms, university departments and private laboratories that use animals for tests, and meat packing plants. Eco-terrorism is rare but Canadians are sometimes involved in acts of sabotage abroad, for example, the Sea Shepherd Conservation Society's attack on whaling equipment in Iceland in November 1986. Alberta farmer and commune leader Weibo Ludwig was involved in over 150 incidents of vandalism against oil installations around his property in 1997 and 1998 as he tried to stop oil companies from polluting the area with sour gas.

In Quebec, the language/nationalist debate provoked a great number of small incidents clustered around political events perceived as endangering French or English in Quebec (depending on the political preferences of the perpetrators). During the 1980 referendum, a few cases of threats against both "yes" and "no" camps were recorded. Tempers flared again in 1982 around the constitutional debate and a new language law. Actions included leaving unarmed dynamite at politically meaningful sites such as Parti Québécois offices, destruction of billboards, attempted arson, and various forms of vandalism against shops and other commercial enterprises displaying English-only signs. In December 1986, a court ruling allowing bilingual signs provoked a new wave of bomb threats, Molotov cocktail attacks, and other forms of vandalism against enterprises that did not appear sufficiently French.

Another ruling in December 1988 triggered attacks, one of which caused $200,000 worth of damage to the Montreal offices of Alliance Quebec (an "English rights" organization). In 2000, ex-FLQ member Rhéal Mathieu was arrested for attempted arson against companies with English names (especially Second Cup cafes) and against a church where an English rights group was to meet. Finally, and more recently, the debate around the amalgamation of municipalities within Montreal became polarized over the language issue and in late 2003 served as the focus for militant threats and acts of vandalism against a former town hall.

Another important area of demand-based terror is the targeting of abortion clinics and their staffs. Actions have included stealing and destroying medical equipment, vandalizing premises with acid, destroying and attempting to destroy premises by arson and bombing, threatening staff (in particular, Dr Henry Morgentaler), and three cases of shooting obstetricians who performed abortions.

Demand-based terror also includes local attempts perpetrated at a micro level such as a 1979 incident in which parents in Langley, British Columbia, set fire to five school officials' homes in a dispute over the admission of their children to the school.

"Private Justice" Terror

Private justice involves a response to an event, situation, or conflict that is intended to obtain retribution as defined by the attacker. In its various guises, it may attempt to obtain reparation and redress, but more often than not its main goal is punishment. It can be a sophisticated response or straightforward revenge, but it is always characterized by a claim of previous victimization.

Examples of private justice terror include the many acts of arson and other destruction committed in British Columbia by members of the Doukhobor Sons of Freedom religious community (the SOF or Freedomites represent a subset of the wider group). Sons of Freedom militants typically reacted against installations or buildings they deemed to be offensive in some way to the religious purity of the physical context in which they lived. Most of these attacks were intended to destroy unholy or sacrilegious buildings and monuments. Others were essentially punitive, targeting the properties of individuals who were perceived to be Doukhobor victimizers. The SOF burned homes, schools, a post office, and municipal buildings and has repeatedly bombed Canadian Pacific rail tracks. SOF arsonists have been far less active during the period under study than they were in the first half of the 20th century, when they burned hundreds of homes and other buildings. Active mainly between 1980 and 1986, when they committed some 40 arsons and explosions, SOF activities are no longer in the news (several members are in jail). One exception was the 2001 burning of a computer lab that caused

$150,000 worth of damage. The arsonist, an 81-year-old woman, was trying to commemorate an important Doukhobor religious anniversary.

This category also includes acts of intimidation carried out by xenophobic groups such as skinheads,* the Ku Klux Klan (KKK), and other groups, some of which have ties to U.S. groups. Many xenophobic attacks have been carried out by *ad hoc* groups that used the KKK symbol to threaten their victims but have no confirmed relations with the Klan. East Indians in British Columbia have been targeted, suffering beatings, murders, arson, bombings, and cross burnings. In April 1981, three Canadian extremist rightwingers were embroiled in a plot to overthrow the government of Dominica and set up a white supremacist utopia on the island, pushing private justice xenophobic terror into revolutionary terror. In 1986, a bomb was placed in a Canadian Immigration Centre in Vancouver, with a note blaming Canadian immigration policy for "dumping third world persons" in Canada. In 1988, five skinheads were caught on tape bragging about their murder of Nirmal Singh Gill, 65, on the grounds of the temple where he worked. In 1992, Austrian police arrested a group of neo-Nazis who were plotting violent attacks in Vienna and found they were financed in part by Canadian-based Ernst Zundel, known for denying the Holocaust.

In 1986 Québecair was sold to CP Air, leading to a series of threats against the flights and planes of both organizations. The sale of the airline, seen as a symbol of Quebec entrepreneurship, was interpreted by some as a loss of economic power to the benefit of Western Canada. The disruption of operations may have been a knee-jerk reaction but may also have been intended to cause financial losses.

This category should include three types of state terror. First are repressive states abroad that attempt to control their dissidents who found refuge in Canada. Libya was at the center of a 1988 FBI investigation into travel agencies used as fronts for Libyan agents. The Manara Travel Agency in Ottawa, which was closely tied to xenophobic groups in Canada and the United States, was dismantled when the FBI arrested some of its operators for plotting to kill Iran-Contra conspirator Oliver North. During the late 1970s, Yugoslavia attempted to control its dissidents in Canada. Some of them reacted by attacking Yugoslavian government targets in Canada and other institutions seen as friendly to the Tito regime.

After the publication of *The Satanic Verses* in 1988, Iran pronounced a *Fatwah* against its author, Salman Rushdie. In Canada this translated into threats and arson attacks on bookstores that carried the book along with counter threats against Iranians in Canada. When the government of Can-

* While being a skinhead can simply be a fashion or symbol of identity, as in other western nations, skinheads in Canada have been associated for a long time with the extreme right.

ada refused to designate the book as hate literature, Revenue Minister Otto Jelinek and Foreign Affairs Minister Joe Clark were also threatened.

Iran also sent agents to Canada, for instance, Mansour Ahani, who was arrested in Italy in 1992 for plotting the assassination of a prominent Iranian dissident, and Djafar Seyfi, who was caught attempting to intimidate Iranians in Canada. A few Canadian-based transnational enterprises support repressive regimes abroad, which may or may not count directly as terrorism but may eventually provoke retaliation in Canada. Former agents of repressive states who migrated to Canada include Léon Mugesera, instigator of the Rwandan genocide, who arrived in 1993.

Revolutionary Terror

Revolutionary terror aims at fundamental changes at the state level. In Canada, such terror is usually aimed at another country, with Canada serving as a base for action elsewhere (e.g., India). One exception is the FLQ, already discussed.

The Armenian Secret Army for the Liberation of Armenia (ASALA) conducted a series of attacks on various targets in the early 1980s. Its overall goals were Turkish acknowledgement of the Armenian genocide during the early 20th century and the creation of an independent Armenia on land ceded from Turkey. The group targeted Turkish diplomats in Canada, newspapers felt to be unsympathetic to its cause, and other Armenians who questioned its approach or refused to fund it. In May 1982, a bomb placed in an Air Canada freight terminal in Los Angeles was defused 15 minutes before it was timed to explode. It was meant as retaliation for the arrests of Armenian extremists in Canada some weeks earlier. The Justice Commandos for the Armenian Genocide (JCAG) assassinated a Turkish diplomat in Canada in August 1982. In 1985, three ASALA gunmen invaded the Turkish embassy in Ottawa, killing a security guard and holding the building for four hours. Two weeks after their arrest, ASALA sent a letter to the Royal Canadian Mounted Police (RCMP) threatening to blow up the Toronto subway if the trio was not released from custody. The Montreal RCMP office received a similar threat targeting the Montreal Métro.

The Provisional Irish Republican Army (IRA) participated in a number of events involving Canadians. In a few cases, Canadian citizens were arrested while trying to smuggle IRA members across the U.S. border. In 1994, a Canadian was arrested in Spain for attempting to deliver weapons to the group. Although we have not investigated the fundraising activities of the IRA in Canada, it is likely such activities have been extensive.

Sikh extremists have been active since 1984 when the Indian government attacked separatists who barricaded themselves in the Golden Temple of Amritsar, Sikhism's most important shrine. The attack left the temple severely damaged and hundreds dead and wounded. Some terrorist attacks were intended as responses to the battle at Amritsar and, to the extent that this was their motivation, could thus be considered private justice. Shortly after the tragedy, a group of Sikhs attacked the Indian high commissioner and another stormed the Indian consulate in Toronto. These attacks, however, only took place because of the pre-existing demands of those who appointed themselves fighters for a future Sikh homeland.

Sikh extremism in Canada ranges from raising funds for violent attacks to intimidation and assassinations. While the overall goal is the creation of an independent Sikh homeland (Khalistan) in India, much violence in Canada occurs around the more immediate concerns of control of local groups and the intimidation (and murder) of vocal dissidents (most notably newspaper editor Tara Singh Hayer, who survived a shooting in 1988 but was finally killed in 1998, while wheelchair bound). However, the Air India Tokyo airport bombings of June 1985 (another Air India plane was scheduled to be bombed in May 1986; the plot was foiled by police in Montreal), Sikh extremism clearly escalated to our next category, restoration terror.

Tamil terrorism in Canada is largely limited to fundraising activities, mostly in Toronto. A handful of exceptions were directed primarily at intra-group dissidence, with damage to property and violent attacks against individuals who failed to conform to group demands. Tamil terrorist financing organizations are particularly adept at disguising their activities, even fooling former ministers Paul Martin and Maria Minna into participating in a fundraising dinner in May 2000.

Direct Action, a small group named after a French extremist organization, targeted capitalism in general as well as certain aspects it considered particularly hateful such as pollution (blowing up a power relay station), the defense industry (blowing up cruise missile sub-contractor Litton), and pornography (torching three X-rated video shops). Its members were eventually arrested in Squamish, British Columbia, and subsequently named the Squamish Five.

When a state of emergency was declared in South Africa in 1986, a few incidents in Canada (and elsewhere) protested against the apartheid government. Some of these, credit for which was claimed by the Azanian People's Liberation Front (APLF), an essentially unknown organization, while ultimately revealed as hoaxes, caused heavy financial losses. The APLF claimed to have poisoned South African fruit that then had to be destroyed; 3,000 bottles of wine were also destroyed when another group using the Direct Action name claimed to have poisoned them.

Canadians Christine Lamont and David Spencer were arrested and tried for the kidnapping of a supermarket chain owner in Brazil in an attempt to finance various leftist revolutionary groups in South America. In 1993, when a cache of weapons and false papers was discovered by accident in Nicaragua, letters by Lamont and Spencer were found with passports in the name of one of the World Trade Center bombers.

Restoration Terror

Restoration terror now occurs mainly within the context of the new terrorism. It involves attempts to re-establish a historical situation. The desired situation may have existed fairly recently or in the distant, sometimes mythical, past and may be pursued through deeds that show such disregard for human life that they are almost impossible to describe objectively. Such deeds may be described as epic, desperate, or self-sacrificial and based on grandiloquent or simply irrational versions of historic misdeeds, or as results of wide-scale victimizations that fuel desires for revenge, reparation, and, ultimately restoration.

One powerful illustration is Osama Bin Laden's references to the Muslim debacle in Spain in the 15th century as a slight that must be remedied. His hortatory discourse about the need for a regained international Muslim dominance is at least in part meant to recruit followers and justify more down-to-earth power struggles. Nonetheless, his efforts manage to inspire some individuals to make the ultimate sacrifices of their lives. Bin Laden's Al-Qaeda network has recruited a few Canadians and others such as Ahmed Ressam who live in Canada but cannot obtain citizenship or resident status.

Visions of historic struggles within millenarian or other eschatological worldviews also fit this category and share an absolutist morality that leaves no room for compromise or negotiation. The Muslim extremists' desire to restore the golden age of the caliphate or their battle against the "apostates" who rule Islam-dominated countries today is one example. Egypt and its "pharaohs," as Islamic fundamentalists refer to Egyptian secular leaders, have been prominent targets. In 1995, the Egyptian embassy in Pakistan was bombed with the financial help of Canadian citizen Ahmad Kahdr (whose son Abdulrahman, at the time of writing, had recently been released from the Guantanamo Bay Naval Base by the U.S. military; Kahdr senior was killed in a firefight with the Pakistani army).

Perhaps the most important example of Muslim extremism in this category is the millennium bomber incident, Ahmed Ressam's attempt to set off a bomb at the Los Angeles airport in 1999 or 2000. The plot failed but the story speaks volumes about the workings of Islamic restoration terror in Canada. Trained in Afghanistan and given seed money to devise an attack on the United States, Ressam was arrested almost by chance—and because he couldn't stay calm under pressure. His connections to terrorists in France, the United States, Afghanistan, Algeria, and Canada reveal a group of individuals falling somewhat short of a network but animated by a powerful overarching mission to strike for the greater glory of Islam at very high cost.

Conventional and "New" Terrorism: Contrasts

Canada has been largely and happily ignored by international history—it has generally been spared from violence, although Canadians have fought in European wars. When leftist terrorism was rampant in Europe (Red Brigades and the Baader–Meinhof Gang) and other groups were motivated by nationalism (the Basque ETA and the IRA in Northern Ireland), Canada also suffered a classic terrorist episode.

Conventional Terrorism: The FLQ as a Canadian Prototype

This terrorist episode took place mainly in the province of Quebec, where a group that called itself the *Front de libération du Québec* (FLQ or Quebec Liberation Front) was active between 1963 and 1973. In October 1970, it generated the greatest political crisis in Canadian history.

The history of the FLQ falls into two periods. From 1963 to 1968, the FLQ's political platform was based on traditional right-wing nationalism and its main demand was the independence of Quebec (Fournier, 1998 :35). Its method can thus be described as demand-based terrorism during the first part of its history. During that time the FLQ perpetrated bomb attacks to get media attention, but it was generally careful not to target people and was in fact responsible for only a few accidental casualties.

By 1968, the police had arrested many members of this first FLQ wave, and the group started to reorganize itself under the leadership of intellectuals who pursued two goals: the traditional goal of Quebec's independence coupled with the goal of emancipating the working class. Both objectives were pursued at the same level of militancy. The FLQ evolved from limited demand-based terror to revolutionary terror and became increasingly violent. The tradition of not endangering people's lives was generally upheld, but FLQ attacks gradually became more vicious. In January 1969, a bomb exploded near the home of the Montreal police chief; in February, another bomb at the Montreal Stock Exchange wounded 20 people, 3 seriously. On 24 June 1970—the National Day of French-Canadians—a bomb exploded at the Department of Defence in Ottawa, killing one person.

The policy of not targeting individuals changed drastically. On 5 October 1970, the FLQ's "Liberation" Cell abducted James Richard Cross, a British diplomat appointed to the consulate in Montreal. The FLQ made several demands, one of which was the public reading of its manifesto on state television. The Canadian government gave in to this demand and the manifesto was read on television by a news anchor on 8 September (it had been read a day earlier over a private radio station). Unexpectedly, the manifesto that denounced the exploitation of Quebec's working class by both the English-

and French-speaking bourgeoisie had a profound impact on Quebec public opinion. Its positive reception transformed what had been perceived as a simple kidnapping into a national issue that became a full-fledged crisis with the dramatic abduction of the Quebec vice-premier, Pierre Laporte, by FLQ's Chénier Cell (it was later learned that the cells did not act according to a coordinated plan).

The police forces in Quebec seemed to be overwhelmed and on 15 October the federal government used forgotten World War I legislation—the War Measures Act—and enacted a set of emergency regulations that abrogated civil liberties in Quebec (Brodeur et al., 1971). The Canadian Forces (CF) were activated in Quebec and on 16 October some 500 citizens were arrested and put in preventive custody.* All were later released without filing of criminal charges.

On 17 October, the body of the abducted minister was found in the trunk of a car and the "October Crisis" reached its climax. One of his abductors, Bernard Lortie, was arrested in Montreal on 6 November. At the end of November, the RCMP finally discovered where Cross was held hostage. His release was negotiated in exchange for safe conduct to Cuba for his five captors and he was freed unharmed on 3 December 1970. The three remaining members of the Chénier Cell who abducted Laporte were arrested on 28 December, bringing the crisis to an end. As we shall see later in this chapter, the FLQ continued its armed struggle from 1970 to 1973 but was ultimately defeated by the police; it was not a threat after 1973.

Contrasting Internal Terror and New Global Waves of Terrorism

Although not as violent as other terrorist organizations that operated concurrently in other parts of the world, the FLQ can serve as a basis for the formulation of hypotheses about the features that define a paradigm of terrorism that started to break down in the 1980s and does not fit the pattern of post-9/11 terrorism. Murderous attempts such as the 1985 bombing of an Air India flight out of Vancouver that killed 320 people and the explosion of a Pan Am flight over Lockerbie in Scotland in December 1988 (270 fatalities) were already anomalies with respect to the conventional terrorism pursued in the 1960s and 1970s (Baader–Meinhof in Germany, Red Brigades in Italy, ETA in Spain, IRA in Ulster and the British mainland, and various Palestinian terrorist groups, although the Palestinian groups never fit the paradigm clearly). Some of the features that we will discuss may seem obvious, but they are important to understanding observable changes in terrorism in Canada.

* Fournier (1998: 507–512) lists 355 names and notes that the list is incomplete.

Territoriality

Most of the conventional movements listed above operated within a single country, with the intent to change its political regime or provoke the secession of territory inhabited by a minority (ethnic, linguistic, or religious) group. The Palestinians, who operated both inside and outside Israel/Palestine, were partial exceptions to this model. Following a suggestion in Mickolus et al. (1989, Vol. 2: xiii–xiv), we make a distinction between *transnational* and *international* terrorism. A transnational terrorist organization is based in one country but operates at times outside its territory. An international organization operates outside a particular territory, is based in several countries, and is comprised of members of different nationalities. Palestinian terrorism is transnational, whereas Al-Qaeda is truly international.

Terrorism as Communication

The literature on terrorism follows two leitmotifs. The first is that terrorism is the weapon of the weak (Laqueur, 1987 and his numerous followers); the second is that it is a form of communication (Crelinsten, 1997; Gressang, 2001; Schmid and de Graaf, 1982; Wieviorka, 1988; Wieviorka and Wolton, 1987). That terrorism thrives on media coverage is true of all its forms. This truism should not, however, blind us to important differences between the old (conventional) and new terrorisms—whether internal or global. Here are some of the main differences.

Signature — Conventional terrorism devoted considerable effort to claiming responsibility and justifying or at least explaining its deeds. The issue of signature plays a lesser role in the new terrorism. For instance, the attacks against the Air India (1985) and the Pan Am (1988) flights were never claimed by any organization, state, or proto-state. Libya belatedly accepted responsibility for the Lockerbie incident. After the longest investigation in Canadian history, charges were finally brought in 2003 against suspects of the Air India bombing, and the motives have finally become explicit. As with more recent attacks, it would seem that the new terrorists purposefully use ambiguous signatures to maximize the terror they seek to provoke.

Dominant feature — Terrorism is a mixture of physical violence and informational content. Terrorist organizations may be categorized based on the balance they strike between violence and information. The FLQ would be at the least violent end of the spectrum as its general strategy was to derive maximum effect from minimal violence through communiqués that spelled out the meaning of the violence (in many cases, sending a threatening communiqué was the only violence). This balance has been reversed in the new terrorism, where maximum violence is not accompanied by discursive explanation.

Words and images — Conventional terrorism communicated mostly through the written word, in a national language understood by all, to an audience generally considered literate. The new terrorism communicates through images of devastation, intended for an international audience that does not share one language and is characterized in some countries by high rates of illiteracy. For the great German sociologist Jürgen Habermas, the collapse of the World Trade Center twin towers was a unique event in the history of terrorism because its enfolding could be watched on television in real time throughout the world (Habermas, Derrida, and Borradori, 2003: 53–78).

Privileged channels — The creation of all-news channels such as CNN, Fox News, and Al-Jazeera brought about a new level of conflict as these news organizations are aimed at a particular audience and in certain instances offer openly partisan coverage. The conflict in the field is now matched by media warfare.

Radicalization — This feature is partly a result of the preceding features and it blends them together. Radicalization is the intensification of a conflict at all levels, including media warfare. More importantly, it also means simplification of the issues underlying the conflict. Conventional terrorism blended physical aggression with an explicit intention to convey its meaning and implications. It utilized reflexive violence: it reflected upon its purpose, which in some instances involved certain levels of complexity (e.g., political independence and social reform), and repeatedly tried to communicate this reflection (Brodeur, 1991). In several cases, terrorists claimed to be military arms of legitimate political movements that attempted to achieve their goals through persuasion. The new terrorism, usually uninterested in conveying an articulate message, instead produces a form of expressive violence that signifies little beyond anger, frustration, and a desire to return to some mythical and glorious past. Some observers have even concluded that the content of expressive violence is so thin that it can regress into nihilism (Glucksman, 2002; Ignatieff, 2004; Wieviorka, 1988).

Interestingly, Canadian law (among others) explicitly defines terrorism as violent action in pursuit of goals, whether political, religious, or ideological. However, one important aspect of extremist terrorism today is the absence of the expected logical connection between tactical means and strategic ends. The means actually used or sought after are at times so catastrophic—up to nuclear terrorism—that they do not allow a distinction between means and goals. They are all instrumentality or all finality, finality being understood here as a generic reference to willful intention (e.g., to harm) without a specific purpose.

Motivation

There is one easily identified difference between conventional and new terrorism. Politics can be said to inspire all conventional terrorism. Indeed, the dominant definition of terrorism is politically motivated violence. However, religion is at the root of the present wave of terrorism. Obviously, religion also played parts in some conventional forms of terrorism. The confrontation between Catholics and Protestants in Ulster comes to mind immediately. In truth, the distinction between politics and religion is often problematic—especially with all forms of fundamentalism. Islam may be easy to narrow down to a religion for people who are not part of it, but its more enthusiastic adepts consider the separation of politics and religion a sin, since the only truly moral politics follows the revealed truths of religion. The connection of religion and politics is also highly problematic in the case of failed state terrorism, for example, Chechnya, Somalia, and the partition of former Yugoslavia, where no stable political institutions serve as backgrounds for differentiating religion and politics.

The best way to model the relationship between politics and religion in trying to understand terrorism is probably to use the dominant feature concept we used earlier to depict the balance between violence and communication. In terms of its dominant feature, fundamentalist terrorism, whether Islamic, Sikh, or Hindu, may be said to be mainly motivated by religion, which we would characterize briefly as a set of beliefs organized around revealed truths and supernatural authority.

This would account for two additional features. First, conventional terrorism rests on a political program that is realized in time determined in identical units such as years. The timeframe of religious terrorism that is embodied in such notions as jihad or holy struggle is much less defined and tends ultimately to blend with timelessness or eternity, as conceived by religion. The second element in modeling the contrast between politics and religion is much more problematic and, for want of a better term, we shall use the word *irrationality* to designate it. Some caution is warranted here: irrationality is a notorious conceit often used to deny an alternative logic of thought to an action that we fail to understand or mean to condemn. Thus, the introduction of an element of irrationality in our understanding of religiously motivated terrorism can also serve as a reminder that much escapes us in considering worldviews that we feel foreign to our own and that we should be cautious in drawing conclusions about them.

Individualization

This last feature can also be seen as forming a spectrum between two extremes. At one end, both terrorists and their victims are individuals with precise identities. In 1975, a terrorist known as Carlos attacked an OPEC conference in Vienna, taking some 70 hostages and killing 3 of them. In this case the victims were targeted for their symbolic value and the terrorist had an elaborate escape plan that worked. Although many forms of conventional terrorism have slipped into violence for its own sake (Wieviorka, 1988), individuals who have not renounced their own identities and who want and plan to enjoy the fruits of victory are nevertheless pursuing it. They generally target individuals who are symbols of what they oppose such as heads of state, diplomats, and bankers.

By contrast, new terrorism is similar to bit-by-bit genocide. It does not discriminate among individual members of its target group and seeks consequences startling in their horror. Not only are civilian men, women, and children indiscriminately killed if they are perceived to belong to an enemy state, nation, ethnic, or otherwise identified group (apostates, Jews, U.S. citizens, Westerners). Recent events have shown that the boundaries of nationality are becoming irrelevant and that even the remotest connection with an "enemy," such as working for the United Nations or the Red Cross in Iraq, qualifies one as a potential target. Importantly, this de-personification is also reflected on the side of the perpetrators who serve as expendable bomb delivery systems and gain fame only for propaganda purposes after their deaths.

Features of Conventional Terrorism and Successful Counterterrorism

One purpose of our comparison of conventional and new terrorism is to lead into a discussion of police strategy, building on our assumption that police counterterrorism tactics must be woven on the distinctive warps of their targets. Canadian police agencies were not prepared for the October Crisis of 1970 and the CF were activated in Quebec in an effort to regain control over what was understood to be a dangerous situation. However, the police soon recovered and fought a winning battle against the FLQ, which ceased to be a threat by the end of 1973. The instrument of this success was infiltration that produced invaluable intelligence information and allowed manipulation of the membership.

The FLQ tried to reorganize after the October Crisis but it was infiltrated by a key police informant and others from 4 November 1970 until its dissolution in 1973 (Québec, 1981a, 1981b).* The informant, Carole de Vault, held a key position of courier among the remaining FLQ cells and was thus able to brief her police handlers extensively on their activities.† Even more crucially, she was entrusted with the task of issuing FLQ communiqués that she eventually wrote under the supervision of her police handler.

* Québec (1981a; Duchaîne Commission) and (1981b; Keable Commission) issued two reports bearing respectively on the FLQ and counterterrorism in Quebec that were commissioned by the provincial government. One of the authors of this chapter (Brodeur) was director of research for the Keable Commission, drafting its report, and served as a consultant for the Duchaîne Commission.

† de Vault became a public figure after her testimony before the Keable Commission and co-authored a book on her activities as a police informant (de Vault and Johnson, 1981).

In November 1971, the Montreal police department counterterrorism unit succeeded in recruiting another informant who operated at the top of the organization. The FLQ became so much of a police colony that when it tried to disband in December 1971 at the call of one of its main ideologues (Pierre Vallières), the RCMP issued a fake FLQ communiqué in the name of a fictitious cell denouncing Vallières as a turncoat and urging the FLQ terrorists to continue to pursue the armed struggle (Québec, 1981b: 91). The FLQ increasingly became an object of derision in Quebec and after 1973 it was replaced as the clandestine group to be reckoned with by the Maoist *En Lutte*, which was not a terrorist organization. One of the two main police informants active in the FLQ pursued his activities within the Maoist group that dissolved after learning that it had been infiltrated.

Keeping the FLQ as a case study of demand-based and revolutionary conventional terrorism, we now look at how the four aspects of terrorism—territoriality, communication, motivation, and individualization—affect the probability of success of counterterrorism strategies.

Territoriality — In cases of national terrorism, terrorists and counterterrorists usually share the same nationality and hence often also share the same physical appearance, language, and culture. As shown by the police struggle against the FLQ, this ethnic homogeneity greatly facilitates infiltration and, more generally, the collection of human intelligence (HUMINT). Differences in physical appearance, language, customs, and other conspicuous features help insulate international terrorist organizations from police and intelligence agencies.

Communication — In the case of the demise of the FLQ, communication was the critical feature. The major strength of this group was communication, not violence. The public approval of the FLQ manifesto generated the October Crisis. With unerring instinct, the police succeeded in infiltrating the FLQ where it mattered most: in writing communiqués.

Motivation — The motivation of the FLQ related directly to its actions. Thus, a clear, direct connection existed between its actions and its goals. This allows identification and protection of likely targets (*target hardening*). Also, negotiation is possible, and with the FLQ it helped resolve at least one issue (liberation of one hostage). In the case of more ambitious revolutionary terrorism, however, where targets tend to be larger and the attacks less discriminating, the resources needed by terrorists become more sizable and/or more difficult to obtain, as is the case with controlled substances (poisons, explosives, CBRN* materials). The obvious police strategy in these cases is to intensify surveillance of the means by which these substances can be obtained.

* Chemical, biological, radiological, and nuclear.

Table 5.2 Strategic Parallelism: Conventional Terrorism

Type of Terrorism	Actionable Characteristics	Possible Responses
Demand-based	Emphasis on message Proximate goals No ethno–cultural disparity	Interference with delivery Target-hardening, strategic negotiation Infiltration
Private justice	High predictability, proximate goals, identifiable targets Self-identification No ethno–cultural disparity	Target-hardening Surveillance/arrest Infiltration
Revolutionary	Emphasis on message More restricted resources needed Communication network needed Proximate goals No ethno–cultural disparity	Interference with delivery Surveillance of procurement Surveillance of communications Strategic negotiation Infiltration

Individualization — Target individualization was a prominent feature of the FLQ. The group abducted a British diplomat and a Quebec government minister who was reputed to be corrupt. Again, this feature permits target protection—all cabinet ministers and British diplomats were put under protection during the October Crisis. Individualization was also a feature of FLQ members. Although its cells were insulated from one another, cells frequently consisted of members of the same family. This facilitated the work of investigators who only needed to identify one member of a cell to discover the identities of others.

Table 5.2 summarizes these conclusions and also covers private justice terrorism, which on the whole does not fit the FLQ but is certainly an aspect of conventional terrorism in Canada. To a large extent it resembles demand-based terrorism, with the added feature that those who engage in it tend to self-identify in the sense that their grievances about specific injustices immediately point to their authors. This greatly simplifies surveillance and investigation.

Finding Correlations between "New" Terrorism and Successful Counterterrorism

It is useful to further clarify the nature of new terrorism because, as with revolutionary terror, its scope places it closer to the boundary where police responses are replaced by military actions. We have already seen how the CF was brought in to deal with what was presented at the time as an insurrection led by the FLQ. In this case, faulty intelligence and political maneuvering were at the heart of the disproportionate response. However, new terrorism on the international level is in fact insurgent terrorism and, at least in part, a military target. This does not mean, however, that the police have no role to play, especially in countries like Canada.

It may be helpful to distinguish between primary and secondary areas of international and transnational terrorist activity. Primary activity areas are where terrorists and terrorist groups conduct their principal operations, i.e., violent attacks. Secondary activity areas serve as bases for support activities such as recruitment, planning, sheltering fugitives, and funding. Secondary areas tend to have low levels of violence in order to minimize political and police attention. Canada, by this measure, is a secondary activity area. While military response may be called for in primary areas due to a certain level of violence or risk of property damage, secondary areas clearly call for police response. Let us consider the same four aspects to see whether we can match them to police strategies that may be more successful for Canadian and U.S. policing and intelligence agencies in their struggles against Al-Qaeda and violent Islamic fundamentalism.

Territoriality —Terrorist activities in Canada, a secondary activity area, generally involve fundraising, organizing, recruiting, intimidating, and other support activities conducted for the most part by foreign nationals or Canadians belonging to minority ethnic groups, which complicates infiltration efforts. Not that infiltration is impossible—recall John Walker Lindh, the "American Taliban." On a less anecdotal note, most ethnic Canadians are not terrorists, are not controlled by terrorists, and many have joined various counterterrorist agencies, thus being in positions to play a part in infiltration. Yet, in our opinion, infiltration in such cases remains especially difficult and probably not the best way to spend limited counterterrorist resources against restoration terrorism, at least in its present form in Canada. Furthermore, infiltrating whole communities on the sole basis that they are mainly comprised of immigrants from a particular part of the world, say, the Middle East, may be tantamount to practicing racial or ethnic profiling on a grand scale. This practice has already been shown to flaunt human rights when applied even on a limited, individual scale.

The problem with infiltration is that it seems trapped in a vicious circle: one must infiltrate in order to identify terrorists, but when terrorists are few or non-existent, infiltration only generates feelings of harassment and dread that may be conducive to retaliation terrorism in unfairly targeted communities.

Communication — We described the absence of an articulated communication strategy with defined targets that characterizes new terrorism—its actions, the spectacular destruction that it wreaks, are its means of communication. However, international terrorists must communicate with one another in order to operate. These communications can be intercepted, as can their money transfers and other logistical and manpower procurement activities. In other words, SIGINT (signal intelligence, as collected in intercepting electronic communications) can take over where HUMINT is too risky for agents or for human rights. It can do so, however—and we cannot emphasize this too much—only to the extent that it is coupled with the adequate capacity for analysis—connecting the dots. Of course, when a government has incontrovertible evidence that a group is dangerous, the group becomes a legitimate target for infiltration.

Motivation — Terrorist motives are too broad and too far removed from actions to help in devising preventive tactics. One may reasonably expect attacks against populated infrastructures (in particular, public transportation) that maximize spectacular destruction and loss of life. This is, however, not descriptive enough to be of any practical use. To the extent that controlled substances may be needed for maximum damage, rigorous monitoring of all means of procuring these substances, as suggested to counter revolutionary terrorism, may be of help but is unlikely to be very effective. Thus, realistically, we believe that resources are better spent on emergency responses.

Individualization — New terrorism de-individualizes both its victims and its agents, with the rare exception of emblematic figures such as Bin Laden. However, membership in organizations that promote a lifestyle in addition to a worldview and the authoritarian imposition of rituals may provide counterterrorist agencies with certain levels of self-identification: potential terrorists may act differently and thus reveal their affiliations. We see this in the case of Ahmed Ressam, who joined a group of extremists already under surveillance by CSIS (Canadian Security Intelligence Service) but were (mistakenly) considered relatively harmless—just a 'bunch of guys' (Sageman, 2004: 101). A stronger analytic capacity might have made it possible to identify the group or some of its members such as Ressam as constituting real threats. The difficulty lies in identifying the line between *talkers* who meet to rant against Israel and call for jihad and *doers*, potential terrorists who are likely to take action. Making this distinction requires background knowledge about terrorism and a strong analytic capability to apply this general background to particular cases.

Table 5.3 completes the categories set up in Table 5.2 by adding restoration terrorism. It should be immediately obvious that counterterrorist strategies that parallel new terrorism may violate the individual rights of Canadians—which is why disproportionate security responses are identified

Table 5.3 Strategic Parallelism: New Terrorism

Type of Terrorism	Actionable Characteristics	Possible Responses
Restoration	More/restricted resources needed Communication network needed Self-identification more likely	Surveillance of procurement Surveillance of communications Surveillance/arrest Improved analysis of surveillance products

as wins for terrorists—one terrorist goal is to undermine the confidence of Westerners in their own governments. Increased interception and surveillance based on suspicion or apparent affiliation are extremely dangerous to our civil liberties and should be considered only when strict accountability and review and overview structures that are now sorely lacking in many police agencies in Canada are put into place.

Conclusion

One last feature of the Ressam affair allows insight into the nature of terrorism prevention. Counterterrorist agencies are often criticized for failing to prevent terrorist attacks that kill hundreds, if not thousands, but the difference between an actual attack and a prevented attack is crucial. We know in all its painful detail what we failed to prevent after an event and its tragic consequences unfold completely. In fact even the terrorists do not always foresee the consequences — such as the collapse of the twin towers of the World Trade Center.

In contrast, when an event is prevented we have only very limited knowledge of what might have occurred. For instance, we know exactly what we failed to prevent on 11 September 2001—we can count the dead and assess the damage. We are in no such position with the failed attack of the millennium bomber, who was intercepted with a trunk load of explosives. We can try to imagine what might have happened if he had been able to set off his bomb at the Los Angeles airport but we cannot know, among the many possible scenarios, what might have happened. For instance, the truck might have been blown up near an underground fuel tank that would also have exploded, setting off a chain of catastrophic events. All we can know for sure is that Ressam was prevented from setting off his homemade bomb at the airport. The cost in lives, property, and social trauma of his success remains pure conjecture. The bottom line is that when considering prevention, it is probable that blame for failure will always be greater than praise for success. This should be remembered when the performance of security services, police organizations, and their individual members is assessed.

References

Brodeur, J-P. (1991) Countering terrorism in Canada, in Farson, S., Stafford, D., and Wark, W. K. (Eds.), *Security and intelligence in a changing world: New perspectives for the 1990s* (pp. 182–200), London: Frank Cass.

Crelinsten, R. D. (1997) Television and terrorism: Implications for crisis management and policymaking, *Terrorism and Political Violence*, 9 (4): 8–32.

De Vault, C. and Johnson, W. (1981) *Toute ma vérité: Les confessions de lagent S.A.T. [Section antiterroriste]* (pp. 945-1071), Montréal: Stanké.

Fournier, L. (1998) *FLQ: Histoire dun mouvement clandestine*, Outremont: Lanctôt Éditeur.

Glucksman, A. (2002) *Dostoïevski à Manhattan*, Paris: Laffont.

Gressang, D. (2001) Audience and message: Assessing terrorist WMD potential, *Terrorism and Political Violence*, 13 (3): 83–106.

Habermas, J., Derrida, J., and Borradori, G. (2003) *Philosophy in a time of terror* (pp. 53–78), Chicago: University of Chicago Press.

Hoffman, B. (1997) The confluence of international and domestic trends in terrorism, *Terrorism and Political Violence*, 9 (2): 1–15.

Ignatieff, M. (2004) *The lesser evil: Politics in an age of terror*, Princeton, NJ: Princeton University Press.

Kellett, A., Beanlands, B., Deacon, J., Jeffrey, H., and Lapalme, C. (1991) *Terrorism in Canada, 1960–1989*, Ottawa: Ministry of the Solicitor General of Canada, National Security Coordination Centre, Police and Security Branch.

Laqueur, W. (1987) *The age of terrorism*, London: Weidenfeld and Nicolson.

Laqueur, W. (1997) *Postmodern terrorism*, United States International Information Program. Retrieved from http://usinfo.state.gov/journals/itgic/0297/ijge/gj-3.htm [Correct September 2007].

Laqueur, W. (1999) *The new terrorism: Fanaticism and the arms of mass destruction*, New York: Oxford University Press.

Laqueur, W. (2003) *No end to war: Terrorism in the twenty-first century*, New York: Continuum.

Mickolus, E. F. (1980) *Transnational terrorism: A chronology of events, 1968–1979*, Westport, CT: Greenwood Press.

Mickolus, E. F. (1993) *Terrorism, 1988–1991: A chronology of events and a selectively annotated bibliography*, Westport, CT: Greenwood Press.

Mickolus, E. F., Sandler, T., and Murdock, J. M. (1989) *International terrorism in the 1980s: A chronology of events. Volume 1: 1980–1983; Volume 2: 1984–1987*, Ames: Iowa State University Press.

Mickolus, E. F. and Simmons, S. L. (1997) *Terrorism, 1992–1995: A chronology of events and a selectively annotated bibliography*, Westport, CT: Greenwood Press.

Pape, R. (2003) The strategic logic of suicide terrorism, *American Political Science Review*, 97 (3): 1–19.

Piotte, J-M., Pichette, M., David, H., Maheu, L., Denis, R., Brodeur, J-P., and de Ipola, E. (Eds.) (1971) *Québec occupé*, Montréal: Parti-Pris.

Québec. (1981a) *Rapport sur les événements doctobre 1970* (Duchaîne Commission), Québec City: Ministère de la Justice.

Québec. (1981b) *Rapport de la Commission denquête sur les opérations policières sur le territoire québécois* (Keable Commission), Québec City: Ministère de la Justice.

Ross, J. I. (1988) Attributes of domestic political terrorism in Canada, *Terrorism*, 11: 213–233.

Sageman, M. (2004) *Understanding terror networks*, Philadelphia: University of Pennsylvania Press.

Schmid, A. and de Graaf, J. (1982) *Violence as communication*, London: Sage.

Vareilles, T. (2001) *Encyclopédie du terrorisme international*, Paris: LHarmattan.
Wieviorka, M. (1988) *Sociétés et terrorisme*, Paris: Fayard.
Wieviorka, M. (1995) *Face au Terrorisme*, Paris: Liana Lévy.
Wieviorka, M. and Wolton, D. (1987) *Terrorisme à la une*, Paris: Gallimard.

Policing Terrorism: A Threat to Community Policing or Just a Shift in Priorities?*

6

JOHN MURRAY

Contents

The introduction of community policing has been heralded as the most significant and progressive change in policing philosophy, and there are good reasons for this claim. Based on its distinctly proactive emphasis, community policing has proven to be a dramatic improvement to the traditional model of policing that is essentially reactive. Characteristically, traditional policing almost invariably depends on a paramilitary structure that tends to distance police from the rest of the community. Community policing, on the other hand, relies on a cooperative community arrangement that reduces both the incidence of crime and also the fear of crime when it works effectively.

It has been frequently said that the terrorist events of September 11 2001 changed the world forever (see Leman-Langlois and Brodeur, Chapter 5 of this volume). To some observers, so too has the public profile of policing. Many countries now show signs of reversion to (or in some cases reaffirmation of) paramilitaristic policing that is more in line with the traditional model and clearly at odds with community policing. The threat of terrorism that exists

* This chapter first appeared in *Police Practice and Research,* 2005, 6(4): 347–361.

today will test the resolve of police commissioners who choose to retain community policing as a dominant philosophy. No doubt, the effectiveness of community policing will be challenged and some will consider it too soft to match the so-called war against terror. While some police forces and services will continue to rely on the community policing model, others will be tempted to return to traditional models and varying degrees of paramilitarism. Williams (2003: 119) notes that in the United States the "effort to incorporate the community policing model into traditional policing operations is faltering."

Another pressure on community policing is governmental influence. In the context of the drive for effectiveness and efficiency and the election value of law and order, some governments will promote the view that police should concentrate on their core business: a focus on crime fighting. This chapter examines and compares traditional policing and community policing, and in particular critiques the paramilitarism of the former to challenge its relevance to policing in general.

Another major consideration in the maintenance of community policing as a dominant philosophy is the prevailing police culture. I comment on the cultural change required by the transition to community policing. While many police forces and services have ostensibly managed the cultural change to accommodate community policing, I warn of the underlying tension that probably still exists in police culture that is likely to prefer the traditional model of policing, a tension also explored in Chapter 2 by Venessa Garcia. Put another way, the dominant police culture dictates that operational police are likely to consider community policing inappropriate for fighting terrorism. Consequently, this presents a real challenge for commissioners who seek to retain community policing, especially in a climate that tends to demand a more visible and aggressive force against terrorism.

It is frequently noted that police alone cannot successfully achieve crime control and that the support of the community is critical. The same principles clearly apply to the prevention of terrorist acts, and prevention should surely be the emphasis. While threats against national security have justifiably shifted the focus of policing priorities to meet this critical demand, I argue that any shift in policing strategies overall should be a shift in emphasis only and not an abandonment of community policing and a total return to the paramilitarism of the traditional model. The shift in focus to counter terrorism will quite rightly involve placing more resources in paramilitary units and providing front-line officers with the necessary skills. However, to do so by abandoning community policing as an overall philosophy will be counterproductive since it takes away the critical facilities of prevention and community cooperation that are inherent in community policing. The two policing philosophies of paramilitarism and community policing can (and in this current environment should) coexist, but under the umbrella of community policing.

Transition from Traditional Paramilitarism to Community Policing

For much of the developed world, the origins of the modern police service can be traced to the creation of the Metropolitan Police in London in 1829 (Reith, 1975). Introduced by Sir Robert Peel, the bill proclaiming the Metropolitan Police Act in England was accompanied by a set of principles for policing that continue to have relevance today. The organizational structure and managerial philosophy that accompanied the establishment of this earliest police organization were consistent with the literal definition of paramilitarism (Auten, 1981; Reith, 1975). The paramilitary stamp was firmly put on Peel's police, evidenced by the facts that: (1) the police were required to be stable, efficient, and organized along military lines (Waters and McGrath, 1974; cited by Auten, 1981); (2) the force had virtually no organizational model other than the military to emulate; and (3) a conscious decision was made to select an inaugural leader who was a military person (Auten, 1981). In fact, the authors of the first manual of instruction adapted their text from an 1803 military manual of the Irish Constabulary Police titled *Military Training and Moral Training* (Reith, 1975).

The move from a traditionally reactive, action-oriented style of policing to a service-oriented community policing model that occurred over the past three decades has arguably been the most significant positive change in policing philosophy. To Bayley (1994: 104), for example,

> ...community policing represents the most serious and sustained attempt to formulate the purpose and practices of policing since the development of the "professional" model in the early twentieth century.

The introduction of community policing followed what were seen as the limitations of traditional policing and the need for change. Moore (1994: 285) neatly summarizes this idea:

> It is not hard to understand the attraction of the new ideas about policing [the community policing movement]. They seem to recognize and respond to what have come to be seen as the limitations of the "reform model" of policing: its predominantly reactive stance toward crime control; its nearly exclusive reliance on arrests as a means of reducing crime and controlling disorder; its inability to develop and sustain close working relationships with the community in controlling crime; and its stifling and ultimately unsuccessful methods of bureaucratic control (Sparrow, Moore, and Kennedy, 1990). In contrast the new ideas point to a new set of possibilities: the potential for crime prevention as well as crime control; creative problem solving as an alternative to arrest; the importance of customer service and community responsiveness as devices for building stronger relations with local communities; and "commissioning"

> street-level officers to initiate community problem-solving efforts. (Sparrow et al., 1990)

Researchers and commentators found that police services that embraced community policing refer to its cornerstone as a collaborative partnership between the community and the police, engaged in a process that identifies and solves problems of crime and disorder (Bayley, 1994; Goldstein, 1990; Rosenbaum, 1988; Sherman et al., 1998). While no single definition appears to apply to community policing, Oliver and Bartgis (1988:491) note a constant theme in the literature:

> The majority of definitions focus on an increase in police and community interaction, a concentration on "quality of life issues," the decentralization of the police, strategic methods for making police practices more efficient and effective, a concentration on neighbourhood patrols, and problem-oriented or problem-solving policing.

Public attitudes about police also determine the success of community policing. A hostile or fearful community, for example, will be disinclined to cooperate with police (Reisig and Giacomazzi, 1998). Police, as Roberg (1994: 251–252) notes, may not be unduly concerned about that because many line officers were "recruited, trained and socialized in a traditional law enforcement orientation and may have a stake in preserving the status quo." Oliver and Bartgis (1988) found line officers had the capability to ignore, circumvent, or sabotage the desires and expectations of the community. Since the transition from traditional policing required a substantial change in culture, it is appropriate to examine the cultural traits of traditional policing and how or to what extent they contrast with those of community policing.

Police Occupational Subculture: Bias toward Traditional Paramilitary Policing?

Based on the extensive authority and discretion held by police, they clearly have the potential to exert dramatic impacts on the lives and liberties of citizens. Reflecting on the importance of maintaining a keen interest in policing, Van Maanen (1978: 311) thought policing to be "possibly the most vital of our human service agencies…too important to be taken for granted, or worse, to be ignored." It certainly follows, therefore, that the ideology, values, principles, and preconceptions generally held by police, and consequently determining police culture, are critical. Unlike most other vocations, the police have the greatest amount of discretion at the lowest level of the organization. While decisions to arrest are open to scrutiny, *most* police decisions involve actions other than arrests and are, therefore, largely without scrutiny or control.

Occupational police culture has been the subject of regular examination by many theorists; the most prominent are Manning (1977) and Skolnick (1966, 1985) in the United States; Cain (1973) and Reiner (1992) in Great Britain; and Chan (1996, 1997, 1999) and Prenzler (1997) in Australia. Many definitions and descriptions of police culture include "developed recognizable and distinct rules, customs, perceptions and interpretations of what they see, along with consequent moral judgements" (Skolnick and Fyfe, 1993: 90) and "an identifiable complex of common culture, values, communication symbols, techniques, and appropriate behaviour patterns" (McBride, 1995: 214). Reiner (1992: 21) equates police culture with the "values, norms, perspectives, and craft rules" that inform police conduct.

Skolnick (1966) refers to the "working personality" that is associated with the police task and is characterized by suspiciousness, internal solidarity, social isolation, and conservatism. Reiner's (1992) subsequent work resulted in similar conclusions. He found that a "central feature of cop culture is a sense of mission [and that to police themselves] policing is not just a job but a way of life with a worthwhile purpose" (p. 111). He also noted that the "core of the police outlook is this subtle and complex intermingling of the themes of mission, hedonistic love of action and pessimistic cynicism" (p. 114). Pertinent to this chapter, he found that "most policemen are well aware that their job has bred them an attitude of constant suspiciousness which cannot be readily switched off [accompanied by a] marked internal solidarity, coupled with social isolation" (pp. 114, 115). These findings are supported to varying degrees by Fitzgerald (1989), Goldstein (1976, 1990), Skolnick and Fyfe (1993), and Wood (1997).

The most interesting aspect of the general findings about operational police culture outlined above is that when summarized they are almost diametrically opposite to what I identified (Murray, 2002) as the appropriate/ideal characteristics of a community police officer, including a genuine belief in community consultation and problem solving; commitment to the notion of equal partnership with the community; creativity and innovation; freedom to exercise discretion at the lowest level of policing; and excellent communication skills so as to be able to develop a rapport with the community, and in turn, win trust and respect. Table 6.1 contrasts these ideal characteristics for a community police officer with cultural traits identified through research.

I suspect, however, the research findings are not as stark as they appear since they tend to ignore the positive aspects of police culture. Chan (1997) believes police culture has become a convenient label for a range of negative values, attitudes, and practice norms among officers. Prenzler (1997) notes that judicial and scholarly references to police culture are almost universally

Table 6.1 Competing Police Profiles

Ideal Profile for Community Police Officer	Research Profile for Operational Police
Commitment to community consultation and problem solving	Sense of mission about police work but distancing from community
Open and accessible in provision of service	Suspiciousness
Creative and innovative in promoting solutions to problems and crime prevention	Pragmatic view that discourages innovation and experimentation
Freedom to exercise discretion at the lowest level so as to incorporate problem solving as an alternative to arrest	Preference for action orientation and arrests
Excellent communication skills to aid in developing rapport with community and win respect and trust	Isolated social life coupled with strong code of solidarity with other officers; cynical or pessimistic perspective about social environment

pejorative. James and Warren (1995: 4) suggest this may be explained to an extent by the fact that:

> The origins of cultural explanations for police behaviour can be traced to attempts by sociologists in the 1960s to explain an enduring anomaly in policing: the breaking of rules by the people whose primary occupation and sole purpose is to enforce rules.

Despite studies repeatedly showing that most police work involves situations in which no crime occurred, police prefer action orientations rather than providing services (Feltes, 1994; Reiner, 1992, 1994; Scott, 1988; Skolnick, 1985; Waddington, 1999). At the same time, some governments rely heavily on response-based performance measures such as numbers of arrests as indicators of police effectiveness since quantitative targets are easy to define and present more convenient solutions to political demands (Redshaw and Sanders, 1995).

Subculture and Alignment to Models of Policing

Traditional policing, which places a heavy emphasis on paramilitarism, and community policing, which is founded on a more democratic model, give rise to very different cultures. Many police services have successfully managed the cultural transition from action to service orientation that accompanied the shift from the traditional to the community policing model, while others experienced resistance arising from the cultural preference for crime fighting rather than problem solving. This tension becomes pertinent in the light of current outside pressures such as the imperative to address terrorism and ensure national security. Some services opted to retain the traditional model of policing, albeit in modified form. As police services around the world address national security, an examination of the differences in police culture that tend to be aligned to traditional versus community policing is appropriate.

Craft or Professional Culture?

Proponents of traditional policing tend to regard it as a craft or trade best learned on the job. This model assumes that most training and mentoring should be undertaken by experienced officers in a master–apprentice arrangement. Certainly in former times, "outside" help was neither requested nor respected. Community policing adopts an open approach for recruitment, training, and development, interpreted by some as a move toward making policing a profession. The meaning of *profession* is, of course, open to different interpretations but is generally considered within policing circles to include the development of a body of knowledge, a strict code of ethics, and working to values rather than rules.

In cultural terms, traditional policing presents a strong preference for the status quo: seasoned officers perpetuate an existing culture, resulting in insularity and an us-versus-them (police versus community) mentality. Community policing culture places a great deal of reliance on community expectations and a willingness to join with and learn from experts outside policing.

Paramilitarism or Democratic Managerial Culture?

Traditional policing, as Auten (1981: 68) notes, promotes a paramilitaristic managerial style that exhibits at least some of the following characteristics:

- Centralized command structure with a rigidly followed chain of command
- Rigid superior–subordinate relationships defined by prerogatives of rank
- Control exerted through the issuance of commands, directives, or general orders
- Primarily vertical communications—from top to bottom
- Initiative not sought or encouraged
- Authoritarian style of leadership
- Us–them division between senior officers and rest of department
- Rule-based and punitive disciplinary measures

Traditional policing relies heavily on these characteristics to both ensure effectiveness and efficiency through command and control and also to maintain discipline. Proponents of community policing never denied the needs for command and control but point out that occasions where they are required are relatively few and that emphasis in the traditional model is disproportionate and counterproductive. Community policing presents a more democratic style of management that relies on personal credibility rather than rank-based authority.

The culture of the traditional model typically manifests expectations of unquestioned acceptance of directions from senior officers and one-way communications. This culture assumes that subordinate ranks must be told what to do, that rank makes the "right" decisions, and that those down the ladder have little to offer. The more democratic style in community policing allows empowerment at the lowest possible level so as to allow greater decision making at the operational level. This gives rise to a culture that supports initiative and problem solving. The culture inherent in community policing also recognizes the need for command and control when required and adaptations appropriate to the occasion.

Authoritarian or Problem-Solving Culture?

Traditional policing emphasizes arrests and the strict enforcement of laws. Little consideration is given to prosecutorial discretion. Interest in the causes of crime is limited and little emphasis is placed on crime prevention. The general assumption is that the police know what is best for the community at large. Community policing, on the other hand, is founded on the primacy of crime prevention and a conscious commitment to joining the community in problem solving. The cultural expectations for these two models are dramatically different. Skolnick (1966) and Reiner (1992), cited above, found that the traditional policing culture demonstrates a tendency for action orientation and a general distancing from the community. Community policing culture tends toward openness, innovation, community interest, service orientation, and a spirit of problem solving.

Compliant or Adaptive Culture?

The traditional model of policing tends to have: (1) a centralized structure with headquarters as the source of orders, rules, and regulations; (2) standardization and uniformity; (3) performance measurements based on quantitative criteria such as number of arrests; (4) excessive specialization; and (5) a narrow definition of the duties of a patrol officer; they are limited to responding to complaints and following predetermined rules and practices. This relatively compliant model meets with problems when confronted with situations not readily covered by existing directives, general orders, or policies and procedures.

Community policing adopts a more adaptive approach through (1) a decentralized structure with the aim to bring the police closer to the community; headquarters serves as the source of support direction, norms, and values; (2) encouragement and support for flexibility; (3) performance measurement based on both quantitative and qualitative criteria such as the achievement of community goals or solving problems; (4) a move from specialization to a balance between versatility and specialization; and (5) the patrol officer as a generalist responsible for attending complaints, solving problems, activating the community, preventing crime, and undertaking preliminary investigations; the discretionary powers of the patrol officer are recognized and developed.

Traditional policing trains officers to work to established rules and regulations. The culture, therefore, tends to be regimented to act on direct orders with the assumption that rank-based authority ensures compliance, efficiency, and effectiveness. Community policing provides a more flexible structure and development of a culture that is more conducive to recognizing that there is usually no single solution to a problem and that by recognizing the valuable contributions from those in the field, a more practical resolution is likely. At operational level, officers will have more confidence to deal with community issues.

Recognizing the Appropriate Model

A shift from traditional to community policing requires a major transition in both managerial and cultural terms. Plainly the characteristics of traditional policing are not suited to community policing. Table 6.2 highlights differences between the two models. After the world changed on September 11 2001, the question to be asked is, are we seeing a reversion to the paramilitarism of the traditional policing model or merely a shift?

Threat of Terrorism and Impact on Community Policing

Prior to September 11 2001, many countries in the developed world had lapsed into a laissez-faire approach to national security. The terrorist attacks on U.S. soil brought that complacency to a dramatic end. Homeland security became a priority in the United States and in many other countries. This required strategic consideration about how military and civil services would reconfigure to address this fresh challenge. While defense forces would obviously feature in the reassessment, policing would also have to meet increased

Table 6.2 Transitions between Traditional and Community Policing

Traditional Policing and Links to Paramilitarism[a]	Community Policing and Democratic Management	Comparison of Cultures
Policing as craft: Traditionally regarded as craft or trade best learned on the job	Policing as profession: Conscious drive to consider policing a profession	Culture developed on job: Traditional policing relies strongly on status quo and learning from experienced officers; community policing develops a more open culture that places a great deal of reliance on community expectations
Paramilitary management style: Traditional policing incorporates managerial style based entirely on military lines or at least draws on military principles	Democratic management style: Command and control are necessary, but relatively few situations require them; management allows all ranks to determine how job is done	Empowered or disempowered culture: Paramilitarism assumes that authority is linked to rank; democratic style empowers all officers
Authoritarian approach: Traditional policing involves strict enforcement of laws, little concern about causes of crime, limited prosecutorial discretion, and less emphasis on preventing crime	Problem-solving approach: Understanding of causes of crime and conscious commitment to joining with community to prevent crime	Linking culture to philosophy: Traditional policing tends toward authoritarianism, defensiveness, cynicism, and action orientation that lead to general distancing from community; community policing fosters open consultative culture geared to solving problems
Inflexible structure: Traditional model tends to have rigid, centralized bureaucracy; officers work to predetermined rules and practices	Flexible structure: Community policing devolves authority and decision making and encourages initiative. Officers work to values and standards	From compliant to adaptive culture: Traditional policing culture tends to be regimented and compliant; community policing is adaptive, recognizing that problems usually do not have single solutions.
Blame culture: Paramilitary model assumes that officers will inevitably do something wrong, and when they do they should be punished	Learning culture: Recognizes failure of punitive model; educates and corrects minor and understandable breaches	From institutional to personal discipline: Punitive model creates apprehension, anxiety, defensiveness, and denial; an us-versus-them culture results; officers in a learning culture work to values; minor breaches are seen as curable mistakes—move from threat to incentive

Table 6.2 Transitions between Traditional and Community Policing (Continued)

Traditional Policing and Links to Paramilitarism[a]	Community Policing and Democratic Management	Comparison of Cultures
Insularity and defensiveness: Traditional policing shows tendency to feel that only police know anything about policing; academics and other commentators are not appreciated	Openness and consultation: Community policing invites outside expert advice; individual police contributions are considered worthwhile	Move toward transparency: Traditional police culture is defense with a tendency toward secrecy; inherent in community policing is the principle that police form part of the community; the desired culture recognizes and works to a model that allows the public to know how and why the police operate as they do

[a] The listing of characteristics of traditional policing and links to paramilitarism are drawn largely from Auten (1981).

responsibilities. In many countries, the changes were dramatic and involved far more than tightening up existing practices. De Guzman (2002: 8), for example, described the U.S. reaction as the "fortification" of the country.

Policing across the world appeared visibly different to the average observer. Not only were more police in view, but they assumed a more aggressive style of dress and manner. Prior to September 11 2001, some writers had already expressed concern about a shift in policing toward paramilitarism. Weber (1999: 2) expressed alarm at the "spawning of a culture of paramilitarism in American law enforcement [with] local police officers…increasingly emulating the war-fighting tactics of soldiers." According to McCulloch (2001a), the threat of terrorism in Australia had been used to justify significant changes in the role of the police and a shift toward paramilitarism. To these writers, the civil–military separation was breaking down and the lines that traditionally separated the military mission from the police were becoming distinctly blurred. Moreover, Weber (1999: 5) contended that:

> Over the last century police departments have evolved into increasingly centralized, authoritarian, autonomous, and militarized bureaucracies, which has led to their isolation from the citizenry.

If Weber is correct, community policing has shifted back to the traditional model or the police have not made the transition at all. It should be remembered she made this comment before September 11 2001. I am concerned that a post–September 11 move would see community policing and all its fine principles undermined by a reversion to the traditional model of policing, rationalized by the need to counter terrorism.

In a reference to Australia, McCulloch (2001b: 4) was more cynical and described "community policing [as] the 'velvet glove' covering the 'iron fist' of more military styles of policing." This is certainly not my observation. While McCulloch and I both accept that paramilitary policing and community policing are actually complementary (McCulloch, 2001b: 4), we do so for different reasons. She considers references by police to community policing as "rhetoric [and] well published strategies designed to counter the negative image and public antipathy arising from the use of coercive paramilitary tactics." I, on the other hand, believe the complement between paramilitary policing and community policing in Australia to mean the maintenance of a capability to counter extreme acts of violence within a genuine community policing model.

As we face the "war on terror," rather than moving away from community policing, police commissioners should look to its qualities and specifically note how the philosophy can be used to their advantage. To abandon or diminish it would be counterproductive and would undo the conscious drive over the decades that has taken policing to the high level of societal acceptance it now enjoys. It follows, therefore, that I cannot accept comments like those of de Guzman (2002: 11) who believes that, "[in] the context of war against terror, some tenets of community policing appear to be inconsistent with the implementation of these new police roles." He continues, "The events of September 11 threaten the utility as well as the continued existence of some community policing ideals on several grounds" (see below). While he concedes community policing should probably not be abandoned, it is appropriate to examine the four points he suggests support the fact that community policing in its present form would be unable to meet the demands introduced by the threat of terrorism.

First, de Guzman (2002: 11) states the philosophical ideal in community policing (winning the hearts and minds of the community) will not be effective against terror because we cannot reason with terrorists. It is futile for police to try, and patrols should be made aware that they should detect and prevent violent terrorist acts, not deter them. I consider this an extremely narrow view. Community–police partnerships work best when they are structured to encourage information sharing from all parts of the community. This *especially* includes groups that tend to be unwilling to assist the police. For de Guzman to refer to this fundamental aspect of community policing as futile in the context of prospective terrorism is unproductive. To exclude or isolate any subgroup from a community policing service amounts to more than failing in a civic duty—it also ignores a most important source of information that would allow police to gauge what they must combat (Bayley and Bittner, 1984). Today, a more thoughtful initiative would involve rebuilding trust with specific ethnic and cultural communities through a genuine commitment by police to protect them and their neighborhoods, workplaces, and places of worship (Lyons, 2002). Community policing that works well will deflect rumors and reduce misinformation and distortion.

Second, de Guzman (2002: 11) believes the introduction of strategies against terrorism will negate assumptions of community cooperation and trust that are implicit in community policing. Terrorists constantly employ deceit, and de Guzman argues that police should be reluctant to invest their trust on such unidentifiable forces. I take a contrary view. Successful detection and prevention of terrorism depend on information. We know from experience that terrorists can successfully occupy positions within conventional communities. A community–police relationship based on mutual trust is more likely to uncover information that will help identify prospective terrorists. A more formal or authoritarian police–community relationship serves to distance police from the community and only genuine law breaking incidents are likely to be reported. However, a good community–police relationship encourages dialogue and is more likely to uncover valuable information about suspicious activities; this can only be brought about by trust and mutual respect. Enlisting the community in its own defense encourages members to take control of their own destiny.

Third, de Guzman (2002: 11) points out that the partnership of community policing in which both parties must reach a consensus about strategies of crime prevention and police operations will fail in today's environment because police cannot reveal their strategies to the community. Furthermore, if the police in their development of counterterrorism strategies hold back information, the community will sense the withdrawal, trust will be breached, and such partnerships will inevitably wither away. Again, I take a distinctly different view. Communities involved in existing policing partnerships never expected police to confide confidential information about investigations or give specific information about operational tactics. Thus dealing with terrorism requires nothing essentially different.

Taking the position that police will decide what is best for a community may be interpreted as arrogant and in breach of a fundamental tenet of public accountability. A community has a right to certain information, and in the context of terrorism, for example, should be made aware of the levels of threats so that individuals can make decisions about their own welfare. A basic assumption of community policing is that police are part of the community (as civilians) and that collaboration is required in addressing crime, terrorism, and other community problems. The contribution community policing can make in this area is extremely positive. In terms of prevention, it can allow the community to focus on the importance of early warning consistent with the spirit of protecting everyone's interests. The community should feel comfortable about coming forward with information no matter how slight its connection to terrorism may appear.

de Guzman's (2002: 12) fourth point is that parochial policing is promoted in community policing but the war on terror necessitates broader collaborative policing. The level of collaboration, he contends, should exist within the department and also include other local departments, state, and federal agencies because the planning for the war on terror may occur far distant from the target phase. Thus, efforts to enhance communications and collaborations among and between police departments should be a constant undertaking. In my view, effective community policing is not parochial and in fact is multidisciplinary on the basis that police alone seldom have all the answers for all community problems. Community policing, therefore, uses a broad rather than a narrow (parochial) approach. Police regularly work with specialists at local and national levels; in the context of the threat of terrorism, they also work at an international level.

Conclusion

The traditional model of policing relies on paramilitarism characterized by rank-based authority and command and control. The organizational structure of this model is hierarchical and inflexible, making it difficult to meet the challenges of a rapidly changing environment. Traditional policing is predominantly reactive and unable to develop and sustain close working relationships with communities in order to control crime. Community policing is eminently sensible because it concentrates on crime prevention.

The transition to community policing has not been easy for most police services because the prevailing culture has shown a distinct preference for action orientation and a lack of interest in "soft" policing with which community policing has been identified. Even in services that successfully made the transition to community policing, it is likely that the tension within the culture remains and that suggestions and movements to revert to the traditional paramilitary style would meet with a great deal of support from the rank and file.

The world certainly changed after September 11, 2001, but that does not mean it is necessary to move away from community policing as a prevailing philosophy. Clearly, a shift of priorities that allows policing strategies to focus on national security is a requirement. To assume, however, that paramilitarism as an overarching model is best suited to achieve this is a serious miscalculation. A reversion to a traditional model of policing will undo decades of great work that has made modern community policing an exemplar of public service in a civil and democratic society. Using the principles of community policing is a much more sensible and effective way of dealing with terrorism.

It is accepted that police cannot fight crime alone and must rely on communities. The same principle applies to terrorism. A community–police relationship built on trust and mutual respect is much more likely to give early warnings about terrorist acts. Rather than move away from community policing, community involvement should be reinforced, especially in light of the police culture that tends to prefer action.

The commitment of police commissioners over the years to make the necessary transitions to achieve this cultural change must not be forgotten. Moreover, as they reconfigure strategies to meet the threat of terrorism (as they must), they should understand that operational police may prefer to move to an action-oriented style of policing characterized by paramilitarism. In their eagerness to reassure the public, politicians may also prefer this model. The road ahead will be demanding for police leaders, but they must resist the temptation to fall back to policing methods that ignore the profound and ethically based principles of community policing.

References

Auten, J. H. (1981) The paramilitary model of police and police professionalism, *Police Studies,* 4 (2): 67–78.

Bayley, D. H. (1994) *Police for the future,* New York: Oxford University Press.

Bayley, D. H. and Bittner, E. (1984) Learning the skills of policing, *Law and Contemporary Problems,* 47 (4): 35–39.

Cain, M. (1973) *Society and the policeman's role,* London: Routledge/Kegan Paul.

Chan, J. (1996) Changing police culture, *British Journal of Criminology,* 36 (1): 109–134.

Chan, J. (1997) *Changing police culture: Policing in a multi-cultural society,* Cambridge: Cambridge University Press.

Chan, J. (1999) Police culture, in Dixon, D. (Ed.), *A culture of corruption,* Sydney: Hawkins Press.

de Guzman, M. C. (2002) The changing roles and strategies of the police in time of terror, *ACJS Today,* 27 (3): 8-13.

Feltes, T. (1994) New philosophies in policing, *Police Studies,* 17 (2): 29–48.

Fitzgerald, G. E. (1989) *Report of a commission of inquiry pursuant to orders in council,* Brisbane Commission of Inquiry into Possible Illegal Activities and Associated Police Misconduct. Queensland Government Printer.

Goldstein, H. (1976) Improving the police: A problem-oriented approach, *Crime and Delinquency,* 25: 236–258.

Goldstein, H. (1990) *Problem oriented policing,* New York: McGraw-Hill.

James, S. and Warren, I. (1995) Police culture, in Bessant, K., Carrington, J., and Cook, S. (Eds.), *Cultures of crime and violence: The Australian experience,* Bundoora: La Trobe University Press.

Lyons, W. (2002) Partnerships, information and public safety: Community policing in a time of terror, *Policing: An International Journal of Police Strategies and Management,* 25 (3): 530–542.

Manning, P. (1977) *Police work,* Cambridge, MA: MIT Press.

McBride, R. B. (1995) Discrimination, in Bailey, W. (Ed.), *The encyclopaedia of police science* (2nd ed.), New York: Garland.

McCulloch, J. (2001a) Paramilitary surveillance: S11, globalisation, terrorists and counter-terrorists, *Current Issues in Criminal Justice*, 13 (1): 23–35.
McCulloch, J. (2001b) *Blue army*, Melbourne: Melbourne University Press.
Moore, M. H. (1994) Research synthesis and policy implications, in Rosenbaum, D. (Ed.), *The challenge of community policing*, London: Sage.
Murray, J. (2002) Police culture: A critical component of community policing, *The Australian Journal of Forensic Sciences*, 34(2): 57–71.
Oliver, W. M. and Bartgis, E. (1988) Community policing: A conceptual framework, *Policing: An International Journal of Police Strategies and Management*, 21 (3): 490–509.
Prenzler, T. (1997) Is there a police culture? *Australian Journal of Public Administration*, 56 (4): 47–65.
Redshaw, J. and Sanders, F. (1995) What does the public want? *Policing*, January 11: 56–60.
Reiner, R. (1992) *The politics of the police* (2nd ed.), Brighton, UK: Harvester.
Reiner, R. (1994) What should the police be doing? *Policing*, March 10: 151–157.
Reisig, M. D. and Giacomazzi, A. L. (1998) Citizen perceptions of community policing: Are attitudes toward police important? *Policing: An International Journal of Police Strategies and Management*, 21 (3): 547–561.
Reith, C. (1975) *The blind eye of history: A study of the origins of the present police era*, Montclair, NJ: Paterson Smith.
Roberg, R. R. (1994) Can today's police organizations effectively implement community policing? in Rosenbaum, D.P. (Ed.), *The challenge of community policing: Testing the* promises, Thousand Oaks, CA: Sage.
Rosenbaum, D. (1988) Community crime prevention: A review of the literature, *Justice Quarterly*, 5: 323–395.
Scott, J. (1998) Performance culture: The return of reactive policing, *Police and Society*, 8: 269–288.
Sherman, L. W., Gottfredson, D., Mackenzie, D. L., Eck, J., Reuter, P., and Bushway, S. D. (1998) *Preventing crime: What works, what doesn't, what's promising*, Washington, D.C.: National Institute of Justice.
Skolnick, J. H. (1966) *Justice without trial: Law enforcement in democratic society*, New York: John Wiley.
Skolnick, J. H. (1985) Suspicion, danger and isolation, in Terry, W. (Ed.), *Policing society: An occupational view*, New York: John Wiley.
Skolnick, J. H. and Fyfe, J. (1993) *Above the law: Police and the excessive use of force*, London: Free Press.
Sparrow, M. K., Moore, M. H., and Kennedy, D. M. (1990) *Beyond 9/11: A new era for policing*, New York: Basic Books.
Van Maanen, J. (1978) On watching the watchers, in Manning, P. K. and van Maanen, J. (Eds.), *Policing: A view from the street*, Santa Monica: Goodyear.
Waddington, P. A. J. (1999) Police (canteen) sub-culture, *British Journal of Criminology*, 39 (4): 765–797.
Weber, D. C. (1999) *Warrior cops: The ominous growth of paramilitarism in American police departments*, CATO Institute Insurance Briefing Paper 50, www.cato.org/pubs/briefs/bp50.pdf [Correct at September 2007].

Williams, E.J. (2003) Structuring in community policing: Institutionalising innovative change, *Police Practice and Research*, 4 (2): 119–129.
Wood, J. (1997) *Royal Commission into the New South Wales Police Services: Final Report (Vols. 1–3)*, Sydney: Government of the State of New South Wales.

Police Strategy and Investigations IV

The Hotspot Matrix: A Framework for Spatio-Temporal Targeting of Crime Reduction*

7

JERRY H. RATCLIFFE

Contents

Increasing Use of Hotspots in Crime Reduction

The use of hotspots to determine policing and crime prevention strategies has grown over recent years. Crime hotspots—areas of high crime intensity—have appeal to both crime prevention practitioners and police managers. The development of planning solutions such as Crime Prevention through Environmental Design (CPTED) (Jeffery and Zahm, 1993) and situational crime prevention (Brantingham and Brantingham, 1990; Clarke, 1992; Ekblom and Tilley, 2000) led to greater claims on the crime prevention budgets of local authorities and city planners. Hotspots allow local councillors to determine the areas of greatest need. Similarly, a considerable shift has occurred toward greater use of hotspots as foundations for problem-oriented policing (Goldstein, 1990) and as focal points for identifying problems that can be resolved with the SARA† technique (Eck and Spelman, 1987; Greene, 2000).

* This chapter first appeared in *Police Practice and Research*, 2004, 5 (1): 5–23.
† Scanning, analysis, response, assessment. A useful guide is presented on the Popcenter website at http://www.popcenter.org/about-SARA.htm [correct as of October 2007].

More recently, hotspot policing has gained prominence as an operational tactic, most notably in the British drive toward intelligence-led policing (Audit Commission, 1993; Heaton, 2000; HMIC, 1997; Maguire, 2000; Ratcliffe, 2002c; Smith, 1997), and also in the United States through the growth of intelligence and crime analysis practice (Andrews and Peterson, 1990; Carter, 1990; Gottlieb, Arenberg, and Singh, 1998) and in Australia (AFP, 2001; CJC, 1996; Seddon and Napper, 1999). Similarly, in Chapter 8 of this volume Per Stangeland gives an account of the geographic profiling of a serial rapist in southern Spain, using a hotspot methodology. In times of fiscal constraint, crime prevention practitioners and police find appeal in a mechanism that allows them to focus resources on the areas of most need and to have a process for explaining their objective decision making to others.

Beyond the immediate practical applications, academic interest in hotspots has come from two directions: different theoretical explanations for hotspots and techniques for the detection of crime hotspots. In the first area, a number of researchers have worked to find theoretical explanations for hotspots, including the development of places as crime attractors or crime generators (Brantingham and Brantingham, 1995a), a better understanding of offender spatial behavior (Brantingham and Brantingham, 1981; Rossmo, 2000), and improved understanding of the spatial dynamics of drug markets (Rengert, 1996). The U.S. National Institute of Justice's Drug Market Analysis Program placed significant emphasis on hotspots of drug activity by mapping the spatial characteristics and police responses with computer programs. The research sites produced a number of papers with implications for spatial policing strategies, including the work of Weisburd and Green (1995) on control strategies for drug market hotspots. A useful summary of environmental criminology can be found in the work of Bottoms and Wiles (2002), while evaluation of some hotspot crime prevention strategies is summarized in the work of Eck (1998).

As the use of geographic information systems (GIS) has grown within the practitioner community, it has also grown in the academic environment beyond the original field of geography, enabling criminal justice professionals and criminologists to explore questions of spatial criminology in greater detail than ever. To answer these more specific questions of crime location has required improvements in the available methods for the description of crime hotspots, and these are discussed below. The chapter then outlines broad categories of spatial and temporal hotspots in the form of a hotspot matrix. Some applications of the hotspot matrix as a practitioner tool in the determination of crime prevention and detection tactics will also be discussed. The chapter begins by outlining the techniques available to researchers for the descriptions of spatial and temporal hotspots.

Spatial Hotspot Identification Processes

Techniques for the detection of crime hotspots have existed for a number of years, but are by no means at the stage where they are both definitive and easily applicable. The real innovations have taken place in recent years with the improvements in computing power associated with the information technology (IT) revolution. Some spatial techniques that have been applied include the use of location quotients (Brantingham and Brantingham, 1995b), the development of kernel surface estimation algorithms (McLafferty, Williamson, and McGuire, 2000), and local indicators of spatial association (LISA) such as Getis and Ord *Gi* and Moran Local *I* (Mencken and Barnett, 1999; Messner et al., 1999).

The limitation is that these techniques are generally applied to administrative areal units such as block groups, police divisional boundaries, and census tracts. Spatial analysis of crime when aggregated to administrative units runs the risk of falling foul of the modifiable areal unit problem (MAUP) that occurs if the result of an analysis changes when the spatial arrangement of the study units is varied (Bailey and Gatrell, 1995; Openshaw, 1984; Unwin, 1996). In other words, an analysis of crime hotspots may look different if the crimes are aggregated to police beats or census tracts.

Some spatial analyses of crime hotspots use an underlying social phenomenon with which to calculate a rate of crime, and this necessitates the use of administrative boundary units such as census tracts or police beats. However, some researchers have also recognized that a simple spatial concentration of crime can also be valuable. For example, although it might be interesting to count the robbery rate per 1,000 residents in an area, this provides little information for the commander of a city center police station. The lack of a residential population in the central business district of most cities negates the value of a rate per 1,000 residents. The operational commander in this situation is therefore simply interested in resource allocation and wants to know where to find the greatest concentration of robberies. Police need does not necessarily coincide with researcher need. A simple map of hotspots can produce great operational policing benefits.

Police adoption of computer mapping processes has been swift in comparison to IT uptake in other areas (Weisburd, 2001). Mapping crime hotspots has been applied to general crime analysis (Canter, 1998; Harries, 1999; LaVigne and Wartell, 1998; Rich, 1995, 2001), vehicle crime analysis (Ratcliffe and McCullagh, 1998a; Rengert, 1997), serial crime investigations (Cook, 1998; Hubbs, 1998; Rossmo, 1995), and gang activity (Kennedy, Braga, and Piehl, 1998). One of the better known techniques for determining crime hotspots is a computer program known as STAC (spatial and temporal analysis of crime). STAC analyses point datasets to determine areas of higher intensity. These are displayed for output as standard deviational ellipses (Harries,

1999; ICJIA, 1996). Although the limitation of output as standard deviational ellipses and the rather arbitrary selection of program parameters have met with some criticism (Bowers and Hirschfield, 1999; Craglia, Haining, and Wiles, 2000; Ratcliffe, 2002b) the program has been utilized by a number of U.S. law enforcement agencies that were attracted by the ability to determine specific hotspot areas, albeit elliptical ones.

A number of other available programs do not dictate specific shapes. They produce hotspot surface maps similar to temperature maps displayed on evening weather reports (McLafferty et al., 2000). These surface maps actually show kernel densities of crime by dividing into a fine grid and calculating a value for each grid cell based on an intensity value calculated from the number and proximity of crime points in the surrounding area. These maps are advantageous because the flow of hotspots mimics the underlying crime patterns and often follows urban geographic features that are known to police officers and other users.

Only a few attempts have been made to establish a methodology that enables users to determine a statistically significant hotspot that does not conform to a predetermined shape, but more closely matches the shape of the underlying crime hotspot. Two groups applied LISA statistics to existing grid patterns. Chakravorty (1995) used local Moran *I* on grid cells of crime in Philadelphia, finding the technique worked in general, but not so well on his example data. Ratcliffe and McCullagh (1999) used Getis and Ord statistics on crime patterns in Nottingham (U.K.) and established basic parameters for determination of statistically significant hotspot regions. Although this appears to be more applicable, the technique still requires custom-written software and an appreciation for the influence of different parameters on analytical outcomes.

While a number of methods can determine crime hotspots, they all have strengths and weaknesses. Location quotients require arbitrary administrative units and are susceptible to the MAUP, but they are also easy to calculate and map. STAC ellipses are tied to one type of shaped output, yet have the advantage of showing definitive hotspot regions. Surface maps are fairly easy to create and interpret, but show a gradual change from a hotspot area to a less dense crime area with no indication of cutoff points. While the use of LISA statistics with grid maps gets around most of these problems by creating fine grid maps with definitive regions that are statistically sound, they are difficult to create. It is clear that considerable research effort has gone into the detection of spatial clusters of crime, but what about temporal factors?

Temporal Hotspot Identification Processes

While considerable research effort has been expended in the search for statistically determined spatial hotspots, much less effort has gone into the temporal dynamics of local crime patterns. Some work examined crime changes over lengthy periods to examine seasonality (Block, 1984) or look at long-term changes (Cohen and Felson, 1979; LeBeau, 1992). Others examined the influence of days or weeks on the risk of repeat victimization (significant bibliography includes Anderson, Chenery and Pease, 1995; Bowers, Hirschfield, and Johnson, 1998; Farrell and Pease, 1993; Johnson, Bowers and Hirschfield, 1997; Polvi et al., 1991; Ratcliffe and McCullagh, 1998b; Robinson, 1998).

Few studies have looked at the changing victimization throughout the day; the work of George Rengert (1997) is a notable exception. The main sticking point appears to be the lack of detail in many police crime databases—the sources of much raw data for crime studies. Because police are rarely in attendance when a property crime occurs, the police are left to record a start (or "from") time when the victim last saw his property and an end (or "to") time when the victim returned to find his property stolen. While crime analysts have been aware of a method of weighting a crime event based on start and end times to determine a possible time of offense (Gottlieb et al., 1998), Ratcliffe and McCullagh (1998a) initially proposed the development of temporal weighting to include a spatial component, an idea further refined for analytical and mapping purposes and referred to as aoristic analysis (Ratcliffe, 2000, 2002a).

The basic premise is that if the time of an event is not known, the start and end times can be used to estimate a probability matrix for each crime event for each hour of the day. The start and end times of crime events are extracted and the probability that an event occurred during each hour (or whatever period the user wishes) is determined. For example, if a victim parked his car at 10 a.m. and returned at 1 p.m. to find it missing, the time span of the theft is 3 hours. Each of the hour blocks is allocated a 0.33 value (one crime event divided by the time span units). This event is combined with others to determine the aoristic signature for vehicle theft in the study region. This process is explained in greater depth in Ratcliffe (2002a), and shown in Figure 7.1.

The figure indicates that crime events with shorter time spans influence the final outcome more than crimes with longer time spans because it is easier to determine the possible times of the offenses. The shorter time span events have higher weightings since the numerator for any weighting is the number of crime events (on an individual basis always one) and the denominator is the time span. If the time span is short, the weighting component for each hour in the analysis will be correspondingly higher. An event of known time of occurrence will have a value of one. Aoristic analysis enables a user to determine a temporal pattern for a crime hotspot (or any study region) based on objective analysis of the data (crimes with known times of occurrence will have greater influence over the final shape of the graph).

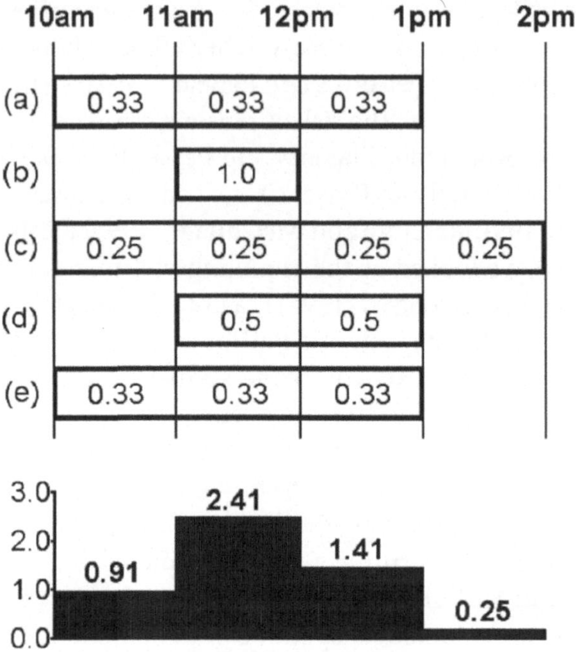

Figure 7.1 Aoristic temporal analysis. The five horizontal bars [(a) through (e)] indicate five vehicle thefts. The times of the offenses run left to right across a timeline split into hour blocks starting at 10 a.m. and ending at 2 p.m. In (a) the owner of the car last saw the vehicle when it was parked at 10 a.m. and the theft was discovered when the victim returned to the car park at 1 p.m., a span of 3 hours. Each hour block is allocated 1/3 (0.33). Offense (b) occurred between 11 a.m. and noon, so this hour block is allocated the full value (1.0). The values of (c) through (e) may be calculated on the same basis. The solid graph at the bottom shows the summed values for all crimes. For example, the 0.91 total represents offenses occurring between 10 a.m. and 11 a.m. determined by adding 0.33 from (a), 0.25 from (c), and 0.33 from (e) and indicates the probability of vehicle crime attributed to this one hour period.

Aoristic analysis lends itself to policing strategies, as crime hotspots are areas of significant police concern, but policing tactics must also reflect the realities of working within a budget. Aoristic analysis allows operational managers the opportunity to determine the best times for patrolling high volume crime areas (Ratcliffe, 2002a). Aoristic analysis also enables the broad categorization of high volume crime hotspots based on temporal characteristics, as discussed in the next section.

Hotspot Matrix

A combination of spatial and temporal techniques allows us to establish a typology of spatio-temporal characteristics of hotspots. The spatial features of crime patterns within the hotspot can be established, and each crime hotspot can be analyzed to determine its aoristic signature (Ratcliffe, 2002a). While a crime hotspot can contain a theoretically infinite number of spatial arrangements of crime events, analytical work in this area over the last few years has established three broad categories of within-hotspot spatial patterns. Similarly, considerable variations surround the temporal patterns that may occur in a given region. This chapter proposes three broad categories of temporal pattern. We start with spatial events.

Dispersed — This is a type of crime hotspot in which the points that generate the hotspot are spread throughout the hotspot area. They are still more concentrated than in other areas of the study (or else they would not constitute a hotspot) but do not cluster or congregate in any particular area. An example might be a housing estate where burglary events are spread throughout the estate due to poor design of the properties. The events within the hotspot do not cluster because all the properties are equally vulnerable.

Clustered — Events occurring at this type of hotspot tend to cluster at one or more particular areas within the hotspot. An example may be a hotspot region that includes a sports stadium. While the stadium may be the focus of vehicle crimes, it does not preclude the possibility that other areas in the vicinity are also victimized by auto crime.

Hotpoint — This is a particular type of crime hotspot generated by a single criminogenic feature that may be considered a crime attractor or generator (Brantingham and Brantingham, 1995a). An example would be a shopping center car park in the middle of a busy city. All the cars available for vehicle crime are concentrated in the parking area, making all of the crime events that generate that hotspot occur in one place. This differs from a clustered hotspot in that clustered events still have high concentrations in one or more areas, but numerous crime events may happen elsewhere in the hotspot.

Figure 7.2 shows examples of these spatial patterns. Each image shows a single hotspot shape involving 12 crime events within the hotspot. In the first two, all 12 points are visible and are respectively dispersed and clustered. Some readers will note that this terminology springs from nearest-neighbor analysis, and there are similarities. However, *dispersed* as used to describe events in a hotspot indicates that the points are dispersed *within* the hotspot and are highly concentrated with regard to the rest of the study area (otherwise there would be no hotspot). In the third image (C) the shape reflects the fact that all 12 points are co-located at the same site within the hotspot. In these circumstances, the hotspots tend to be circular. Temporal events can be broadly distinguished in three ways.

Diffused — These are crime hotspots where the crime events could happen at any time over the 24 hours of a day or because the time span of events is so large that it is not possible to determine significant peaks of activity. This does not preclude a diffused hotspot from having peaks and troughs;

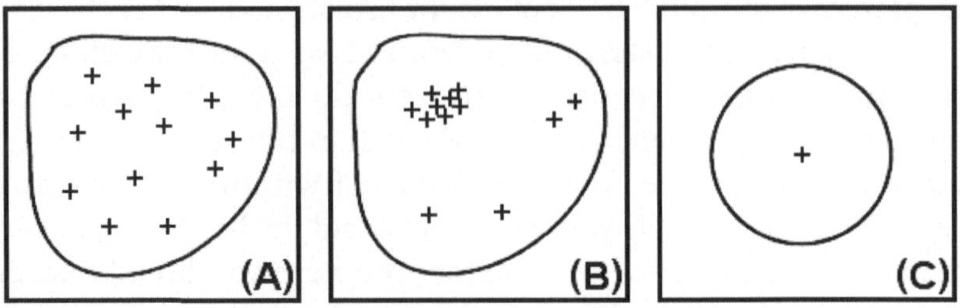

Figure 7.2 Dispersed, clustered, and hotpoint types of spatial hotspots. Each image shows 12 crime points located within a hotspot. In (A), the points are dispersed throughout the hotspot. In (B), the points are spread throughout the hotspot but clustering is evident at top left. In (C), all 12 points are co-located in the center of a circular hotspot.

it means that they are not significant enough to be considered useful from a crime prevention perspective.

Focused — Crimes in a focused hotspot may occur throughout a day, but certain times are more subject to significant activity than other times. The determination of significance may be statistical or may be judged on its value from a crime reduction perspective. In other words, a police inspector examining the aoristic signature of a crime pattern may determine that the peak over a 3-hour period is strong enough to warrant the deployment of extra officers at that time.

Acute — This is a rare group of hotspots. The temporal activity is confined to a small period of time or the aoristic signature almost negates the possibility of criminal activity during certain times. This does not mean that some events cannot occur in other periods, but unlike the focused hotspot, few events occur outside the acute time.

Figure 7.3 depicts these types of temporal hotspots. Vertical bars indicate the level of risk for each hour of the day, from midnight to the following mid-

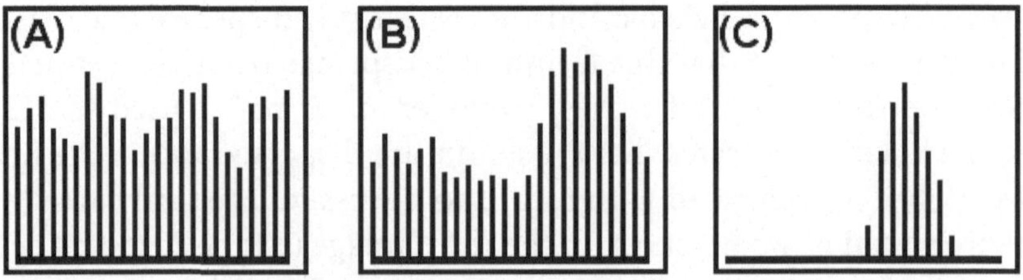

Figure 7.3 Three temporal hotspot categories. The probabilistically weighted offense times are shown as vertical bars. Each bar represents hour, running left to right from 00:00–00:59 to 23:00–23:59 hours (hourly from midnight to midnight). The three temporal hotspot types are diffused (A), focused (B), and acute (C). In (A), the risk of crime rises and falls throughout the hours of the day and night. Although (B) represents a general level of risk, significantly higher risk is present during the evening. In (C), the risk of crime is most acute in the early evening only.

night. (A) shows a general level of crime risk throughout the day and night, suggesting a diffused temporal hotspot. Although (B) shows times of general risk, it also shows a period of heightened risk during the evening, suggesting a focused temporal hotspot. Finally, (C) portrays concentrated risk in early evening, suggesting an acute temporal hotspot.

Examples of Hotspot Types

To demonstrate some of the hotspot types described, this section shows two examples based on real data. This chapter describes spatio-temporal crime hotspots by first discussing the temporal component, followed by the spatial component. Figure 7.4 shows a burglary hotspot based on an analysis of all burglaries at shops in the city of Canberra, Australia, for 1999 and 2000. This analysis generated a number of statistically significant hotspots, one of which was located in the commercial area of Fyshwick in the southeast of the city. The figure shows the hotspot and a breakdown of the 197 relevant crime events. The regular sides of the hotspot are functions of the grid cell sizes used to determine the area. Further details of the technique can be found in Ratcliffe and McCullagh (1999).

The sizes of the grey points vary based on the number of repeat victimizations at several locations. While a few locations were targeted more than others, the events are spread throughout the hotspot. This suggests a spatially *dispersed* range of events within the hotspot. The chart showing times of day when incidents occurred indicates little activity during daytime. After midnight (indicated by the first vertical bar), the high level of activity reduces rapidly by the time the shops open, then returns to higher values again after closing time and into the evening. This suggests a temporally *focused* crime hotspot. This hotspot is therefore best described as *focused* and *dispersed*.

The map and graph of Figure 7.5 show a different type of hotspot. Analysis of patterns of thefts of motor vehicles in the Eastern Beaches area of Sydney revealed a number of statistically significant hotspots, one of which involved a car park at the East Gardens shopping center. The hotspot includes other crime points near the car park, but is dominated by the car park. This suggests a *hotpoint* spatial pattern. The graph below the map shows a temporal pattern of offenses occurring at the car park. This aoristic analysis shows an acute period of 5 to 6 hours when most thefts take place. It could be argued that the graph may also represent a focus type temporal hotspot, but the lack of crime at certain times suggests an acute pattern. Had significant numbers of crimes occurred at other times, with a strong peak in the afternoon, a focus type temporal hotspot might have been appropriate. The area shown is therefore best described as an *acute hotpoint* hotspot.

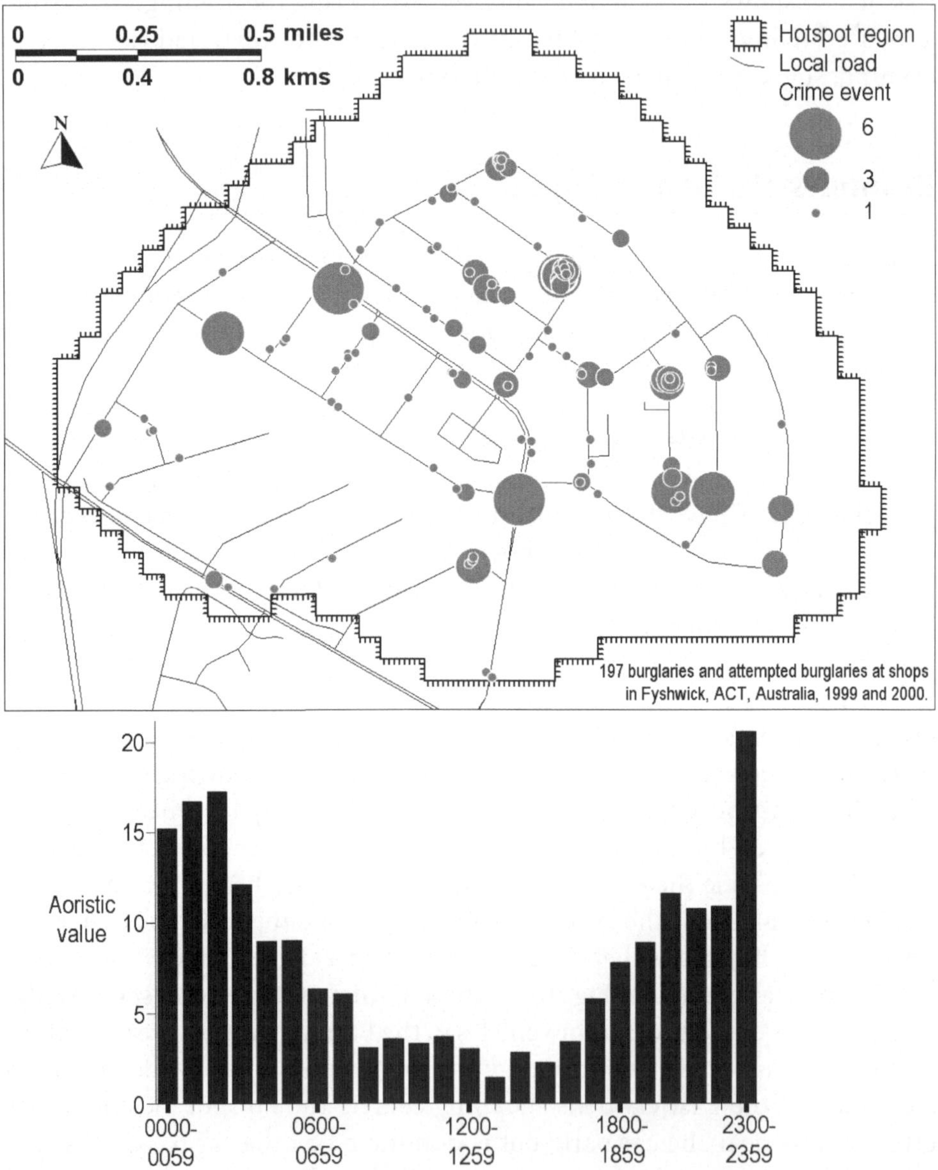

Figure 7.4 Focused, dispersed hotspot of burglaries and attempted burglaries at shops in the Fyshwick area of Canberra, Australia, 1999–2000. The map shows the locations of affected properties over a 2-year period. Repeat incidents are indicated by larger symbols. The chart shows the aoristic signature of the events in Fyshwick, suggesting a strong incidence of overnight offenses and little burglary activity during the day.

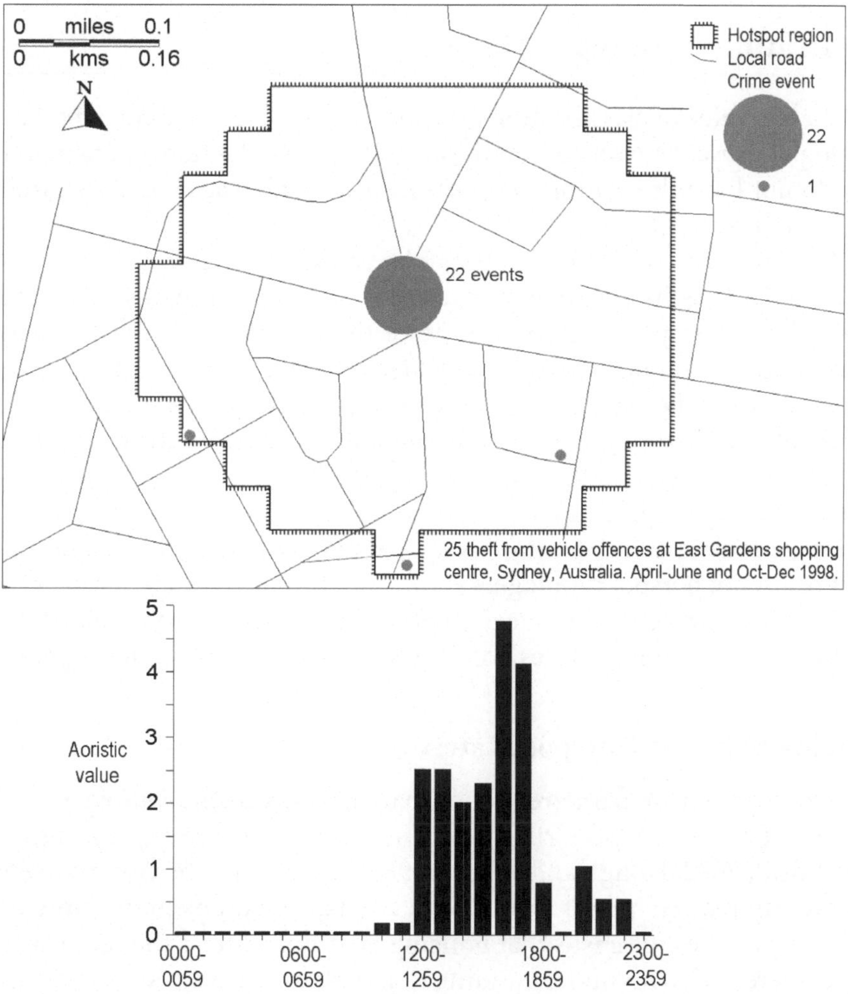

Figure 7.5 Acute hotpoint hotspot of thefts from vehicles at a shopping center in the Eastern Beaches area of Sydney, Australia. Data drawn from 2 periods (April–June and October–December 1998). The hotspot is dominated spatially by a shopping center. A few other points exist, but the shopping center is the single most important site and suggests a *hotpoint*. The temporal pattern in the graph shows a significant block of 6 hours during which most incidents occur. Although it could be argued that this block could be interpreted as a focus, activity outside the 6-hour period is negligible, indicating an *acute* temporal hotspot.

These real examples demonstrate two types of hotspots found in the matrix, and individually show two of the three types of spatial and temporal hotspots. The next section discusses practical applications of the hotspot matrix.

Application of Hotspot Matrix

What is the value of classification systems such as the hotspot matrix? Simple typologies present advantages in the area of crime reduction where practitioners do not have the training opportunities afforded academic researchers, who have time to explore fine points.

A simple typology of hotspots can be created alongside a list of possible remedies. This technique may be easier to teach as a limited set of systems, rather than attempting to communicate the complexity of environmental theory and the gamut of prevention literature such as the extensive *What works?* report of the National Institute of Justice (Sherman et al., 1998). While this chapter does not claim that every possible hotspot structure may fall easily into three spatial and three temporal patterns, the simple typology allows future researchers and practitioners to discuss practical crime reduction with regard to a specific, commonly agreed upon view of hotspots. Establishment of a set of hotspot typologies allows practitioners the ability to evaluate specific crime prevention strategies applicable to different types of hotspots. The following section explores how one such hotspot matrix may operate.

Policing Solution Hotspot Matrix

The development of crime reduction partnerships in the United Kingdom resulting from the 1998 Crime and Disorder Act (Bowers, Jennings, and Hirschfield, 2002; Hough and Tilley, 1998) suggests that the law enforcement community realizes that it is unable to combat the problem of crime on its own. Despite the consensus that policing does not address the root causes of crime, there is also an understanding that certain policing tactics may influence the short-term patterns of crime. Indeed, local community partnerships can take some time to coordinate and organize, and some law enforcement tactics can be implemented at short notice to fill the gap. These include crackdowns (Sherman, 1990), intelligence-led operations (Ratcliffe, 2001), and problem-oriented policing (Goldstein, 1990; Leigh, Read, and Tilley, 1996).

These strategies are part of a whole toolbox of possible tactics that an operational commander can employ, including flooding an area with uniform patrols, deploying surveillance units, using car patrols, and in some countries deterring offenders by setting up random breath tests in high crime areas. Some of these tactics are geared more toward crime prevention, while others (such as the use of surveillance units) focus on crime detection.

		Spatial		
	Policing Hotspot Matrix	**Dispersed** 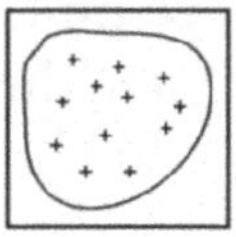	**Clustered** 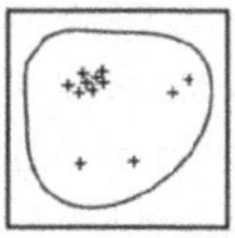	**Hotpoint** 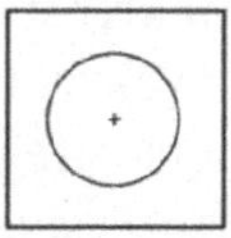
Temporal	**Diffused** 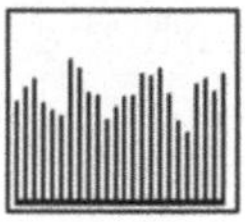	Uniform vehicle patrols, architectural changes, public education campaign	Random breath tests, foot patrols, architectural changes, publicity campaigns	Roadblocks, plain clothes patrols, random breath tests, private security, CCTV
	Focused 	Uniform vehicle and foot patrols, improved lighting, public education campaign	Vehicle and foot patrols, random breath tests, private security, improved lighting	Surveillance units, plain clothes foot patrols, CCTV, surveillance of entry/exit points
	Acute 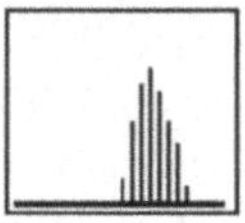	Unmarked vehicle patrols, private security, improved lighting	Surveillance and plain clothes patrols, CCTV	Surveillance, arrest squads, CCTV, unmarked police units

Figure 7.6 Example hotspot matrix for a housing estate. Strategies indicated are examples only and are not indicative of strategies evaluated for these types of spatio-temporal hotspots.

All these tactics involve outlays of funds. The job of the operational commander is to balance the potential results with the specific costs. Successful tactics can be shared so that particular types of hotspots can be tackled with strategies that were successful elsewhere. Alternatively, police commanders can try a number of tactics and establish what works best for a particular hotspot type.

Figure 7.6 shows one potential hotspot matrix that could be created to combat the different types of hotspots explained earlier. The solutions shown could, for example, be applied to a crime hotspot on a problem housing estate.* Choice of appropriate measures would clearly be decisions for operational commanders based on a variety of factors including

* The strategies populating the matrix here are examples only, and do not necessarily represent empirically evaluated crime reduction tactics.

availability of units, costs, and likelihood of success. Figure 7.6 illustrates shifts in tactics as the hotspots become more temporally and spatially concentrated—a movement from visible uniform patrols and high visibility tactics such as roadblocks and breath testing to tactics more likely to result in arrests, including surveillance units and unmarked patrols. This shift moves from prevention to detection. The figure shows suggestions for policing strategy, allowing the police to choose between prevention and more aggressive measures.

The hotspot matrix also considers longer term strategies that could be put into place in conjunction with short-term operations. A number of police agencies have experimented for years with the inclusion of a crime prevention officer as part of their sworn staffs. Some U.K. police operations established crime prevention officer positions many years ago. Again, cost and likelihood of success affect the decision to employ a crime prevention officer. The hotspot matrix will have the same shape and composition, but the range of options for a crime prevention officer may be different.

Longer term options may include closed circuit television (CCTV) systems, increased guards, and improved lighting and architectural changes to enable better natural surveillance of the housing estate. Again, decisions regarding cost may be made in the light of the spatial and temporal signatures of the hotspot. For example, installation of CCTV throughout the estate may be prohibitively expensive, thus negating the use of CCTV for a *temporally diffused* and *spatially dispersed* hotspot. CCTV may, however, be an option to prevent problems at a key location, and the introduction of one CCTV camera may fit within the available budget. CCTV therefore may be a viable option for an *acute hotpoint* hotspot.

Discussion

For many readers, the introduction of the temporal component will be a new feature, but many readers may be familiar with the various techniques for establishing spatial hotspot areas. This chapter has not sought to provide detailed explanations of spatial hotspot techniques. These methods are more thoroughly explained elsewhere and references cited earlier in this chapter provide further information. The temporal component has received less research attention, but it is arguably of equal value to an operational police commander or crime prevention officer.

One significant resource of a police commander is personnel, but personnel cost money. This cost is a factor in hiring extra officers and providing additional patrol time. Understanding the spatial dynamics of hotspots enables a commander to limit the spatial area of patrol, thus reducing the number of officers. Greater understanding of the temporal dynamics of hotspots will enable the commander to limit the time costs of extra patrols. Most usefully, the aoristic analysis method for temporal analysis cited in this chapter is not required for all crime types. Victims of assault generally know when they were assaulted and police start and end times tend to be the same. It would appear, from statistical tests shown in Ratcliffe (2002a), that the aoristic method is applicable primarily to high volume property offenses such as burglaries and vehicle thefts. Assault and robbery incidents can be easily analyzed based on the time of offense.

Spatial and temporal categorization of crime hotspots is subjective to a degree. It may be argued that a significant distinction may exist between a focused and an acute temporal hotspot, but the degree of subjectivity that may creep into such analyses is recognized. The main point, however, is that this type of analysis enables operational police officers to include spatial and temporal factors in their thinking. Although officers may disagree about the exact nature of a crime hotspot, chances are that discussions will still generate positive thinking about the best operational tactic to employ to combat the particular hotspot problem. Within the framework of SARA (Eck and Spelman, 1987; Greene, 2000), the hotspot matrix may be useful as a method of determining the most appropriate response.

This chapter has been a first attempt to describe a typology of crime hotspots in a spatiotemporal manner. It is possible that some types such as acute dispersed hotspots may be rarely encountered. Subsequent work by other researchers may reveal additional types of hotspots by adding, deleting, or modifying the spatial and temporal typologies.

The aim of this chapter is to describe hotspots in a practical way so that practitioners such as crime analysts, police managers, and crime prevention officers can discuss and evaluate crime reduction strategies targeted to the spatial and temporal characteristics of a problem. It would be possible to describe myriad hotspot shapes and patterns, but significant additions to the relatively simple typology presented here may prove counterproductive to the intent to provide a simple tool for collaboration and crime reduction. This chapter attempts to reduce the complexity of the effects of interactions of space, time, and volume to a practical level.

Finally, the strategies proposed in the matrices merely represent examples. Empirical evaluation of strategies employed in the past is likely to yield a more beneficial list of options. The move in Figure 7.6 from prevention to detection is likely to remain a part of most policing matrices because of the high costs of maintaining plain clothes unit surveillance in large areas over long periods. Certain strategies such as roadblocks and random breath tests are not available or legal in some jurisdictions. The onus is therefore on the practitioner reading this chapter to replace such tactics with more acceptable local strategies.

Conclusion

Any discussion of crime hotspots is of clear interest to police managers because of the need to devise suitable strategies for crime reduction in high crime areas. As gatekeepers (Ericson and Haggerty, 1997) of most crime knowledge for the rest of the criminal justice system, they are at the forefront of providing pertinent information to other agencies in digestible form and are required to formulate operational policy to combat crime hotspots. While most previous discussions of crime hotspots focused entirely on spatial characteristics, the introduction of a methodology for examining temporal characteristics provides an additional dimension and this additional feature has clear benefits for policing strategies applicable to hotspots.

Resources are usually required to combat crime problems and resources bring costs. Law enforcement managers may wish to identify both temporal and spatial patterns of crime hotspots to better utilize their resources at the most appropriate times. Little value accrues from having night-duty officers perform high visibility patrols on overtime in a crime hotspot if the temporal pattern suggests that the highest incidence time is the middle of the day. In times of fiscal constraint when police must accomplish the same tasks with the same or fewer resources (Ratcliffe, 2001), justifying a strategy based on objective analysis of spatial and temporal characteristics of high crime areas is an attractive option. While the choice of appropriate strategy is somewhat subjective now, a bank of knowledge regarding the best strategies for different scenarios within a hotspot matrix will grow over time and provide objective ammunition for operational police commanders to present to holders of the departmental purse strings. A well considered crime reduction policy based on an objective assessment of crime hotspots combined with an objective choice of crime reduction strategy is a difficult principle to argue against.

References

AFP [Australian Federal Police]. (2001) *Anchorage: An excellent example of intelligence-led policing, 592/2001*, ACT Policing media release, Canberra.

Anderson, D., Chenery, S., and Pease, K. (1995) *Biting back: Tackling repeat burglary and car crime*, Police Research Group: Crime Detection and Prevention Series Paper 58, London: Home Office.

Andrews, P. P. and Peterson, M. B. (1990) *Criminal intelligence analysis*, Loomis, CA: Palmer Enterprises.

Audit Commission (1993) *Helping with enquiries: Tackling crime effectively*, London: HMSO.

Bailey, T. C. and Gatrell, A. C. (1995) *Interactive spatial data analysis*, London: Longman.

Block, C. R. (1984) *Is crime seasonal?*, Chicago: Illinois Criminal Justice Information Authority.

Bottoms, A. E. and Wiles, P. (2002) Environmental criminology, in Maguire, M., Morgan, R., and Reiner, R. (Eds.), *Oxford handbook of criminology*, 3rd edition, London: Oxford University Press.

Bowers, K. J. and Hirschfield, A. (1999) Exploring the link between crime and disadvantage in northwest England: An analysis using geographical information systems, *International Journal of Geographical Information Science*, 13 (2): 159–184.

Bowers, K. J., Hirschfield, A., and Johnson, S. D. (1998) Victimization revisited, *British Journal of Criminology*, 38 (3): 429–452.

Bowers, K. J., Jennings, J., and Hirschfield, A. (2002) The crime and disorder audit process: A post-mortem on the first round, *Crime Prevention and Community Safety*, 4 (2): 19–32.

Brantingham, P. L. and Brantingham, P. J. (1981) *Environmental criminology*, Prospect Heights, IL: Waveland Press.

Brantingham, P. L. and Brantingham, P. J. (1990) Situational crime prevention in practice, *Canadian Journal of Criminology*, 32 (1): 17–40.

Brantingham, P. L. and Brantingham, P. J. (1995a) Criminality of place: Crime generators and crime attractors, *European Journal of Criminal Policy and Research*, 3 (3): 5–26.

Brantingham, P. L. and Brantingham, P. J. (1995b) Location quotients and crime hotspots in the city, in Block, C., Dabdoub, M., and Fregly, S. (Eds.), *Crime analysis through computer mapping*, Washington, D.C.: Police Executive Research Forum.

Canter, P. R. (1998) Geographical information systems and crime analysis in Baltimore County, Maryland, in Weisburd, D. and McEwen, T. (Eds.), *Crime mapping and crime prevention* (pp. 158–190), Monsey, NY: Criminal Justice Press.

Carter, D. L. (1990) *Law enforcement intelligence operations: An overview of concepts, issues and terms*, Washington, D.C.: National Institute of Justice.

Chakravorty, S. (1995) Identifying crime clusters: The spatial principles, *Middle States Geographer*, 28: 53–58.

CJC [Criminal Justice Commission] (1996) Intelligence at work inside the CJC., *Criminal Justice Commission Issue Paper Series*, 3 (1): 12.

Clarke, R. V. (1992) *Situational crime prevention: Successful case studies*, Albany, NY: Harrow and Heston.

Cohen, L. E. and Felson, M. (1979) Social change and crime rate trends: A routine activity approach, *American Sociological Review*, 44: 588–608.

Cook, P. (1998) Mapping a murderer's path, in LaVigne, N. and Wartell, J. (Eds.), *Crime mapping case studies: Successes in the field* (pp. 123–128), Washington, D.C.: Police Executive Research Forum.

Craglia, M., Haining, R., and Wiles, P. (2000) A comparative evaluation of approaches to urban crime pattern analysis, *Urban Studies*, 34 (4): 711–729.

Eck, J. (1998) Preventing crime at places, Chapter 7, in *Preventing crime: What works, what doesn't, what's promising?* Washington, D.C.: National Institute of Justice.

Eck, J. and Spelman, W. (1987) *Problem solving: Problem-oriented policing in Newport News*, Washington, D.C.: Police Executive Research Forum.

Ekblom, P. and Tilley, N. (2000) Going equipped: Criminology, situational crime prevention and the resourceful offender, *British Journal of Criminology*, 40 (3): 376–398.

Ericson, R. V. and Haggerty, K. D. (1997) *Policing the risk society*, Oxford: Clarendon Press.

Farrell, G. and Pease, K. (1993) *Once bitten, twice bitten: Repeat victimisation and its implications for crime prevention*, Police Research Group: Crime Prevention Unit Series Paper 46, London: Home Office.

Goldstein, H. (1990) *Problem-oriented policing*, New York: McGraw-Hill.

Gottlieb, S., Arenberg, S., and Singh, R. (1998) *Crime analysis: From first report to final arrest*, Montclair: Alpha Publishing.

Greene, J. R. (2000) Community policing in America: Changing the nature, structure, and function of the police, in Horney, J. (Ed.), *Criminal justice 2000: Policies, processes, and decisions of the criminal justice system* (pp. 299–370), Washington, D.C.: National Institute of Justice.

Harries, K. (1999) *Mapping crime: Principles and practice*, Washington, D.C.: National Institute of Justice.

Heaton, R. (2000) The prospects for intelligence-led policing: Some historical and quantitative considerations, *Policing and Society*, 9 (4): 337–356.

HMIC (1997) *Policing with intelligence*, London: Her Majesty's Inspectorate of Constabulary.

Hough, M. and Tilley, N. (1998) *Auditing crime and disorder: Guidance for local partnerships*, Police Research Group: Crime Detection and Prevention Series 91, London: Home Office.

Hubbs, R. (1998) The Greenway rapist case: Matching repeat offenders with crime locations, in LaVigne, N. and Wartell, J. (Eds.), *Crime mapping case studies: Successes in the field* (pp. 93–97), Washington, D.C.: Police Executive Research Forum.

ICJIA (1996) *STAC user manual*, Chicago: Illinois Criminal Justice Information Authority.

Jeffery, C. R. and Zahm, D. L. (1993) Crime prevention through environmental design, opportunity theory, and rational choice models, in Clark, R. V. and Felson, M. (Eds.), *Routine activity and rational choice* (pp. 323–350), New Brunswick, NJ: Transaction Publishers.

Johnson, S. D., Bowers, K., and Hirschfield, A. (1997) New insights into the spatial and temporal distribution of repeat victimization, *British Journal of Criminology*, 37 (2): 224–241.

Kennedy, D. M., Braga, A. A., and Piehl, A. M. (1998) The (un)known universe: Mapping gangs and gang violence in Boston, in Weisburd, D. and McEwen, T. (Eds.), *Crime mapping and crime prevention* (pp. 219–262), Monsey, NY: Criminal Justice Press.

LaVigne, N. and Wartell, J. (1998) *Crime mapping case studies: Successes in the field*, Washington, D.C.: Police Executive Research Forum.

LeBeau, J. L. (1992) Four case studies illustrating the spatial–temporal analysis of serial rapists, *Police Studies*, 15: 124–145.

Leigh, A., Read, T., and Tilley, N. (1996) *Problem-oriented policing*, Police Research Group: Crime Detection and Prevention Series 75, London: Home Office.

Maguire, M. (2000) Policing by risks and targets: Some dimensions and implications of intelligence led crime control, *Policing and Society*, 9 (4): 315–336.

McLafferty, S., Williamson, D., and McGuire, P. G. (2000) Identifying crime hot spots using kernel smoothing, in Goldsmith, V., McGuire, P. G., Mollenkopf, J. H., and Ross, T. A. (Eds.), *Analyzing crime patterns: Frontiers of practice* (pp. 77–85), Thousand Oaks, CA: Sage.

Mencken, F. C. and Barnett, C. (1999) Murder, non-negligent manslaughter and spatial autocorrelation in mid-South counties, *Journal of Quantitative Criminology*, 15 (4): 407–422.

Messner, S. F., Anselin, L., Baller, R. D., Hawkins, D. F., Deane, G., and Tolnay, S.E. (1999) The spatial patterning of county homicide rates: An application of exploratory spatial data Analysis, *Journal of Quantitative Criminology*, 15 (4): 423–450.

Openshaw, S. (1984) The modifiable areal unit problem, *Concepts and Techniques in Modern* Geography, 38.

Polvi, N., Looman, T., Humphries, C., and Pease, K. (1991) The time course of repeat burglary victimization, *British Journal of Criminology*, 31 (4): 411–414.

Ratcliffe, J. H. (2000) Aoristic analysis: The spatial interpretation of unspecific temporal events, *International Journal of Geographical Information Science*, 14 (7): 669–679.

Ratcliffe, J. H. (2001) Policing urban burglary, *Trends and Issues in Crime and Criminal Justice*, 213.

Ratcliffe, J. H. (2002a) Aoristic signatures and the temporal analysis of high volume crime patterns, *Journal of Quantitative Criminology*, 18 (1): 23–43.

Ratcliffe, J. H. (2002b) Damned if you don't, damned if you do: Crime mapping and its implications in the real world, *Policing and Society*, 12 (3): 211–225.

Ratcliffe, J. H. (2002c) Intelligence-led policing and the problems of turning rhetoric into practice, *Policing and* Society, 12 (1): 53–66.

Ratcliffe, J. H. and McCullagh, M. J. (1998a) Aoristic crime analysis, *International Journal of Geographical Information Science*, 12 (7): 751–764.

Ratcliffe, J. H. and McCullagh, M. J. (1998b) Identifying repeat victimisation with GIS, *British Journal of Criminology*, 38 (4): 651–662.

Ratcliffe, J. H. and McCullagh, M. J. (1999) Hotbeds of crime and the search for spatial accuracy, *Geographical Systems*, 1 (4): 385–398.

Rengert, G. F. (1996) *The geography of illegal drugs*, Boulder, CO: Westview Press.

Rengert, G. F. (1997) Auto theft in Philadelphia, in Homel, R. (Ed.), *Policing for prevention: Reducing crime, public intoxication and injury* (pp. 199–219), Monsey, NY: Criminal Justice Press.

Rich, T. F. (1995) *The use of computerized mapping in crime control and prevention programs*, Washington, D.C.: National Institute of Justice.

Rich, T. F. (2001) *Crime mapping and analysis in community organization in Hartford, Connecticut*, Washington, D.C.: National Institute of Justice.

Robinson, M. (1998) Burglary re-victimization: the time period of heightened risk, *British Journal of Criminology*, 38 (1): 78–87.

Rossmo, D. K. (1995) Place, space, and police investigations: Hunting serial violent criminals, in Weisburd, D. and Eck, J. E. (Eds.), *Crime and place* (pp. 217–235), Monsey, NY: Criminal Justice Press.

Rossmo, D. K. (2000) *Geographic profiling*, Boca Raton, FL: CRC Press.

Seddon, K. and Napper, R. (1999) *Integrated crime management model discussion paper*, unpublished, Sydney: New South Wales Police Service.

Sherman, L. W. (1990) Police crackdowns: Initial and residual deterrence, in Tonry, M. and Morris, N. (Eds.), *Crime and justice: An annual review of research* (pp. 1–48), Chicago: University of Chicago Press.

Sherman, L. W., Gottfredson, D., MacKenzie, D., Eck, J., Reuter, P., and Bushway, S. (1998) *Preventing crime: What works, what doesn't, what's promising?* Washington, D.C.: National Institute of Justice.

Smith, A. (1997) *Intelligence led policing*, International Association of Law Enforcement Intelligence Analysts, Inc.

Unwin, D. J. (1996) GIS, spatial analysis and spatial statistics, *Progress in Human Geography*, 20 (4): 540–551.

Weisburd, D. (2001) Translating research into practice: Reflections on the diffusion of innovation in crime mapping, *International Crime Mapping Research Conference*, Dallas, TX, December 2001.

Weisburd, D. and Green, L. (1995) Policing drug hot spots: The Jersey City drug market analysis experiment, *Justice Quarterly*, 12: 711–735.

Catching a Serial Rapist: Hits and Misses in Criminal Profiling*

8

PER STANGELAND

Contents

This chapter discusses a "live" case of geographic profiling in a cultural setting outside the United States and Great Britain. It was developed on request from police to aid their investigation of a case of serial rape.

The first 18 assaults occurred in the west part of Malaga, a historical city of approximately 600,000 inhabitants located on the southern coast of Spain. DNA and fingerprints found at the crime scenes indicated that the same offender committed them and that he had no previous criminal record. Four victims contacted the Victim Assistance Service in Malaga and we† were asked to collaborate with the National Police to help track down the perpetrator and prevent future crimes.

After the rapist was apprehended, we interviewed him during several long sessions in prison. This chapter concentrates on the geographic profile we developed and compared with the rapist's explanation of how he sought out his victims. Comparing this real case with the theory of geographic profiling, we present recommendations that may assist future police investigations of serial crimes.

* This chapter first appeared in *Police Practice and Research*, 2005, 6 (5): 453–469.

† The author served as director of the Victim Assistance Service in Malaga and coordinated the criminological profile described. All employees of the office (Carmen García Ferrer, Maria Victoria Rosas Lozano, Miguel Angel Román Florido, and Maria Cheli Shaw) participated. José Antonio Hernández Sánchez, a forensic psychologist from the Madrid tribunals, elaborated most of the psychological profile.

Literature Review

Criminological research has shown that most offenders tend to commit crimes fairly close to where they live. Through Shaw and McKay (1942), Wikström (1991), and Hesseling (1992), we have seen proof of this phenomenon in various cultures and countries.

We have several ways to put this knowledge to practical use. Urban planning and crime prevention projects are obvious targets. However, applying this knowledge during an ongoing criminal investigation is a different matter altogether. Instead of using data on offenders' residences to analyze crime rates, we use a reverse process in which the known factor is the location where a crime or a series of connected crimes were committed. The factor to be determined is where the offender lives. This reversal of criminological research also implies a shift from aggregate data about groups of offenders toward individual assumptions about a specific person. Error margins on these kinds of predictions are obviously high and they increase when important information is missing. Geographic profiling presents, at best, a way to assign priorities to time-consuming police investigations, and recommends the investigative paths that will most likely produce results. The technique has provided constructive suggestions in several important criminal cases (Canter, 2003).

The theory behind such profiling is based on environmental and geographical theories on crime and the routine activity approach in criminology (Felson, 1994). Brantingham and Brantingham (1981) stipulate that criminals, like everyone else, have awareness spaces or mental maps of areas where they live. Such maps are based on personal observation, recommendations from friends, or other sources of information, and indicate where to find specific shops, restaurants, or train stations. Within the awareness space, we find activity spaces centered on home, workplace, and leisure activities.

The theory stipulates that crimes tend to occur when offenders are en route between anchor points in their activity spaces. This is a familiar area, a comfort zone where they know what they seek, how to get there, and how to get away. Turner (1969) was the first to suggest that a safety zone or buffer zone existed around a criminal's home base where he or she is not likely to commit a predatory offense because of the likelihood of being recognized. Rossmo (2000: 139), in a study of serial offenders, suggests four kinds of predatory strategies:

- The **hunter** sets out specifically to search for a victim, starting from a home base.
- The **poacher** sets out specifically to search for a victim, but starts from another activity site.

- The **troller**, while involved in other activities, opportunistically encounters a victim.
- The **trapper** creates a situation to encounter victims within locations under his control.

Canter and Larkin (1993) tested some specific hypotheses on serial rapists. They used police data from the 1980s covering 45 sexual assaulters in Southeast England including their home bases and the distances to the aggression sites. Initially, the researchers worked on two alternative hypotheses. The *commuter hypothesis* was that the rapists traveled into different areas from where they lived to commit their crimes. The crime area may have been familiar but it was distant from his normal activity space. The alternative was the *marauder hypothesis*, where the home base was more or less at the center of the assault. Drawing a circle and placing the two types of offense sites as far away from each other as possible within the circle (one site at each end of the diameter) means a home base is likely to be inside the circle. Crimes are less likely to be committed inside a buffer zone near the home base. We can expect to find that the crimes are more spread out, the further they are from the home base. Clusters of crimes with shorter distances between them would be closer to the home base.

A later analysis of the same material (Canter and Gregory, 1994) found different patterns for the group of serial rapists. Rapists older than 25, with easier access to motor vehicles, traveled longer distances. The younger, more impulsive, and socially deprived traveled shorter distances. The researchers found an average buffer zone of 0.61 mile around home bases and an average minimum distance of crime to home of 1.53 miles. They also found that 87% had bases within the circle hypothesis prediction area. Of the 45 cases, only 6 were "commuters" who operated from bases outside the circles described by their offenses. Consequently, the study indicated a fairly high probability of locating serial rapists in an area slightly askew of the center of activities. This circle hypothesis was tested through a series of studies involving circles drawn around the two offenses furthest apart. They found offenders' home bases inside the circles in at least half the cases (Kocsis and Irwin, 1997; Warren et al., 1998).

The operative usefulness of the circle hypothesis for the police investigator is not very clear. The investigation of a serial crime usually starts with two or three cases, but the police cannot sit back and wait until a sufficient number of cases allow them to draw a circle. Also, the area encompassed by two crime sites may be fairly large. In big cities, several million inhabitants may live in a circled area. Most investigations on serial criminals focused on offenders in the United States or England. Awareness space and traveling distances may be different in other kinds of urban areas.

The initial theory development and the first field tests were based on police files or newspaper clippings of solved cases (Canter, 2000; LeBeau, 1987; Rossmo, 1995a, 1995b), although later works also contained several examples of profiles developed to direct police investigations (Canter, 2003; Garrido, 2003; Rossmo, 2000).

Case Details

The first rape in the series studied occurred in 1997. As a married woman returned home after shopping at midday, a man waiting near her apartment door assaulted her. He dragged her into the bedroom and raped her. She had no opportunity to see his face.

A series of similar attacks occurred over the next 3 years. The victims were always married, young, and attractive. All assaults took place in their homes and matrimonial beds. DNA and fingerprint proofs found at the crime scenes indicated that the same offender, a person with no previous criminal record, committed the assaults. The physical descriptions of the rapist were minimal. He was dark haired, tall, and strong. On some occasions he brandished a knife found in the kitchen, but he usually inflicted no bodily harm to the victims apart from the rape. If victims screamed and strongly resisted, the assailant fled.

His habits changed in 2000. He stopped hiding his face, and pretended to be a plumber repairing a water leak. He also changed his assault area. While all previous cases occurred west of the city center, the rapist moved his activities to the more affluent eastern suburbs. His victim preferences also changed. He sought younger girls, primarily Scandinavians and Germans, 16 to 22 years old. Most of them were taking Spanish courses in language schools east of the city center. He made sure that each victim was alone at home, pulled a knife, and raped her in her own bed. His skill at controlling his victims increased with practice, and on some occasions, he committed multiple rapes, tying up one girl while he raped the other. The suspected perpetrator of 29 sexual aggressions was arrested in February 2002.

Methodology

We joined the police investigation of this case in September 2001 and obtained access to all pertinent information about the 22 incidents known. Our continuous contacts with four victims were also of great help. For the geographical part of the profile, we concentrated on the area circumscribed by the first 18 cases, assuming that these first assaults gave the best clue to the rapist's activity space. We walked through the area, searching the apartment blocks for clues as to where he first spotted his victims, how he had been able to surprise his victims on their doorsteps, and how he could enter and leave the building without being noticed.

The computer analysis utilized a geographic information system set up at our institute to analyze crime patterns and hotspots in the city of Malaga (see also Jerry Ratcliffe's Chapter 7). We had already introduced some 80,000 police reports and emergency calls generated in 1998 and 1999 (Stangeland and Garrido, 2003). The police searched their archives for possible links to other crimes. We made similar searches of their data but found no further clues. However, the system served as a platform for geographic profiling.

The system is not dedicated like the Rigel program set up by Rossmo (2000: 222) and the Dragnet system used by Canter et al. (2000). We used the spatial analyst module of the ArcView program to analyze the density of events in a uniform fashion. We later cross-checked our results by introducing the same data in a dedicated geographic profiling program (Dragnet) and found basically the same pattern as the one presented as Figure 8.2.

The theory behind hotspot analysis is different from the one behind criminal geographic targeting, but the methodologies have many similarities. After individual crime sites are introduced on a city map, the program calculates the density of events in the surrounding area. The user can adjust the grid size and the circle that describes it. One can, for example, set the grid cell size to 50 square feet and the search radius to 1 mile. The radius determines the distance to search for points from each cell in the grid. Each grid cell is assigned a color that corresponds to the number of neighboring points inside the specified search radius.

The results we presented to the police included a map with colors to indicate the probabilities of finding the offender's home base in different areas (see Figure 8.3). However, the parameter for distance decay (*search radius* in the ArcView program) is chosen by the user and not pre-set by the program. It should represent an estimate of how far from his home base an offender would be likely to travel to commit a crime. Different parameters can, as we will show, give strikingly different results.

After the arrest of the suspect,* we carried out a series of interviews with him in prison. He had by then confessed to the sexual aggressions and was willing to describe his routine activities and how he located his victims.

Criminal Profile

We submitted a criminal profile of the suspect to the police in October 2001. The main points are summarized in tabular form in Table 8.1, with our predictions in the center column and data about the arrested suspect on the right.

* At the time of writing, the presumed rapist was a suspect. He was convicted in 2005 of 24 rapes or intents to rape and sentenced to 271 years of imprisonment.

Table 8.1 Comparison of Criminal Profile and Suspect Data

Topic	October 2001 Criminal Profile	Data on Suspect Arrested February 2002
AGE	28 to 30 years at start; 32 to 34 now	29 years
HEIGHT	1.78 to 1.83 m	1.84 ms
APPEARANCE	Nearsighted, 2 to 4 diopters; wears glasses with black frames; strongly built, corpulent	Not nearsighted. Glasses worn as camouflage; slightly taller, stronger, and less corpulent than predicted
RESIDENCE	Works in southern area; lives inside circle marked North (see Figure 8.3)	Lives half a mile from the center of the south circle
WORK	Probably works days, has much liberty regarding working hours or works shifts with days off; may shower and change clothes at workplace; not a manual worker; no knowledge of firearms	Gymnastics teacher at a college; has time off between classes. Opportunity to shower and change clothes at workplace
SEX	Experienced sexual problems during adolescence or youth; possible exhibitionist or voyeur acts at age 17 to 18; frustration about adolescent sex object (young Swede myth); uses pornography and possibly occasional prostitute; sex fantasies based on domination and passive consenting women	According to his own declarations, was a victim of homosexual assault at age 23; aggressions were attempts to create sexual situation in which he was in control; never an exhibitionist or voyeur
FIRST VICTIM	May be acquaintance from adolescence	No previous relationship
EDUCATION	Secondary school, A level or more likely higher vocational training	Higher studies in physical education
LANGUAGE	Correct, shows education and Andalusian origin without strong Malaga accent	Correct
SOCIAL ADAPTATION	Socially adapted, but few social skills	Basically correct
MARRIAGE	After several years of formal courtship, probably married in 2000	Correct; in 2000 married girl with whom he went steady since adolescence

Table 8.1 Comparison of Criminal Profile and Suspect Data (Continued)

Topic	October 2001 Criminal Profile	Data on Suspect Arrested February 2002
PERSONALITY	Timid, trifling personality, educated, clean, not violent; has low self-esteem; not impulsive; obsessive with psychopathic traits; personality features evolving from insecurity of adolescence toward hardness and stronger ego; sensation of invulnerability (no longer hides his face)	Correct
DRUG USE	Does not consume drugs or go to discotheques	Correct
FAMILY	Probably not of Malaga origin; protective mother; absent and masculine dominating father; member of working middle class	Basically correct; born in Malaga; family comes from a different Andalusian province; both parents absent during infancy; father is plumber

We should stress that a profile of this sort is not a psychological or psychiatric diagnosis. Its only purpose is to yield clues that may assist the police to identify a criminal still at large and thus prevent future crimes. The information in the right column is based on preliminary data that came to light after the arrest of the offender. It is not meant as a clinical evaluation of his mental state or sexual habits. The criminal profile was correct on most points. One error was the suggestion that the rapist might have known the first victim before the attack that caused us to increase the age estimate by a couple of years to match the age of that victim and led to false leads. The best hit that may have achieved an early arrest was the suggestion that the rapist married in 2000. That was based on his change in scenarios from the fantasy world of being the husband of a pretty woman to the fantasy of having affairs with Swedish students 10 years younger than he was. It was also based on the testimony of one victim in late 2000 who stated that he wore a wedding ring.

However, a fairly good description of the kind of person who commits such acts may be of little help. Clues about where he lives are more useful than clues about his personality traits. We therefore also supplied a geographic profile.

Geographic Profile

Figure 8.1 shows the locations of the first 20 attacks. This map is similar to the pin maps police used during the investigation. We see that the assaults are concentrated on the west side of the city center, to the left on the map.

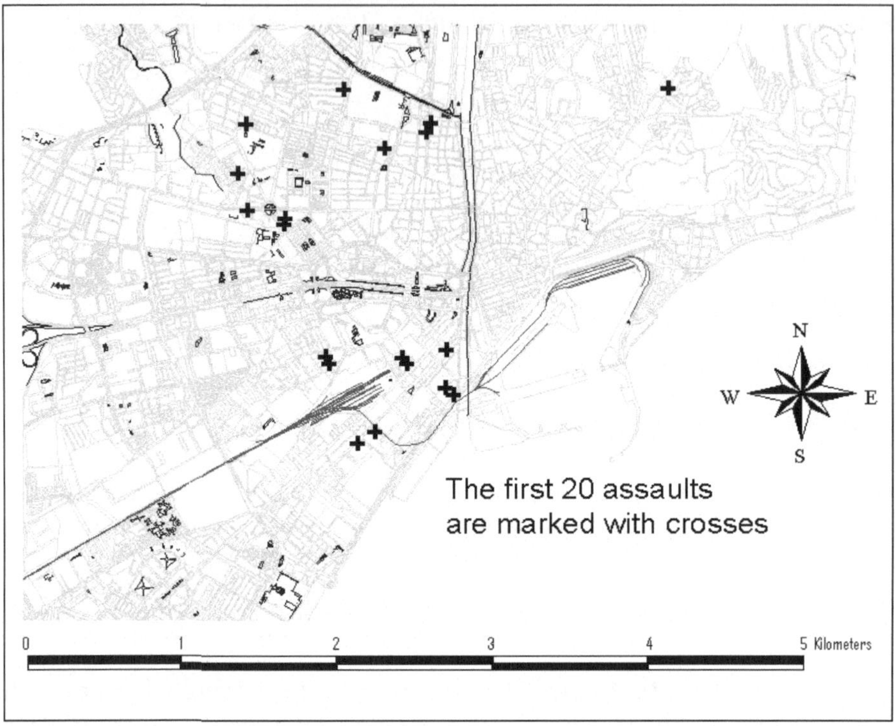

Figure 8.1 Geographic distribution of first 20 rapes.

Later rapes took place in the eastern suburbs, off the map on the right side. We did not include these crimes in our geographical analysis because we were convinced that the first 3 years of operations revealed his base. Our assumption was that this offender, like most other serial criminals, ventured into wider areas as time passed. This assumption was later shown to be correct; his home base had not moved.

Figure 8.2 is a density map that draws a circle around the first 18 rapes and attempted rapes. The circle can be considered a safe guess. We now know that his two residences and the sport stadium where he worked during the afternoons were inside the circle. His other workplace, a college where he worked in the mornings, was 2 km outside the circle. However, this map would not have been very useful to police. The population within the circle was about 100,000 inhabitants. The police knew already that the rapist probably lived in this area, but had not identified him during their 3-year investigation.

Figure 8.3 is the density map presented to the police. It offers a more ambitious interpretation of the data in Figure 8.2, and suggests that the rapist operated in two well defined zones. The crime data and the calculating algorithm are the same as in Figure 8.2. The only difference is the search radius parameter or distance decay function. While Figure 8.2 calculates the density of events within a 2,000-m radius, Figure 8.3 reduces the radius

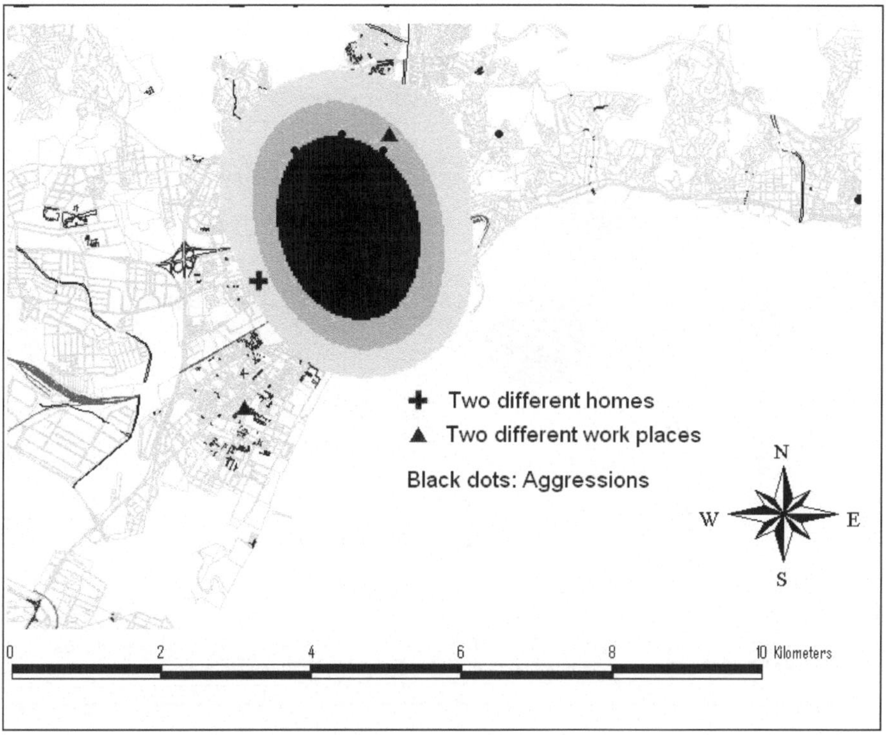

Figure 8.2 Geographic profile according to circle hypothesis.

to 1,000 m, a more typical walking distance range. We gave a base for that assumption in the profile submitted to the police:

> The victims coincide in describing the aggressor as a clean person. He has an agreeable smell, not from hair lotion but rather as coming straight from the shower. However, he sweats easily, and cannot have walked long distances from his base to the crime site. If he had come by car, his hunting zones would have been more oblong, along an avenue etc. (Translated extract from original offender profile, October 15, 2001.)

We now discover what looks like a "bimodal pattern with crime clusters centered around two anchor points" (Rossmo, 2000: 195). The main railway station of Malaga appears in the center of the lower cluster (Zone South) on the map. The events appear to form a circle around that station at convenient walking distances. All events occurred on weekdays during morning hours, many of them between 9 and 10 a.m. or during the last hour before lunch, 1 to 2 p.m.* Our main hypothesis was that the rapist worked inside this zone.

* The midday break at most shops and offices in Malaga is from 2 to 5 p.m. They reopen from 5 to 8 p.m.

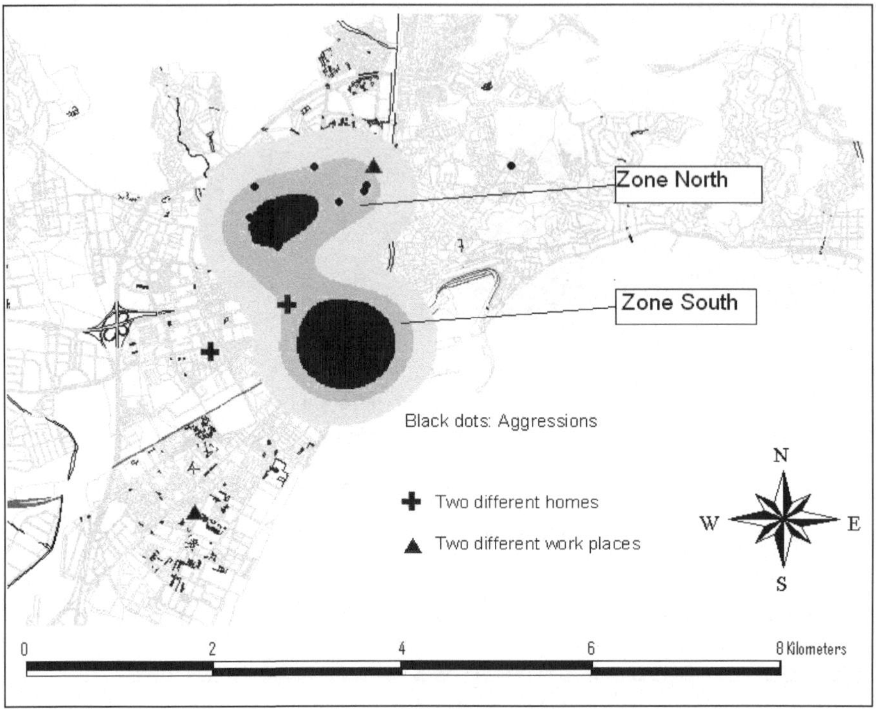

Figure 8.3 Geographic profile with narrower range.

The circle also contains a bus terminal, central offices of the regional government, a big shopping center, and other facilities.

A mile further north, we find a second cluster of crime scenes. Several of these aggressions had occurred between 5 and 8 p.m. In the center of Zone North, we find a circle with a diameter of half a mile inside which no attacks occurred. This is a residential area containing middle-class apartment blocks of four to eight stories that may represent a buffer zone around the rapist's home. Our recommendation was to concentrate police investigations in this area. According to our profile:

> All assaults in the southern zone occur during daytime. A person who works from 8 to 3 PM, with great liberties at his work place, could dedicate himself to search for victims during the first and last hours of work. Aggressions in the northern zone show more temporal variation, including two events late at night. In the northern zone there is a circle that the offender appears to avoid. Searches should be concentrated in that area, given that he might live there. (Translated extract from original offender profile, October 15, 2001.)

Zone North has a population of 15,000, a much more manageable number than the zone indicated by Figure 8.2. The police, based on this recommendation, carried out discreet inquiries in every building. The search was fruitless.

The profile produced no direct results and the offender raped four more young girls, all of whom were language students from other countries and lived on the east side of the city. The police, in cooperation with our victim service, concentrated on preventive work, advising all language schools about the danger and giving students a hotline number they could call in case someone pretending to be a plumber tried to enter their apartments. The last four rape victims attended language schools that failed to warn their students.

The suspect behind 29 sexual assaults was arrested in February 2002. His error was making a second approach to a girl he visited some months earlier. During the first visit, he pretended to be a plumber and made no suspicious moves because the girl's boyfriend was present. However, when he returned 3 months later, she had been warned. She did not open the door and called the police. The suspect eluded the patrol that soon arrived, but a policewoman noted the license plate number. The suspect left his car in a no-parking zone.

After Arrest: Contrasting Profile with Behavior

Figure 8.3 is identical to the map we gave the police along with a criminal profile except for one vital difference. We have added the locations of his home and workplace. They are marked with a cross and a triangle, both in the peripheries of the circles. After the suspect's arrest, we learned that he lived in Zone South, 700 m "as the crow flies" from the center of our circle. The second cross further to the left indicates a home where the suspect grew up. The hypothesis that he lived in the northern zone was incorrect. The rapist committed the crimes in Zone North while in transit between his home and a sport club where he worked in the evenings. Contrary to what we expected, he did not seek out his victims on foot. On several occasions, he left his car double parked while he sought a victim. That behavior contributed to his arrest.

The distance between his home and the first rape was 1,800 m—a bit more than a mile. That fits well with the analysis of Canter and Gregory (1994: 172) of serial rapists in southern England. Because the suspect was white, older than 25, and perpetrated his rapes during workdays, we would expect a buffer zone of at least a mile. There was little dispersal. The first 18 rapes were committed in a relatively limited zone, with a distance of only 2.5 km between the two sites most remote from each other.

The concentrated pattern led us to conclude that the rapist traveled on foot. This was the most serious error in our geographic profile. He used a car. Based on Rossmo's classification, he was a *troller* who sought potential victims while he drove his car from one workplace to another. The map of crime sites clearly revealed his area of routine activities. The theory behind criminal profiling was, in fact, validated, but, like most other criminal profilers, we were not able to interpret the clues with sufficient precision to lead to his arrest. We therefore conducted a series of interviews with the suspect in the local prison to better understand his motivation and his methods.

During 5 years of criminal activity, he taught physical education at two colleges and worked as a trainer for a football team. We saw no indications of sexual harassment or aggression in relation to his pupils or in his large circle of acquaintances.

The rapist drove 3 to 4 km several times daily, crossing the western part of the city. Traffic in Malaga is highly congested and involves frequent stops at traffic lights. He observed women walking as he drove. When he saw someone who appeared to be a pretty housewife on her way home carrying shopping bags or taking children to a kindergarten, he hurriedly parked and followed her on foot. He often reached the apartment block just behind her, and climbed the stairs while she took the elevator, and determined where she lived. Later, perhaps the next day, he arrived around the same time and waited for her to open the door.

In our deliberations with the police during the investigation, we discussed at length the rapist's method of finding victims. Since we found it likely that he spotted them in the street, we ruled out the possibility that he was motorized. We would have expected a wider hunting area along a main road for motorized killers or rapists. That was not the pattern we found. We also found it improbable, especially in zones where parking was scarce or non-existent, for a rapist to park a car and then follow his victim without losing track of her. Parking illegally in front of a garbage container or in the middle of a pedestrian crossing would certainly attract attention, but that was exactly what he did.

If he had committed a rape closer to his main workplace, the college, the hunting zone would have been more elongated, and the motorized transport more evident. He explained that in our interviews. He did not know the part of the city where the college was located sufficiently well to hunt for victims there. He did not commit any rapes in the buffer zone where he grew up for the opposite reason: he was too well known there. It is shown to the left of Zone South in Figure 8.3.

At the start of our second interview with him in prison, we gave him a large blank sheet of paper and asked him to draw a map of the city of Malaga. His sketch (Figure 8.4) indicates his awareness space. It shows that he drove a car. Most main roads in the western part of the town are included with great precision and a fairly accurate scale. Landmarks shown on the map include shopping centers (Eroski, Carrefour), a popular bakery (La Canasta), the bus and train stations (Estación Autobuses, Estación Tren), and probably as a reflection of later events, the central police station (Comisaria). The map also shows two sports centers, the university, and two hospitals (Carlos Haya and Hospital Clinico).

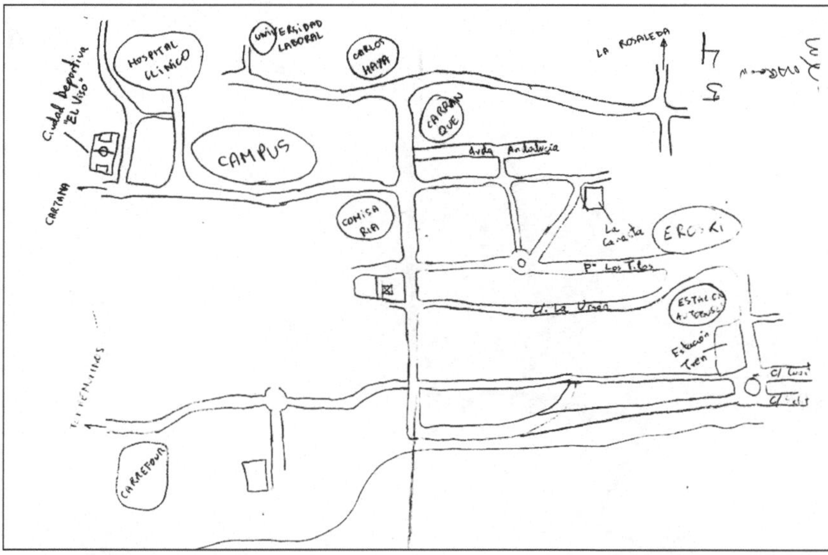

Figure 8.4 Map drawn by presumed rapist.

Comparing this map with maps drawn by a control group revealed striking differences. The rapist's map completely neglects the city center. He is familiar with a western suburb and thus omitted tourist landmarks such as the cathedral and the Moorish castle. Also, Avenida Andaluciá, the main traffic artery that leads downtown, is misplaced and unfinished on his map. He rarely used that road in his daily movements and did not go downtown very often. He probably indulged in hunting fantasies about potential victims whenever he went driving, and preferred busy streets with traffic lights and many pedestrians.

Later, we gave the suspect a city map and asked him to trace the roads he used on his way to work. Figure 8.5 shows the result and the proximity to the first 18 crime sites. The figure gives the key to the bimodal pattern we believed to have found in Figure 8.3. One-way traffic regulations made him choose one path northward and another one southward. Since he traveled to his workplace in the upper part of the map in the afternoons, these assaults tended to occur later in the day. Had we seen the relation of crime sites to these throughways, the last four victims may have been spared. Had we known that he traveled by car, the parameter for distance decay (search radius) on the density map would have been higher. Figure 8.2 was, in hindsight, a safer guess than Figure 8.3, although it would not have helped the police much. Figure 8.5 would have put them on the right track.

The rapist denies having committed the two incidents noted in the upper left corner. Both were frustrated night assaults that may have been perpetrated by someone else. We may also exclude the crime noted on the right side of the map. It corresponds to a rape committed at a later stage, when

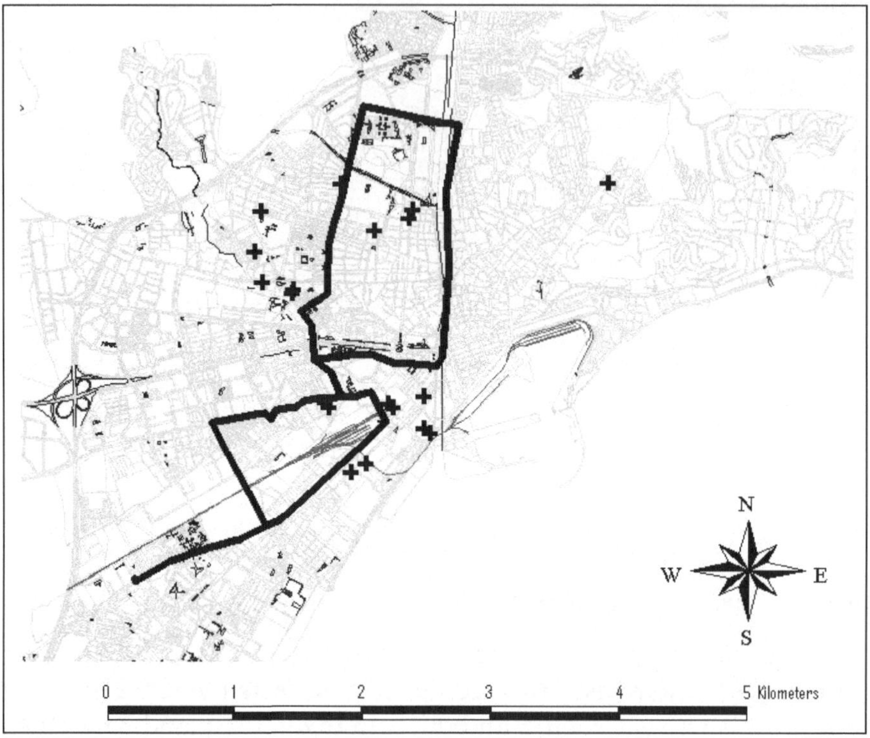

Figure 8.5 Roads used by presumed rapist.

his search patterns became different. Excluding these incidents, we find a median distance of 75 m between the road traced on the map and the crime sites. The minimum distance is 20 m and the maximum 500 m, which gives a mean distance of 180 m. The rapist probably verged from his normal route and took a parallel road when he approached victims who lived 500 m from the track traced in Figure 8.5. We find that all victims were spotted from his car as he drove by them. He then followed them on foot, normally no further than 100 m.

Police Investigation: Review and Discussion

In Spain, the police achieve high clearing rates for homicides and rapes (Ministerio del Interior, 2001: 138). Suspects are arrested in nine of ten cases. However, this is based on previous links between offenders and victims, thus reducing the number of suspects. Another reason is that most serious offenders have criminal records and their descriptions and fingerprints can be checked in police files.

When both these conventional investigation methods fail, police investigations run into serious problems. This is when they may benefit from behavioral science in the form of criminal profiling. Any clues that may reduce the number of suspects from a million (tall, strong, dark haired Andalucian men, 25 to 35 years old) to a couple thousand may lead to an arrest.

The purpose of scientific criminal profiling is to give priorities to multifaceted investigations. A successful investigation may not depend on individual brilliance and intuition, but rather on systematic evaluations of probabilities. The traditional haphazard way of conducting investigations based on a combination of meticulous work and good luck may, as suggested by Canter et al. (2000), be assisted by a scientifically designed decision support system. Criminal investigations of serious crimes usually start with many inconsistent scraps of information. Investigators, according to the resources they can allocate to a case, follow up many leads simultaneously. Most of them lead up blind alleys, but the more extensive an investigation, the more likely one of the tracks will lead to an arrest. Investigative psychology or criminology claims the ability to assist investigators with priorities. Some leads are more likely to give results than others.

Figure 8.6 summarizes the police investigation in this case. Investigation leads are presented in the left column. Most yielded no results. One lead developed early in the investigation led to the arrest of a suspect who was later cleared of charges. The culprit was finally arrested because he approached a potential victim twice.

An intelligent criminal of middle-class background is less likely to be the subject of a police file. However, the possibility of tracking him down through other kinds of records increases. Because he lives a normal life, he is more likely to be a homeowner registered on local census rolls and have a mobile phone, credit cards, and a car in his name. The possibility of combining two or more known facts about a person and performing a computer search of public or private registers can reduce the circle of suspects. We knew that the rapist described in this chapter was about 1.80 m tall. Computerized military records listing recruits 1.78 to 1.85 m tall could have been cross-checked with civil registers of marriages in Malaga during 2000. This strategy did not produce results. Lack of computerization and the deficient states of most public registers made them almost useless.

The police manually checked civil records of marriages during 2000. They collected the names from registers and visually checked the identity photographs of all males married that year to identify those who showed similarities to the Identi-Kit image. An official Spanish identity card includes a print of the right index finger. Such prints of dark haired married males were compared to a fingerprint found on a cupboard at one crime site and presumably belonging to the the rapist. No match was found. As was later discovered, he had married in 2000 and appeared in the marriage register. However, the right-hand index fingerprint on the cupboard was not his.

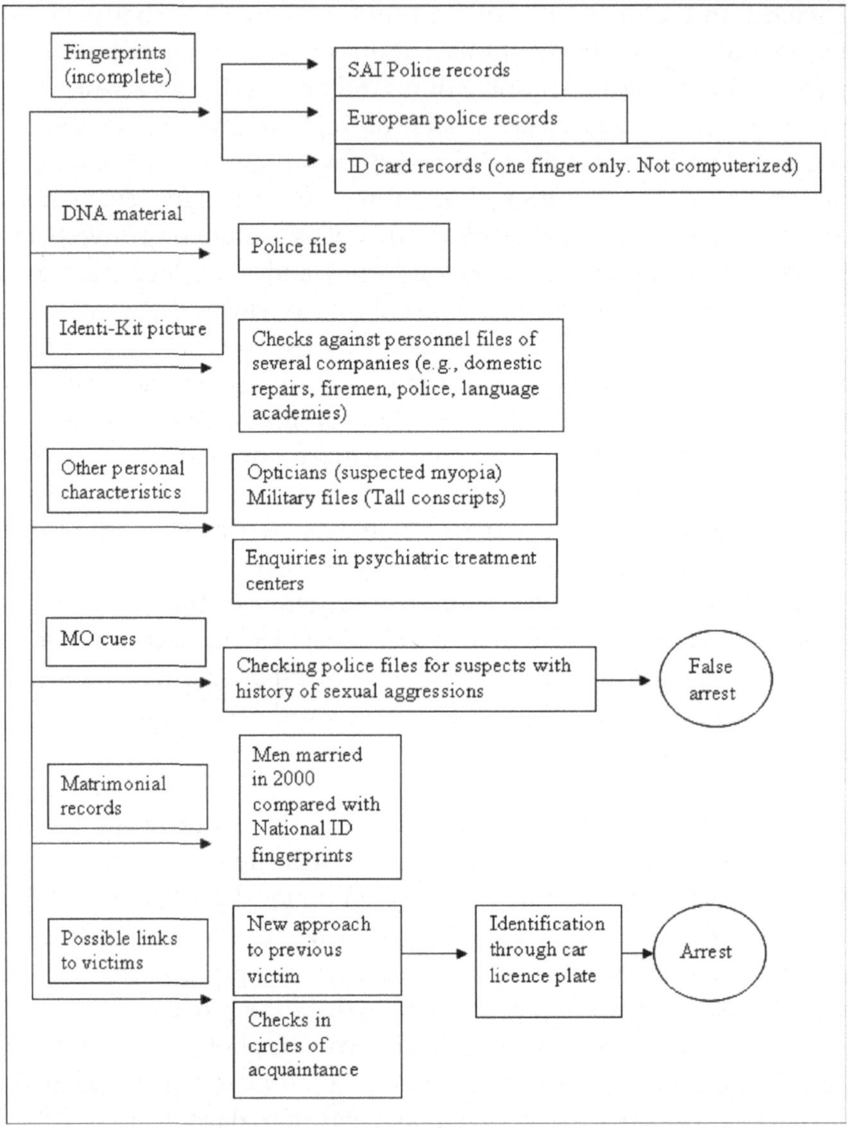

Figure 8.6 Summary of police investigation.

Cross-checking huge manual registers requires resources beyond the capacity of the police. Thirty police officers worked on this case in peak periods. Usually this case was one of several handled by a team of eight officers and the manpower was insufficient to allow extensive archive checks. Clearing complicated cases like this depends on the volume of resources that can be allocated to a police investigation. The lack of computerized population data may be a reason that serial offenders in Third World countries can operate unchecked for long periods. They can be found sooner in countries that have accurate computerized public registers and the capacity to dedicate hundreds of investigators to a single case.

One line of investigation we did not pursue was arranging a press conference to request public assistance. Media coverage was not sought for two reasons. First, publicity may have caused the offender to hide, then reappear with a disguise in a new area. It is easier to catch a perpetrator if he feels confident. Second, the rapist began to target a very specific group of young foreign girls. They were recent arrivals, did not speak Spanish, and would not have been warned by reports in local newspapers or television. The best way to protect them would have been via specific warnings from the language schools they attended. The police managed to keep the case out of the media. A single press report about the uncleared rapes appeared in March 2000. Our interviews with the rapist after his arrest confirmed that he was aware of this publicity, and that it contributed to his change of target and operating area later that year. More media coverage at later stages might have made him change tactics again.

In hindsight, the decision to keep the case confidential proved correct. The rapist led a perfect double life, his arrest came as a shock to all who knew him, and no one would have come forward with a useful tip based on the Identi-Kit portrait. Neither did previously unreported cases appear when the case finally reached the media after his arrest.

In the future, a case like this may be solved through medical registers that, in special cases, authorized by a judge, permit police access to DNA profile data. In this case, a register that included only DNA identifications of previously convicted persons would not have helped. However, police access to a register of the total population would have helped. Sexual aggressions could be reduced drastically if DNA patterns could be compared to nationwide medical databases. Such access might be considered an infringement of civil liberties, but cases like this reveal how the absence of such general registers infringes in a very cruel way on the most basic liberties of rape victims.

Conclusions

The theory behind geographic profiling clearly explains the patterns found. This rapist was intelligent, well educated, calculating, and able to live a double life. No one suspected that he was a serial rapist in his spare time. However, he revealed his activity space through his crimes. He lived half a mile from the center of one of the two circles on a computer map. The problem shared by most profilers is that this information was not precise enough to identify the rapist.

Geographic profiling, combined with the possibility of cross-checking information in computerized registers, may be a powerful tool in difficult cases. This case study shows the potential of computerized registers and illustrates some of the problems encountered in real-life situations. It suggests that a geographic profile must take into account actual traffic flows and street systems of areas under study. Such analyses must be based on accurate assumptions about transport. In this case, the input parameter for calculating distance decay was 1,000 m, a typical walking distance. It should have been higher because the rapist moved around by car. Had we seen the connection between the streets he used and the crime sites, several victims may have been spared.

References

Brantingham, P. J. and Brantingham, P. L. (1981) *Environmental criminology*, Thousand Oaks, CA: Sage.

Canter, D. (2000) Offender profiling and criminal differentiation, *Legal and Criminological Psychology*, 5: 23–46.

Canter, D. (2003) *Mapping murder. The secrets of geographical profiling*, London: Virgin Books.

Canter, D., Coffey, T., Huntley, M., and Missen, C. (2000) Predicting serial killers home base using a decision support system, *Journal of Quantitative Criminology*, 16 (4): 457–477.

Canter, D. and Gregory, A. (1994) Identifying the residential location of rapists, *Journal of the Forensic Science Society*, 34 (3): 169.

Canter, D. and Larkin, P. (1993) The environmental range of serial rapists, *Journal of Environmental Psychology*, 13: 66–69.

Felson, M. (1994) *Crime and everyday life*, Thousand Oaks, CA: Pine Forge Press.

Garrido, V. (2003) *Psicópatas y otros delincuentes violentos*, Valencia, Spain: Tirant lo Blanch.

Hesseling, R. B. P. (1992) Using data on offender mobility in ecological research, *Journal of Quantitative Criminology*, 8: 98–114.

Kocsis, R. N. and Irwin, H. J. (1997) An analysis of spatial patterns in serial rape, arson and burglary: The utility of the Circle Theory of environmental range for psychological profiling, *Psychiatry, Psychology and Law*, 4 (2): 195–206.

LeBeau, J. L. (1987) The methods and measures of centrography and the spatial dynamics of rape, *Journal of Quantitative Criminology*, 3: 125–141.

Ministerio del Interior (2001) *Anuario estadístico*, available at www.mir.es.

Rossmo, D. K. (1995a) *Geographic profiling: Target patterns of serial murderers*, dissertation, Simon Fraser University, Vancouver, Canada.

Rossmo, D. K. (1995b) Place, space and police investigations: Hunting serial violent criminals, in Eck, J. E. and Weisburd, D. (Eds.), *Crime prevention studies*, Vol. 4 (pp. 217–235), New York: Willow Tree Press.

Rossmo, D. K. (2000) *Geographic profiling*, Boca Raton, FL: CRC Press.

Shaw, C. R. and McKay, H. (1969) *Juvenile delinquency in urban areas*, Chicago: University of Chicago Press.

Stangeland, P. and Garrido, M. J. (2003) *El lugar del crimen. Herramientas geográficas para policías y criminólogos*, Valencia: Tirant lo Blanch.

Turner, S. (1969) Delinquency and distance, in Wolfgang, M. E. and Sellin, T. (Eds.), *Delinquency: Selected studies* (pp. 11–26), New York: Wiley.
Warren, J., Reboussin, R., Hazelwood, R., Cummings, A., Gibbs, N., and Trumbetta, S. (1998) Crime scene and distance correlates of serial rape, *Journal of Quantitative Criminology*, 14 (1): 35–59.
Wikström, P-O. (1991) *Urban crime, criminals and victims*, New York: Springer.

Restorative Policing

V

Restorative Policing in Canada: Royal Canadian Mounted Police, Community Justice Forums, and Youth Criminal Justice Act*

9

JHARNA CHATTERJEE
LIZ ELLIOTT

Contents

At a time when the meaning and capacity of the criminal justice system are in question, it is not surprising that an idea like restorative justice has captured the attention of communities and criminal justice systems. Indeed, a recent Canadian study has demonstrated that restorative justice has been more successful than the retributive system in achieving victim and offender satisfaction, increasing offender compliance with restitution, and decreasing recidivism (Latimer, Dowden and Muise, 2001: 17). Like many new ideas, however, the implementation of restorative processes has required growth, the direction of which appears to depend on adherence to the restorative philosophy of peacemaking. The suitability of restorative justice for "peace officers" seems logical, but it presents a number of potential obstacles to effective police-based restorative practices (see also Bazemore and Griffith, Chapter 10).

This discussion examines the roles of the Royal Canadian Mounted Police (RCMP) in the development of one restorative practice model in Canada. It includes a brief history and a discussion of restorative justice practice

* This chapter first appeared in *Police Practice and Research*, 2003, 4(4): 347–359.

in Canada, the practice of which can be traced to two general origins and models: the dyadic restorative mediation of the Mennonite* tradition and the peacemaking circles of aboriginal peoples. The police introduced a third model to Canada via New Zealand and Australia.

The restorative justice approach of family group conferencing was first adopted by the RCMP in British Columbia in 1995, and since then it has been used across the country. The implementation of the Youth Criminal Justice Act (YCJA) in April 2003 provides for the use of restorative approaches in certain cases, creating the potential to expand police participation in alternative community-based justice processes. The YCJA's impact on police practices is one consideration of this chapter. Finally, we suggest some concerns or variables that may require attention in the implementation of conferencing.

Restorative Justice in Canadian Context

Modern conceptions of non-retributive justice approaches (collectively called *restorative justice*) began to surface in the mid-1970s. The first criminal justice process shift in the direction of restorative justice was manifested in Canada in what was to become known as the Victim–Offender Reconciliation Program (VORP), in Kitchener-Waterloo, Ontario. Responding to the vandalism of 22 properties by two young men in nearby Elmira, a probation officer and a staff member from the local Mennonite Central Committee arranged for the young men to meet with the victims to negotiate restitution for the damage.† From these beginnings in 1974, a modern restorative approach was launched.

The term *restorative justice* was created by Albert Eglash (Llewellyn and Howse, 1999: 4) in the specific context of restitution (Eglash, 1977). Howard Zehr of Eastern Mennonite University in Virginia later produced what has become known as one of the seminal works in the development of restorative justice thought (1990) and suggested that a paradigm shift in ways of thinking about justice was in order. In contrast to the conventional understanding of crime as a violation of the state through lawbreaking, the premise of restorative justice was that crime is primarily a violation of people and relationships. Over a decade later, Zehr refined these concepts, summarizing the principles in three pillars of restorative justice: a focus on harms and needs, accountability through attention to obligations, and engagement or participation of those with legitimate interests or stakes in the offense (Zehr, 2002: 22–24).

The Mennonite influence on modern developments in restorative justice extended beyond the early attempts in southern Ontario. One promi-

* A Christian church that emphasizes "peace building" (see www.mennonitechurch.ca).

† A more detailed description of VORP's experimental stages is found in Zehr (1990). For a personal account of this story, see *From Scoundrel to Scholar...The Russ Kelly Story* (Kelly, 2006).

nent example is the Fraser Region Community Justice Initiatives Association (CJIA), founded in 1981 in Langley, British Columbia. The CJI developed the VORP concept in 1989 to include affected parties in serious crimes of violence, providing them with post-sentence counseling and mediation services under the umbrella of the Victim Offender Mediation Program (VOMP).* This project well demonstrates the capacity of restorative justice for meaningful and significant intervention in cases of serious crime—a domain thought by some to be out of the purview of this harm-focused approach to justice.

These contributions significantly shaped the processes of restorative mediation. This process focuses mainly on dyadic relationships, primarily relationships of those harmed and the harm doers. In this model, mediators are caretakers and diplomats. Attention to the wellbeing of both parties is at the heart of the model's success and indicates the role of spirituality in this restorative approach. Originally, dyadic mediations such as VORP and VOMP were based on the beliefs of the Mennonites, who practice a peace-oriented faith. Successful mediations are not gauged merely by diplomatic agreements between the parties, but also by the healing experienced.

Other primary contributors to the modern understanding of restorative justice are the traditional practices of aboriginal communities. Community and relationships are central concepts in aboriginal ways of understanding the world. Traditional processes to address conflict, apart from everyday ethics and guidelines for social interactions (Brandt, 1990), tend to be inclusive of the wider community. The collective is seen as the source of an individual's pain and their healing. Individuals are seen as reflections of the whole; the wrongdoer, in Navajo terms, "acts as if he has no relatives" (Yazzie and Zion, 1996: 162).

Key to understanding the integrity of aboriginal justice is the focus on the medicine wheel. In aboriginal traditions, good medicine is a practice that "helps to restore balance in human beings and their communities" (Bopp and Bopp, 2001: 22). The medicine wheel is a way of seeing and knowing oneself in relation to one's Creator and the world, with implications for responses to conflict. The wheel is composed of four interrelated areas of life: mental, emotional, physical, and spiritual, which exist in individuals and in the collective. The hurt of one is considered to be the hurt of all (Four Worlds Development Project, 1984).

In Canada, several aboriginal communities reclaimed their traditional conflict processes to address crimes and other harms. A prominent example is Hollow Water, a Manitoba village that began to tackle sexual abuse prob-

* A 1995 evaluation of VOMP by the Fraser Region Community Justice Initiatives Association reported "unanimous support for the program by all victim and offender respondents" interviewed. In total, 22 offenders and 24 victims in 24 matched victim-offender cases constituted the sample. See Roberts (1995).

lems within families in 1984. Using teams from various social services, the Hollow Water project involved various stages leading to a Special Gathering and the creation of a Healing Contract, and ending with a Cleansing Ceremony.* Belief in healing is a cornerstone of aboriginal justice. Patricia Monture-Angus of Saskatchewan described healing as "learning to act in a good way" (1995). Healing also suggests that this process is facilitated with affirming support for both the harmed and the harm doer.

Aboriginal approaches to justice in Canada are also found in circle sentencing, particularly in the Prairies and Northern Territories. Circle sentencing is not a wholly aboriginal practice. It was created as a hybrid model by criminal court judges and aboriginal communities. The court officers sit with the accused, victim(s), and other community members in a circle, often in a venue outside the formal court. Everyone in the circle is asked for input in the case, and the group usually makes the sentencing decision. A central feature of this process is the role of the community, whose members are knowledgeable about the context of the offense and are likely to be involved in the subsequent sentencing agreement.†

Circle processes may also be used outside the purview of criminal justice. One advantage of this process is its flexibility: a circle may be used for community dialogues about larger issues, for healing, and for coming to agreements. The circle is also an apt metaphor for restorative justice values, many of which are also reflected in the dyadic model of restorative mediation. These values, as articulated by former Chief Justice of the Yukon Territory Barry Stuart, Tlingit (Yukon) land claims negotiator Mark Wedge, and Kay Pranis of the Minnesota Department of Corrections, include: respect, trust, honesty, humility, sharing, inclusivity, love, empathy, courage, and forgiveness (Pranis, Stuart and Wedge, 2003).

Restorative justice philosophy is described as a balance between an ethic of justice and an ethic of care (Sharpe, 1998: 7). The ethic of justice is "a powerful moral intuition that something must be done" (Llewellyn and Howse, 1999: 37); the ethic of care speaks of practices intended to heal people and relationships. Together, they imply that we are called to respond to acts that cause harm to people and the environment and that that response should facilitate healing. The process used in response to harm should model the values of restorative justice (Elliott, 2002). Restorative justice practices what it preaches through values-based processes.

* Rupert Ross describes the Hollow Water experience in *Returning to the Teachings* (1996). Ross was a crown attorney who developed an interest in aboriginal perspectives of justice in northern Canadian communities in which he practiced law and conducted research.

† A more detailed discussion of aboriginal sentencing alternatives is found in Ross Green's *Justice in Aboriginal Communities: Sentencing Alternatives* (1998).

Contemporary restorative justice philosophy in Canada has been built primarily from two sources: Mennonite mediation initiatives and aboriginal justice. A third process model known as conferencing is the subject of the remainder of this discussion. This model may or may not embody the values and principles of restorative justice, depending on the knowledge and perspectives of the conference facilitators.* In Canada, conferencing has been the RCMP's tool of choice.

Conferencing and Police

Since New Zealand introduced the Children, Young Offenders and Families Act in 1989, most relatively serious offenses are referred directly to family group conferences that include the offenders, victims, facilitators, and community representatives whose aim is restorative resolution of an offense. Police are reported to use informal cautioning instead of conferencing for less serious cases. The ratio of cases of informal police caution to those dealt with through family group conferences is 4 to 1 (O'Connell and Moore, 1992). Maxwell and Morris (2000) reported that 82% of the cases were dealt with by police warnings and diversions, and about 8% were dealt with by a family group conferences in which police tended to play prominent roles. Only 10%—a substantial reduction—were handled by youth courts. According to these authors, the rate of youth court appearance dropped from 64 per 1000 before the act to 16 per 1000 after the act was introduced. They also observed that police prominence in family group conferences was not unanimously viewed as desirable. Later, the role of police was seen to be in supporting the victim by presenting information about the offense and the offender's history and representing the interests of the community.

According to O'Connell and Moore (1992), the Wagga Wagga model† introduced in Australia in 1991 utilizes family group conferencing as a tool for formal police cautioning. The primary difference between the New Zealand and the Wagga Wagga models is that the victim is central in the latter approach and the former emphasizes reform of the offender rather than

* Zehr (2002) refers to degrees of restorative justice practices on a continuum (pp. 54–57), from pseudo/non-restorative, through potential/partial/mostly, to fully restorative. Conferencing is offered in 2- or 3-day training sessions. It is not necessarily true that facilitators in training will have made paradigm shifts in thought from punishment to healing. Therefore, a conference—a restorative tool in itself—can be facilitated in ways that are non- or partially restorative (e.g., an offender is deliberately or unconsciously shamed, conference outcomes are punitive rather than logically tied to the harm). This speaks to the hazard of offering training of conferencing mechanics, without substantial education first of the values and principles of restorative justice.

† Wagga Wagga is a rural city in New South Wales, Australia.

restoring the victim. The Wagga Wagga model includes a follow-up process emphasizing remedial skills for offenders. Follow-ups are coordinated by the Police and Community Youth Clubs (PCYC).*

These conferences operate within the guidelines of the police commissioner's instructions requiring a panel of sergeants to decide the appropriateness of the use of police discretion in each individual case. The seriousness of each offense is considered, not on legal or technical grounds, but in terms of a continuum of harmful consequences. Reducing juvenile offender recidivism is a major objective. It is believed that this can be accomplished by ensuring that young offenders understand the consequences of their actions by facing their victims. The Australian Federal Police in Canberra began using the conferencing program studied under the Reintegrative Shaming Experiments (RISE; Sherman and Strang, 1997). Restorative conferences are practiced in school settings in Queensland as well. Howard and Purches (1992) commented:

> Initiatives in Juvenile Cautioning currently being implemented in Wagga Wagga by the local Police Patrol are innovative; they reflect the progressive nature of policing in this rural city. The Family Group Conferences have the potential to steer young offenders away from the court system, and in the long term may contribute to a decline in recidivism.

However, they point out two major potential problems: net widening and interventions in children's lives without proper safeguards. This suggests needs for careful screening to avoid over-processing minor matters and realistically assessing community capacities.

A somewhat different philosophy of transformative justice† evolved from the initial conferencing work in Australia. Its proponents, John McDonald and David Moore (1999), used it to deal with conflicts in workplaces as well as in communities. The key difference between the earlier conferencing activities that McDonald and Moore considered consistent with the theory of re-integrative shaming (Braithwaite, 1989) and the philosophy underlying transformative justice is that the experience of shame is said to be *collective*—for all conference participants, and not for the offender alone. This collective shame results in an emotional transformation and forgiveness—the most important sociological element in the entire process. McDonald and Moore suggest that conferencing is an appropriate tool for transforming conflicts "defined as criminally harmful" (1999: 22), and recommend a reformulation

* See www.pcycnsw.org.

† Ruth Morris (2000), a Canadian, created the *transformative justice* term in response to the inadequacy of *restorative justice* to address distributive injustices: "[Restorative justice] still accepts the idea that one event now defines all that matters of right and wrong—it leaves out the past, and the social causes of all events: (p. 4).

of the theory and practice from crime, shame, and reintegration to conflict, acknowledgment, and transformation.

In England, the Thames Valley Police experimented with and gradually expanded their use of restorative cautioning with youth since 1998. The cautioning takes the form of restorative conferences facilitated by trained police facilitators; all individuals affected by the offense are invited. The researchers found a substantial reduction in recidivism (14% as compared with twice that rate for conventional cautioning) in police records for youths aged 10 to 17 who experienced restorative cautioning. One of the encouraging findings was that the cautioning sessions adhering most closely to restorative justice principles produced the most positive results (Hoyle, Young and Hill, 2002).

Canadian Experience

In 1997, the RCMP officially adopted a restorative justice approach as a discretionary option for dealing with non-violent offenses. This is a version of the family group conference called a *community justice forum* (CJF) based on the Wagga Wagga model—although not all CJFs are police-facilitated. *Community* has a wide range of meanings. CJF's definition of *community of impact* covers the people affected by an offense.

In 1995, RCMP Sergeant Jake Bouwman and lawyer Glen Purdy were encouraged by Judge Heino Lilles to read a booklet about a new approach practiced in Sparwood, British Columbia, and known as restorative justice. The two men were sufficiently impressed to start applying the approach unofficially with local youths. In 1996, a delegation led by the Canadian Department of Justice that included representatives from other departments such as the RCMP visited Australia and New Zealand to learn first-hand about this new approach, based on ancient Maori traditions.* The RCMP found this method of handling appropriate offenses consistent with its already embraced community policing philosophy and officially launched its Restorative Justice Initiative in early 1997 by hosting train-the-trainer sessions at several sites across the country. The 50 trainees included members of the RCMP and other provincial and municipal police departments, and key members of communities such as social workers, school board members, volunteers, and teachers.

Although the RCMP chose the CJF as its preferred restorative tool, it also supports other forms of restorative justice such as victim–offender mediations, community justice committees, and circle sentencing. The RCMP pre-

* These practices of dealing with crime and conflict through community-based discussions and sanctions have been practiced for hundreds of years in traditional cultures worldwide, including aboriginal peoples in Canada.

fers to see itself as a catalyst that trains key community members to become trainers or CJF facilitators and encourages and helps communities to solve their own problems by utilizing CJFs and other restorative options whenever possible in appropriate cases.

A case handled successfully via a CJF is cited in an RCMP evaluation* of its restorative justice initiative (Chatterjee, 1999). A senior student in a college was confronted about his sexual harassment of several female students. A CJF was convened and included two college deans, house parents from male and female dormitories, the senior student, his friend, six female students, a college social worker, and two CJF facilitators. The male student admitted the abuse and initially did not appear resentful. In expressions of strong emotion, the female students told him how the abuse affected them. Their supporters spoke of their inability to help the young women. The male student's friend suggested that he would have stopped the actions if he knew about their impacts. The student made a sincere apology and volunteered to talk to the other young men in the dormitories to ask them to change their behavior. His friend agreed to accompany him and they followed through with the commitment. Later, the female students noted that sexual harassment at the college had been almost eliminated. The CJF follow-up data indicated that the male student appeared "different" and "happier" (Chatterjee, 1999: App. A).

The evaluation revealed that, by the end of 1998, the RCMP trained about 1700 individuals across Canada to conduct CJF sessions. The facilitators who conducted CJFs reported handling at least 30 different types of offenses including thefts (26%), assaults (21%), mischief (7%), drugs (6%), property damage (5%), break-and-enter incidents (5%), sexual abuse (4%), and harassment or bullying (4%). Seventy-nine percent of active facilitators reported dealing with offenders who were 19 years old or younger. The most frequently reported age range for offenders who participated in CJFs was 14 to 16 years (38%); 15% were 17 to 19 years old; 2% were people over 50; and 7% involved offenders under age 11.

The responses (based on surveys and structured interviews) of a total of 487 participants indicated that the mean ratings of overall satisfaction and levels of satisfaction for procedural and outcome fairness were high. Ninety-eight percent of all participants expressed at least moderate overall satisfaction, over 87% of whom were quite or very satisfied. Ninety-four percent of all participants (but 100% of the victims) perceived the CJF process to be very or quite fair. Most participants indicated their CJF participation was voluntary (100% of offenders and victim supporters and more than 95% of victims and offender supporters). Satisfaction with agreement or outcome

* Data were collected and analyzed up to March 2001, even after the first and second evaluation reports were published.

was consistently high; 90% of participants reported outcomes as quite or very fair. Most acknowledged having opportunities to provide input into agreements without undue pressure. Ninety-four percent of victims and 82% of offenders found the agreements to be quite or very fair (Chatterjee, 1999).

Ninety-eight percent of offenders said that CJF participation helped them understand the harmful impacts of offenses on others and also helped them to take responsibility for their actions. In most cases, the offenders complied with the agreements; the failure to do so was usually beyond their control. Most victims felt that the CJFs helped their sense of healing and regaining control over their lives. The mean response to a question about the extent to which justice was done was 4.2 (highest possible rating was 5); 95% of the sample endorsed at least a moderate rating. Supporters of both offenders and victims indicated that harmony was restored (Chatterjee, 1999).

These findings are consistent with those of the Australian RISE studies as well (Sherman and Strang, 1997). Certain critics, however, believe that without any empirical evidence on recidivism, the benefit of restorative justice is doubtful. It must be noted that restorative justice (and CJF in particular) is a relatively new concept in most countries. At the time of writing, conclusive empirical data on recidivism are yet to be gathered. The satisfaction of participants with the fairness of the process and outcome, nevertheless, should not be discarded as soft evidence. The satisfaction of people who experience the justice system validates it and affords them faith in the system.

YCJA: Police Role and Conferencing

In April 2003, the Government of Canada implemented the Youth Criminal Justice Act (YCJA). It addresses some of the concerns cited in the 1984 Young Offenders Act (YOA) by clearly stating the objectives of the youth justice system: prevention of crime; rehabilitation and reintegration of youth into society; and providing young wrongdoers fair, timely, and meaningful consequences within the boundaries of proportionate accountability.

The act also emphasizes that interventions should reinforce respect for societal values and respond to the needs of the youth; encourage harms to be repaired; respect gender, ethnic, cultural, and linguistic differences (with special consideration for the circumstances of aboriginal youth), while guaranteeing protection of all young people; parents, families, and communities, where appropriate, are to be encouraged to participate in the process; and, finally, the most serious interventions such as incarceration should be utilized as a last resort for the most serious offenses. The YCJA prescribes more specific principles for various key points in the justice system: extrajudicial measures, youth sentencing, and custody and supervision. The police are usually the first contacts in the youth justice system. Thus, the provisions relevant to policing are those concerning extrajudicial measures. The explanatory material produced by the Department of Justice (2002) instructs that:

> Extrajudicial measures should be used in all cases where they would be adequate to hold the youth accountable.
> Extrajudicial measures are presumed to be adequate for first-time, nonviolent offenders.
> Extrajudicial measures may be used if the young person has previously been dealt with by extrajudicial measures or has been found guilty of an offence.
> The objectives of extrajudicial measures include: (i) repairing the harm done, (ii) opportunity for the victims to participate, (iii) measures be proportionate to the seriousness of offense, and (iv) families or support persons be encouraged to get involved whenever possible.

One of the major objectives of the YCJA is to reduce the use of courts for less serious offenses of youth. It requires police officers to first consider extrajudicial options instead of charging and to provide early interventions where such measures can adequately hold youths accountable and provide them with meaningful consequences. The responses are intended to be graduated, according to the seriousness of the offense and adequacy to hold the young person accountable. Extrajudicial measures include (1) taking no further action, (2) warnings, (3) police cautions, (4) Crown cautions, (5) referrals (with consent of young person) to community programs or agencies that address the root causes of the offense, and (6) extrajudicial sanctions (to be used only when a youth admits responsibility and the Attorney General is sure of the evidence to proceed with prosecution and authorizes such programs). Thus, extrajudicial sanctions (known as alternative measures under the YOA) are the most formal measures, and should be used only if the other less formal measures such as warnings, cautions, and referrals are judged inadequate. Extrajudicial sanctions must be consistent with the YCJA principles such as proportionality and reduced accountability of youth—an acknowledgment that young persons lack the maturity of adults.

The YCJA defines a conference as "a group of people convened to give advice to a decision maker under the Act (Section 19)." It encourages the advisory use of conferences by the police, judge, prosecutor, or any other decision makers within the youth justice system. Conferences may take place at various decision points in the criminal justice process, such as at the front end (to charge or not; to choose the most appropriate extrajudicial measure), pre-trial detention (conditions for judicial interim release), sentencing (type of sentence), and reintegration (planning to assist rehabilitation into the community after custody). Different participants are considered relevant at different decision points. For example, victim, counsel, family, and support persons may be the most appropriate participants at a front-end conference;

teachers, social workers, and mental health workers for a reintegration planning conference; and social workers, counsel, and family for conferences convened at the pre-trial detention stage.

The objective of a conference is to gain "a wider range of perspectives, more creative solutions, better coordination of services, and increased involvement of the victim and other community members" (Department of Justice, 2002: 7). Conferences may be formal (for more serious and complex cases) or informal, based on the circumstances and perceived needs of the person calling the conference (police officer, judge, youth worker, justice of the peace, prosecutor, or provincial director). Under the YCJA, a restorative justice conference (e.g., family group conference) is one of the two general types. The other is a professional case conference, where the objective is to discuss the best way to handle a case. Sentencing circles, youth justice committees, and community justice panels are other examples of conferencing.

A police officer would usually convene a restorative conference or a case conference, with a view to seeking advice regarding a minor offense involving a youth. However, under the YCJA, a province *may* establish rules for conferences called by police, prosecutors, provincial directors, or youth workers. If a province chooses not to establish rules for conferences, the police, prosecutor, youth worker, or a provincial director still has the authority to call a conference but must ensure that it is consistent with the Act.

Most YCHA principles are consistent with the principles of family group conferencing (or CJFs) as practiced in other countries. However, the most important difference is that a conference is not a decision making body; a decision maker may or may not accept the advice or recommendation of a conference, depending upon its consistency with the other principles of the YCJA such as proportionate accountability.

Discussion

One issue of contention with the conferencing model is its focus on shame. Premised on the earlier work of John Braithwaite (1989), the centrality of shame in conferencing has been a significant detractor to some community groups. Braithwaite argued that "potent shaming directed at offenders is the essential necessary condition for low crime rates" (1989: 4), with the caveat that shaming must be based on a reintegrative rather than a disintegrative premise. Several concerns arise with this approach. Notwithstanding careful attempts to explicate this important difference in premises, criminal justice agents and community members more comfortable with retributive approaches can quickly adopt the disintegrative approach.

The difficulties with the emphasis on shaming in the dominant conferencing models can be explained by the differences arising from the use of *shame* as a noun or a verb. When used as a noun, *shame* describes a self-derived *emotion*. If a harm doer hears community members speak about their own feelings and relationships to others, he or she will remember his or her own relationships with others and feel shame about the harm the offense brought to the community. This volitional experience of shame—recognizing responsibility for another's pain, perhaps as a reflection of conscience—may be expected and does not compromise the integrity of restorative justice processes, but it requires skilled facilitators who know how to help a group manage shame in an integrative way. If shame is felt by the collective, as proposed by McDonald and Moore (1999), the transition to a constructive process resulting in healing becomes the responsibility of the collective (the forum participants), who may be expected to ensure harm reduction by the offender.

Some conferencing facilitators encourage the use of *shaming*. When used as a verb, *shaming* connotes the active efforts of others to shame a harm doer into taking responsibility for his or her actions. This deliberate effort to make another person "feel bad" (shame is a negative emotion) puts the "shamer" in the position of deliberately creating new harms. Conference facilitators, therefore, may want to ground their pre-conference discussions with participants in restorative values, to minimize subsequent disintegrative shaming. As noted earlier, restorative justice is about *healing* harms, not creating new ones, even for "good" reasons. As a values-based process, restorative justice is predicated on the notion that we cannot "get to a good place in a bad way."* Shaming, as an active disintegrative process, creates a contradiction between process and values.

It is important to note that carefully facilitated conferencing manages shame in a good way—many examples of community conferencing models are careful to create the safe spaces needed to accommodate difficult conversations.† The concern about shaming, however, must be upheld for valid reasons. One, the contradiction between process and values, has already been raised. Another reason is that shaming may inadvertently increase violent behavior. James Gilligan, of the Department of Psychiatry at the Harvard Medical School,‡ speaks of the attendant shame of punishment as a source of violence (2000: 767):

* Credit for this expression of values-based processes goes to Molly Baldwin, Executive Director of ROCA Inc, Chelsea, MA; see www.rocainc.org.

† Examples of this in Lower Mainland, British Columbia, are models employed by the North Shore Restorative Justice Society and the Fraser-Burrard Community Justice Society.

‡ Gilligan also directed mental health services for the Massachusetts prison system for many years and is director of the Center for the Study of Violence, immediate past president of the International Association for Forensic Psychotherapy, author of *Violence: Reflections on a National Epidemic* (1997) and *Preventing Violence* (2001), and a member of the Academic Advisory Council of the National Campaign Against Youth Violence, to which he was appointed by President Clinton.

> It is understandable…why punishment would stimulate violence rather than inhibiting it. Punishment increases feelings of shame (it is humiliating to be punished, as it is intended to be) and decreases feelings of guilt (as it is intended to do)…[V]iolence is most likely when shame is maximized and guilt is minimized—exactly the conditions created by punishment.

In *Preventing Violence* (2001), Gilligan concludes, "The basic psychological motive of violent behavior is the wish to eliminate the feeling of shame and humiliation." In this analysis, violence is a means of self-defense and an attempt to force respect from others.*

In addition to calling our attention to the inducements for exacerbating violence by disintegrative shaming, this connection of shame and violence through punishment also speaks to the content of conferencing agreements. Agreements that focus on healing, personal accountability, and meaningful restitution may be considered restorative. Indirect consequences and punitive measures are not restorative. Expressly punitive measures can heighten shame and an offender's need to respond to humiliation in defense of his honor.

Conferencing is appealing to the formal criminal justice system including the police for a variety of reasons. It can potentially reduce court costs, include a variety of affected parties, and help knit individual offenders back into communities. In New Zealand, Australia, the United States, and Canada, conferencing is usually institutionally based. The inference is that conferencing is recognized by the courts, police, and schools as an efficient restorative justice tool that can be deployed in a timely fashion. Cases are usually offender-based, and must be processed within a timeframe set by law or institutional governance.

An offender-centered, time restricted process generates potential difficulties for restorative justice. Restorative justice (Zehr, 2002: 21) asks, who has been hurt, what are his or her needs, and whose obligation is the hurt? These questions present obvious problems for an offender-centered process. Institutionally-based conferencing models tend to privilege their mandates, which in the conventional system are based on what laws were broken, who did it, and what does the person who did it deserve? The victim in these conferencing models—which are certainly more accommodating than processes in the conventional system—is still a secondary party. An evaluation of the

* In his treatise on humiliation, William Ian Miller (1993) argues that "[s]hame depends on the failure to measure up to the external standard imposed by the honor group.… Shame requires membership in a society, a community of people sharing norms of right action and caring deeply about what others in their community think of them" (p. 118). Braithwaite's (1989) notion of reintegrative shaming comes to mind: the community has a corollary obligation to provide opportunities for the shamed individual to reconnect. Absent this opportunity, shaming is but a degradation of a status that existed before the particular failing (p. 157).

New South Wales Youth Justice Conferencing Scheme* in Australia provides data that support this concern. While it is noted that 72.5% of victims and 87.4% of offenders' immediate families attended approximately 1,800 conferences over the 17-month study period, it is assumed that *all* offenders attended because of statutory necessity (Trimboli, 2000: viii).

The evaluation also noted weak adherence to statutory time periods by the conferences. Only about 8% were held within the 21-day limit; approximately 60% were held in twice that time (Trimboli, 2000: viii). This suggests that the demands of conflict do not fit conveniently into institutional time schedules, particularly if the needs of the victims and offenders are great and conference facilitators must also contend with limited resources. Pressures to focus on the offender and meet within specific time limits will usually compromise the volume and quality of pre- and post-conference meetings that are critical to the process. Failure to help the parties begin to have their immediate needs met *before* they participate in an all-party conference increases the vulnerability of both offender and victim to disintegrative shaming.

Another potential fallout from the statutory imposition of restorative justice is the subtle compromising of community development. One of the most promising features of restorative justice is that it is forward looking (Sharpe, 1998: 7). Conferences facilitated with sufficient attention paid to pre- and post-conference meetings tend to produce greater awareness in communities of their capacities to handle the problems uncovered in the process. For example, a community organization offering conferencing may discover that available resources to handle treatment of substance abuse are not adequate to the needs identified in conferencing. Crime prevention through social development is a significant benefit of restorative justice. Timelines that prevent communities from learning important lessons about their assets and deficits and acting on them responsibly may require more flexibility.

Much discussion has focused on the exact roles of the RCMP and other police departments in conferencing and extrajudicial measures. This relates to the previous concern about the role of a community in handling its own problems. Should the police act as facilitators in conferences, attend as interested parties (arresting officers), or not attend? Under the YCJA, the police may do nothing, issue warnings, make referrals to other agencies, or convene conferences. Despite the efforts of the Department of Justice to disseminate information and explanatory material nationwide, it is not yet clear how individual officers will use their judgment to decide which cases warrant

* This comprehensive study by Lily Trimboli (2000) focused on the "participants' satisfaction with both the conferencing process and the agreements or outcome plans developed by the conferences," as well as determining compliance with statutory requirements regarding timeframes (p. 1).

conferences or warnings. This will likely become a matter of ongoing dialogue between police and community restorative justice agencies.

These concerns are not indicators of the implausibility of restorative approaches to justice and do not suggest that the police cannot play significant roles in restorative justice approaches. They are, however, reminders of the potential hazards of implementing programs without solid groundings in restorative values and principles. They also suggest the significance of suitable facilitators—people who clearly understand restorative justice, receive ample and ongoing training, and have the capacity to help participants manage shame in helpful ways, among other attributes.

The police role in restorative justice, as front-end referral agents and supporters of community-based justice, is significant. It also marks a return to an original goal for police: to act as "peace officers." Creating peaceful communities begins with fostering peaceful relationships among individuals (Elliott, 2003). The police, as key components of communities and the criminal justice system, can potentially play significant roles in these efforts.

References

Bopp, M. and Bopp, J. (2001) *Recreating the world: A practical guide to building sustainable communities*, Calgary, Alberta: Four Worlds Press.

Braithwaite, J. (1989) *Crime, shame and reintegration*, New York: Cambridge University Press.

Brandt, C. C. (1990) Native ethics and rules of behaviour, *The Canadian Journal of Psychiatry*, 35: 534–539.

Chatterjee, J. (1999) *A report on the evaluation of RCMP restorative justice initiative: Community justice forum as seen by participants*, Ottawa: Research and Evaluation Branch, Community, Contract and Aboriginal Policing Services.

Department of Justice (2002) *The Youth Criminal Justice Act: Summary and background.*

Eglash, A. (1977) Beyond restitution: Creative restitution, in Hudson, J. and Galaway, B. (Eds.), *Restitution in criminal justice* (pp. 91–99), Lexington, MA: Lexington Books.

Elliott, E. (2002) Con game and restorative justice: Inventing the truth about Canada's prisons, *Canadian Journal of Criminology*, 44 (4): 459–474.

Elliott, E. (2003) When justice means restoring the moral bond of community, *The Vancouver Sun*, Wednesday, May 7.

Four Worlds Development Project (1984) *The sacred tree: Reflections on Native American spirituality*, Lethbridge, Alberta: Four Worlds Development Press.

Gilligan, J. (2001) *Preventing violence*, London: Thames and Hudson.

Gilligan, J. (2000) Punishment and violence: Is the criminal law based on one huge mistake? *Social Research*, 67 (3): 745–772.

Gilligan, J. (1997) *Violence: Reflections on a national epidemic*, New York: Vintage Books.

Green, R. G. (1998) *Justice in Aboriginal communities: Sentencing alternatives*, Saskatoon: Purich Press.

Howard, B. and Purches, L. (1992) A discussion of the police family group conferences and the follow-up program (stage 2) in the Wagga Wagga Juvenile Cautioning Process, *Rural Society,* 2 (2). http://www.csu.edu.au/research/crsr/ruralsoc/v2n2p20.htm [Correct October 2007].

Hoyle, C., Young, R., and Hill, R. (2002) *Proceed with caution: An evaluation of the Thames Valley Police initiative in restorative cautioning,* York: Joseph Rowntree Foundation.

Kelly, R. (2006) *From Scoundrel to Scholar...The Russ Kelly Story,* Fergus Ontario: Russ Kelly Publishing. http://www.volumesdirect.com/detail.aspx?ID=2955 [Correct October 2007]

Latimer, J., Dowden, C., and Muise, D. (2001) *The effectiveness of restorative justice practices: A meta-analysis,* Ottawa, Ontario: Research and Statistics Division, Department of Justice.

Llewellyn, J. and Howse, R. (1999) *Restorative justice: A conceptual framework,* Ottawa, Ontario: Law Commission of Canada.

McDonald, J. and Moore, D. (1999) *Common Ground Newsletter,* October. Munn Conflict Resolution Services. http://www.munncrs.com/COMMON_GROUND/MCRSOctober1999.pdf [Correct October 2007].

Maxwell, G. and Morris, A. (2000) *Police diversionary actions in the New Zealand youth justice system,* Wellington: Institute of Criminology, Victoria University of Wellington.

Miller, W. I. (1993) *Humiliation, and other essays on honor, social discomfort and violence,* Ithaca, NY: Cornell University Press.

Monture-Angus, P. (1995) Thinking about change, *Justice as Healing,* Saskatoon: Native Law Centre of the University of Saskatchewan. Summer, p. 3.

Morris, R. (2000) *Stories of transformative justice,* Toronto: Canadian Scholars Press Inc.

Nathanson, D. L. (1987) *The many faces of shame,* New York: Guilford.

OConnell, T. and Moore, D. (1992) Wagga Wagga juvenile cautioning process: The general applicability of family group conferences for juvenile offenders and their victims, *Rural Society,* 2 (2). http://www.csu.edu.au/research/crsr/ruralsoc/v2n2p16.htm [Correct October 2007].

Roberts, T. (1995) *Evaluation of the victim offender mediation project, Langley, BC.* Final Report for Solicitor General of Canada.

Ross, R. (1996) *Returning to the teachings: Exploring Aboriginal justice,* Toronto: Penguin Books Canada.

Sharpe, S. (1998) *Restorative justice: A vision for healing and change,* Edmonton: Mediation and Restorative Justice Centre.

Sherman, L. and Strang, H. (1997) *The right kind of shame for crime prevention,* RISE Working Paper 1, Canberra: Australian National University.

Trimboli, L. (2000) *An evaluation of the NSW youth justice conferencing scheme,* Sydney: New South Wales Bureau of Crime Statistics and Research.

Yazzie, R. and Zion, J. W. (1996) Navajo restorative justice: The law of equality and justice, in Galaway, B. and Hudson, J. (Eds.), *Restorative justice: International perspectives* (pp. 157–173), Monsey, NY: Criminal Justice Press.

Zehr, H. (1990) *Changing lenses,* Waterloo, Ontario: Herald Press.

Zehr, H. (2002) *The little book of restorative justice,* Intercourse, PA: Good Books.

Police Reform, Restorative Justice, and Restorative Policing*

10

GORDON BAZEMORE
CURT T. GRIFFITHS

Contents

When not focused on addressing corruption and allegations of bias, harassment, and brutality, much police reform since the 1960s can be characterized as a slow movement away from the professional model (Kelling and Moore, 1988). Much of this reform can be seen as an attempt to escape the rigidity associated with the paramilitary organizational structure and overcome the limits bureaucratic structures have imposed on flexible, effective, long-term solutions to crime. One area of focus is the promotion of greater citizen participation and community partnerships in crime resolution and prevention, in essence fostering new relationships between police departments and the communities they serve (Skolnick and Bayley, 1986; Bayley, 1994). Such reform has moved along two separate but related problem-oriented and community-oriented policing tracks.

In the 1970s, team policing appeared to challenge the idea that guided officer discretion was a bad thing. This innovation promoted the view that decentralized decision making offered benefits to police effectiveness in addressing real problems at the community level. While team policing con-

* This chapter first appeared in *Police Practice and Research*, 2003, 4 (4): 335–346. This was a special edition about restorative justice. In this chapter, the authors cite a number of other papers appearing in this special edition. http://www.tandf.co.uk/journals/titles/15614263.asp.

tained some of the seeds of what was later known as problem-oriented policing (Eck and Spellman, 1987; Goldstein, 1990), the commitment to localized problem-solving processes grounded in close relationships with community members also paved the way for the more potentially revolutionary vision of community policing (Kelling and Moore, 1988; Rosenbaum, 1994). Specifically, problem solving offered officers discretion to develop tactical response alternatives that rejected incident-driven 911 policing (Sparrow, Moore, and Kennedy, 1990). Although problem-oriented officers sought input and information from community members and to a degree took such input and opinions seriously, problem-oriented policing for the most part left key decisions to police professionals.

In contrast, at least some visions of community policing were arguably more radical in their implications for a true co-production of safe communities (Kelling and Moore, 1988; Skogan, 1990) and in ambitious statements about democratization of decision-making authority that could produce a shift of power to neighborhood groups and citizens (Skolnick and Bayley, 1986; Bayley, 1994). Debate continues about the extent to which such power-sharing ever really occurred (Buerger, 1994), whether communities were willing and able to assume responsibilities for social control in the absence of substantial and systematic community building (Rosenbaum, 1994), and whether the vision of community policing was ever more than a vision (Taylor, Fritsch and Caeti, 1998). Questions remain about the extent to which community policing was truly understood in the deeper sense of the community–police partnerships and whether such conceptualizations were linked logically to implementation strategies and practices consistent with such an understanding (Maguire and Katz, 2002; see also Chapter 2 and Chapter 6 of this volume).

The most optimistic assumptions about a widespread understanding of this vision and the will to move forward with potentially transformative reforms implied in some community policing literature are not, however, sufficient for effective implementation. Reformers must still confront police agency organizational structures and cultures that present significant barriers to implementing such reform (Taylor et al., 1998; Mastrofski and Ritti, 2000). Moreover, the continuing focus on community policing as a programmatic rather than systemic reform and the apparent fear of sharing power with communities arguably continue to erect barriers that remain difficult to overcome.

Restorative Justice and Restorative Policing

Restorative policing (McCold and Wachtel, 1998; Nicholls, 1998) appears to offer new hope for reform, new tools, a new value framework, and new challenges (see also Jharna Chatterjee and Liz Elliot, Chapter 9). While it shares some values and strategies with those associated with community justice generally (Clear and Karp, 1999) and community policing specifically (Pranis and Bazemore, 2001), restorative justice as an international movement operates from a distinctive normative theory and prioritizes new intervention strategies and practices (Van Ness and Strong, 2001; Braithwaite, 2002). Specifically, restorative justice values offer a challenge to the traditional goals of intervention—punishment and treatment of an offender after completion of a court-based, adversarial process. In doing so, restorative justice advocates may thereby raise questions about one unspoken primary goal of most policing strategies, including those informed by problem-oriented and community-oriented values: to turn all lawbreakers over to such a process.

First, the principled focus on doing justice by repairing the harm of crime, rather than simply punishing or treating an offender (Van Ness and Strong, 1997; 2001), gives a new meaning to intervention objectives. This focus in turn has implications for critical perspectives on what is likely to be achieved as a result of an adversarial process whose end result is often unsatisfying to victims, offenders, and communities. Although courts and the adversarial system have their place, such a result is also in direct conflict with the second core principle of restorative justice: that a plan for repairing harm (or resolution in the aftermath of a crime) is best developed with maximum input from victim, offender, and their supporters through a non-adversarial process. This process, in turn, has value in its own right, for example, as a means of promoting stakeholder ownership of the problem created by the crime in question. The principles of repairing harm and maximizing involvement of those harmed in the decision-making process also have implications for what the police might do if invested in the goal of allowing offenders to make amends or to seek to rebuild relationships harmed by crime by giving stakeholders voices and meaningful roles in crafting solutions.

While such approaches do not seem inconsistent with community- and problem-oriented policing, they are not spelled out or even necessarily assumed in these models. A community may be involved in crime prevention and public safety activities in a number of ways that do not require involvement of citizens in case decision making. Restorative obligations that repair harm to victims and communities have not been spelled out as objectives of community policing intervention, although officers may informally engage stakeholders in processes that allow offenders to make amends and/or seek to repair relationships damaged by crime.

Ultimately, what some view as the third core principle of restorative justice (Van Ness and Strong, 1997; Bazemore and Walgrave, 1999) comes closest to full compatibility with the vision of community policing in its most ambitious form. This principle suggests a need for a transformation of the relationship between the governmental criminal justice system and a community that gives the community a much more active role in promoting both public safety and justice. In this new relationship, the justice system is acknowledged as playing a vital role in preserving *order* while the community is viewed as promoting *peace* (Van Ness and Strong, 1997).

To support the community in assuming this role, police committed to this vision and to restorative principles would focus significant attention on *community building* aimed at mobilizing and enhancing citizen and community groups' skills and confidence in informal responses to crime, harm, and conflict. More generally, community building of this type aims to promote the exercise of informal social control (Hunter, 1985) and social support (Cullen, 1994; Bazemore, 2001) grounded in social capital as relationships of trust and reciprocity based on shared norms and values (Putnam, 2000). It also focuses on the skill sets associated with informal social control. Tapping into, revitalizing, and rebuilding such social capital and collective efficacy (Sampson, Raudenbush and Earls, 1997) after years of telling communities to leave crime control to the experts is no easy task. The level of difficulty, coupled with past failures of most community policing efforts to focus strategically on community capacity building, is certainly one reason that some critics concluded that community policing failed to deliver on its promises (Rosenbaum, 1994; Taylor et al., 1998).

At the level of specific practice, what restorative justice brings to community- and problem-oriented policing is a set of tools or "levers" for building social capital and efficacy around direct responses to incidents of crime, conflict, and harm. While generic community policing offers opportunities for citizen participation in determining police priorities and invites community involvement in organized group events (neighborhood watches, cleanups), restorative policing provides at the case level a decision-making role for citizens in informal sanctioning and the effective resolution of individual incidents of crime that has traditionally been the province of courts and professional court group decision makers (e.g., prosecutors, defenders). Through application of restorative conferencing techniques (Bazemore and Umbreit, 2001), affected parties along with police officers as facilitators, conveners, or participants develop agreements that outline offender obligations such as community service, restitution, other informal reparative sanctions, apologies, peacemaking pacts, and relationship building approaches that allow for concrete repair of harm without recourse to adversarial processing. Such agreements are developed using a process that promotes collective community ownership of the resolution, as well as individual stakeholder (victim and offender) satisfaction, and ultimately builds or rebuilds community skills.

Police involvement in such functions has raised concerns about conflicts of interest or inappropriate stretching of roles, also known as boundary erosion (Friel, 2000), which place police in the roles of prosecutor and judge in addition to enforcing laws. Some restorative justice advocates have raised questions about police involvement in decision making that—when not handled formally by court professionals—should be left to juvenile justice professionals who are more oriented toward social work (White, 1992; Umbreit and Stacey, 1996). Another question is whether police can serve as useful facilitators or participants in restorative processes; this raised cautions that officers may quickly revert to their law enforcement roles (e.g., using conferences to gather evidence) (Young, 2001). Others, however, find that police can be effective facilitators and may even help participants reach decisions and resolutions more consistent with community views (and hence more sustainable) than those driven by social work perspectives (Moore and O'Connell, 1994; McCold and Wachtel, 1998). In any case, *some* primary police role in restorative decision making appears essential if restorative justice is to genuinely return the conflict resolution task to communities (Christie, 1977).

How well might police do in the general role of returning crime prevention and conflict resolution to communities? How will they function in new roles consistent with restorative justice? Because officers who participate most actively in restorative justice processes usually choose to do so, police have thus far shown a great deal of competency in several roles. Viable options for police agency involvement in restorative decision making and other restorative programs include (1) taking an active role as primary sources of referral to free-standing restorative conferencing programs; (2) sponsoring such programs within their agencies, whether or not they use officers as facilitators; (3) asking officers to convene or participate in conferences facilitated by others; and (4) designing and operating other in-house restorative programs focused on victim needs, youth reparation, and other special needs (Schwartz, Hennessey and Lavitas, 2003).

Perhaps the least obvious and most important role for individual police officers in restorative justice practice is informal. Specifically, when officers apply restorative justice principles in response to harm and conflict on the street, with families in their homes, and at schools and workplaces, they expand the application of restorative solutions and expose more community members to these practices than would ever be possible through reliance on a single program. In addition, such street level applications are likely to minimize the use of more formal and expensive court and other diversion resources. The approach should also promote more appropriate and cost-effective use of formal restorative programs, especially when officers are encouraged not to send cases to the program when they can accomplish restorative objectives and principled problem solving less formally (Hines and Bazemore, 2003).

Finally, police executives and law enforcement organizations appear to be at least as effective as other criminal justice decision makers such as judges, prosecutors, and corrections professionals in leadership roles that require them to initiate and win broader system and community support.

Law enforcement leaders face many of the same and some unique dilemmas when it comes to implementing and sustaining these programs. On the one hand, based on the traditionally rigid, paramilitary structures that continue to characterize police bureaucracies, leadership may confront even great organizational and interorganizational obstacles to implementing restorative programs. On the other hand, with regard to sustainability, police may also have some unique advantages as a result of their generally closer connections to community and local agents of informal social control.

Emerging literature in restorative justice (O'Brien, 1999; Carey, 2001; McLeod, 2003) is concerned with what for years was called the Achilles heel of policy reform: implementation (Pressman and Wildavsky, 1973). This chapter does not address specific issues of implementation. However, it proposes a single implementation principle and suggests several levels of implementation that police administrators should consider in efforts to move forward with restorative justice reforms.

Value of Systemic Reform: Theory to Practice

Based on lessons learned from community policing (Rosenbaum, 1994; Taylor et al., 1998) and from restorative justice implemented to date (Bazemore and Schiff, 2001), our general principle of implementation is by no means original. However, it remains a neglected feature of strategic reform efforts, both in restorative justice and community policing. This principle is that successful implementation of restorative justice reforms requires a *systemic vision and focus.* The converse of this is that sustainable restorative justice cannot be built on programs alone. Put another way, while a restorative justice vision alone will not produce restorative policing, the *absence* of a restorative vision is virtually guaranteed to lead to practice and policy that have little to do with restorative justice.

Restorative justice programs are of course essential to demonstrate what restorative policing looks like. One lesson of community policing, however, is that programs alone are not sufficient. Indeed, as tactics such as foot patrols, citizen advisory groups, neighborhood watch programs, specialized officers, and neighborhood police centers came to be seen as *equivalents* of community policing, a once holistic reform agenda became viewed in many police departments as minimally related to the policing mission (Maguire and Katz, 2001). Like programmatic criminal justice efforts such as community corrections that provide small case examples of reform but do not spill over to impact mainstream practice (Maloney, Bazemore and Hudson, 2001), community policing as a program simply was not viewed in many jurisdictions as having implications for what most police officers did. In reality, community policing practices in many jurisdictions affected some small fraction of cases in a few targeted neighborhoods (Rosenbaum, 1994).

Systemic Reform and Restorative Policing

Systemic reform begins with a vision of change in all sectors of the criminal justice system and changes in professional roles. At the agency or organizational level, when police leaders implement restorative justice reform systemically, they envision transformative change that begins at the departmental level and moves outward (Nicholls, 1998).

The *goal* of systemic reform, if restorative policing is the vision, is to conceptualize a response to all incidents of crime based on restorative principles and then ensure that a full menu of restorative options is available to police and to community members and groups that bring them cases. This of course implies program development and great attention to program quality hopefully assessed by adherence to principles allowing adaptation to different police functions and different neighborhoods. Indeed, a systemic vision includes programmatic reform. The difference is that programs and tactics serve to achieve the goals of the mission and vision instead of displacing these goals with no overarching value framework. The vision ensures that restorative programs will not suffice. Saturating communities with a range of restorative practices is an important means of supporting and expanding a systemic vision.

The second feature of systemic reform is the idea that restorative policing should change (1) the way officers think about conflict resolution, sanctioning, and community involvement (as in restorative conferencing programs) and (2) the way they think about and perform *all* police functions. In essence, one could envision a more or less restorative justice approach to crime prevention, order maintenance, service functions, surveillance, conflict resolution, and law enforcement. The core concept at play in such a vision is perhaps best portrayed by the warden of a correctional facility who had committed to systemic reform in his facility by agency-wide training in restorative justice principles that included janitors, cooks, transportation staff, clerical workers, professional correctional officers, and treatment staff. He described the systemic goal of changing agency functions as building "restorative justice into the bricks."

We have no guarantees that the systemic vision will bring success in implementing restorative policing. Indeed, the danger of "loose coupling" (Weick, 1976) of an ambitious vision and actual practice has recently been documented in the community policing movement in studies that indicate sweeping changes in mission and vision, with little accompanying implementation of practice. For the most part, however, at least in the United States, widespread implementation of a range of community-oriented policing (COP) practice options, according to one recent national study, appears to be closely linked to general visionary claims expressed in mission statements (Maguire and Katz, 2002). In other words, with a few exceptions related to mid-level management changes, it appears that police organizations whose leaders support the mission of community policing are more likely to implement practices that support this mission and vision. It is rare to see a full array of community policing practices in departments not committed to a vision and mission.

Domains of Action for Systemic Change

To support the systemic vision and mission of restorative policing, we suggest four domains or sectors critical to effective implementation and sustainability.

Legislation and Policy Domain

Restorative justice reform should never be envisioned as a top–down strategy implemented only because it is required by legislation (which often also implies access to funding). However, internationally, the governments that can boast widespread use of restorative practices including adoption of these practices by police agencies and their participation in multiple aspects of implementation for use in cases beyond those involving low-level offenses are characterized by clear legislation (Morris and Maxwell, 2001; Braithwaite, 2002).

Such policy statements give preference to mandate, or make funding contingent on the use of restorative practices. Except for a few states that have loosely tied eligibility for certain federal funding streams to implementation of restorative practices, most of the United States serves as an important case study in how the absence of specific legislation is associated with relatively minimal implementation of restorative practices. Notable exceptions cited by Hines and Bazemore (2003); McCold (2003); and Schwartz, Hennessey, and Levitas (2003) reflect the reality that development and referrals to restorative programs require changes in thinking, practice, and incentives that are not usually forthcoming in the absence of policy and statutes.

Chatterjee and Elliott (2003; Chapter 9 of this volume) specifically address the vital role of legislation in the successful early implementation of restorative policy. A prominent feature of Canada's 2002 Youth Criminal Justice Act is that it directs that all means should be explored in attempts to reduce the numbers of youth sent to custody. This provides a framework within which the Royal Canadian Mounted Police and other police forces across the country can become more extensively involved in restorative policing practices, although the specific nature of this involvement has yet to emerge.

Organizational Domain

Two dimensions of organizations require attention in restorative justice reform: structure and culture. The structural dimension includes job descriptions that reconfigure policing role definitions, incentive structures that support restorative practices, and management/leadership structures that facilitate the discretionary decision making required for restorative problem solving and widespread application of principles. Organizational culture is considered even more important by a number of restorative justice advocates in what remains a relatively new movement (Carey, 2001). This dimension is concerned with agency-wide values that prioritize peacemaking, conflict resolution, and community building over aggressive patrol and coercion. More subtly, departmental artifacts exemplified by informal interactions, jokes officers tell, and attitudes toward community members and groups are important indicators of a culture supportive of or incompatible with restorative policing values.

Although it is possible to identify conceptually the stages of organizational reform required for a department to develop the capacity for restorative practices, the specific form such practices take will necessarily depend on the environment and community within which the police deliver services. Griffiths, Parent, and Whitelaw (1999: 42) note that determining how to best implement community policing, measure whether objectives have been achieved, and define the specific police and community initiatives required is best achieved on a community-by-community basis, depending on community needs and the outcomes of dialogues between the police and residents. So too should the implementation and assessment of police restorative practices be measured within the framework most sensitive to the environments and contexts within which the police operate.

To allow a police service to develop the capacity to effectively carry out restorative practices, it is empirically and theoretically important to pay attention to the organizational level. Colleen McLeod (2003) notes that this will require that departmental transition from a traditional police bureaucracy to a restorative community model of police organization. The experience of community policing over the past two decades has indicated clearly that, in the absence of organizational reform, it is very difficult to alter the manner in which police departments carry out their mandate and line level officers exercise their discretion. McLeod makes the important point that, for a department to become a restorative organization, "leadership…must clearly understand what restorative justice is, what the commitment to change is, and what the change process requires." This places the onus on police leaders to create the organizational structures and environments within which officers have the authority and autonomy to explore alternatives to dispute resolution, experiment with various restorative practices, and take the necessary risks and assume ownership of restorative practices and outcomes.

Paul McCold (2003) has illustrated conclusively that it is possible for police officers to conduct restorative conferences that require accountability on the parts of offenders and are viewed as fair by victims, offenders, and other relevant parties. Further, police-sponsored conferencing can gain acceptance in a community while at the same time producing outcomes as or more favorable than other restorative approaches such as victim–offender mediation. At the organizational level, McCold raises cautions about overly optimistic expectations and notes that even highly successful programs may exert little impact on the attitude and culture of a police department as a whole.

Individual Officer Domain

Traditional police officers who become restorative advocates often report "conversion experiences" that produced significant, self-identified, transformations in their thinking about the job of policing. Such transformations in the authors' experience almost never transform tough cops into social workers. Indeed, personality types highly invested in restorative policing run the gamut of policing and personal styles.

For most officers committed to restorative policing, such commitments do not mean as a community policing officer recently told us, "that we are wimps." Restorative policing does require a commitment to a more holistic vision of policing that prioritizes certain principled goals, for example, resolving conflict by repairing harm in a way that maximizes stakeholder involvement and builds community. Part of the basis for what may begin as a difficult persuasion effort in the case of resistant system professionals is best characterized as a kind of experiential theory of change. Anecdotally, many restorative justice practitioners and activists have become convinced that the easiest way to persuade resistant criminal justice professionals of the value of restorative practices (especially key decision makers such as judges, prosecutors, and police) is to convince them to participate in restorative conferencing or another decision-making process.

On this personal level, reportedly hardened police chiefs and resistant judges may soon become zealous advocates. Other authors identified additional implementation issues within the individual officer domain. In a study by Abramson (2003) some police officers were reluctant to refer cases to a restorative justice program, and others showed a lack of understanding. In an investigation of more traditional justice practices and the interface between Navajo Nation Peacekeepers and the Navajo Nation Police, Nielsen and Gould (2003) identified an inherent conflict between European-style law enforcement taught at police academies and the traditional healing approaches of peacemakers.

Community Domain

The community domain of restorative policing provides both the greatest challenge and the greatest opportunity for transformative systemic impact. Community involvement and community building are in essence key parts of the solution to many of the implementation problems noted above. A prominent emergent theory of change is that a community, when involved and engaged, brings the system along with reform efforts and helps sustain commitment (Stuart, 1996; Pranis, 2001). This implies involvement of community members and groups beyond levels of participation in restorative processes as victims, offenders, community members, or supporters. It also implies strategic use of volunteers and community building strategies that enable community members and groups to demonstrate their competence and willingness to exercise acquired skills to provide ongoing informal social control in the response to neighborhood crime.

Although one missing link in the reform effort thus far has been widespread implementation of restorative conferencing (plans for moving forward with conferencing programs at the neighborhood level are currently on the drawing board), the agency-wide commitment to core principles and the focus on interface with community in reentry programming offers great promise for community building.

Of direct relevance to the community domain in restorative policing, Hines and Bazemore (2003) provide an account of experiences in implementing and expanding what is now one of the more long-standing police-based restorative conferencing programs in the United States. They describe how Hines was able to strike a vitally important agreement with a local prosecutor that allowed the police department to choose the cases to be diverted to the conferencing program. The agreement effectively meant that the program was able to include a significantly greater number of chronic and serious young offenders than was formerly typical of conferencing in the United States (75% felony referrals in a recent year). Taking the program to the next level and sustaining the already high levels of commitment within the department and county criminal justice system meant expanding community involvement implemented in recent years through the use of volunteers. Most notably, moving the program forward meant paying attention to often serendipitous incidents of community building as outcomes of restorative group conferences. This led to a more strategic focus on maximizing opportunities to use these processes to build trust and relationships, as well as competencies of community groups and citizens for exercising informal social control. Future learning from this case study should be based on examination of the extent to which more strategic efforts to increase community capacity (rather than simply program capacity) become the true keys to the sustainability of restorative policing.

Summary

Restorative policing appears to represent the next logical step in community policing and police reform. The restorative justice model offers both new tools and new principles of intervention that assist police in the tasks of engaging communities, forming meaningful partnerships, and building community capacity. Despite many success stories in the short history of restorative policing, challenges to implementation abound. Effective principled implementation of restorative policing depends on a holistic, *systemic* vision that seeks to incorporate restorative justice principles in all aspects of the profession. Goals for this systemic vision include developing restorative resolutions to crime and harm to the greatest extent possible and promoting community ownership of crime and conflict.

References

Abramson A. M. (2003) Sustainable relationships and competing values: restorative justice initiatives and the police: a case study, *Police Practice and Research*, 4 (4): 391–398.

Bayley, D. H. (1994) *Police for the future*, New York: Oxford University Press.

Bazemore, G. (2001) Young people, trouble, and crime: Restorative justice as a normative theory of informal social control and social support, *Youth and Society*, 33 (2): 199–226.

Bazemore, G. and Schiff, M. (Eds.) (2001) *Restorative and community justice: Repairing harm and transforming communities*, Cincinnati, OH: Anderson.

Bazemore, G. and Umbreit, M. (2001) A comparison of four restorative conferencing models, *Juvenile Justice Bulletin*, Office of Justice Programs, U.S. Department of Justice.

Bazemore, G. and Walgrave, L. (1999) Restorative justice: In search of fundamentals and an outline for systemic reform, in Bazemore, G. and Walgrave, L. (Eds.) *Restorative juvenile justice: Repairing the harm of youth crime*, Monsey, NY: Criminal Justice Press.

Braithwaite, J. (2002) *Restorative justice and responsive regulation*, New York: Oxford University Press.

Buerger, M. E. (1994) The limits of community, in Rosenbaum, D. P. (Ed.), *The challenge of community policing*, Thousand Oaks, CA: Sage.

Carey, M. (2001) Infancy, adolescence, and restorative justice: Strategies for promoting organizational reform, in Bazemore, G. and Schiff, M. (Eds.) *Restorative and community justice: Repairing harm and transforming communities*, Cincinnati, OH: Anderson.

Chatterjee, J. and Elliot, L. (2003) Restorative policing in Canada: The Royal Canadian Mounted Police, Community Justice Forums, and the Youth Criminal Justice Act, *Police Practice and Research*, 4 (4): 347–359 (reproduced as Chapter 9).

Christie, N. (1977) Conflict as property, *British Journal of Criminology*, 17 (1): 1–15.

Clear, T. and Karp, D. (1999) *The community justice ideal: Preventing crime and achieving justice*, Boulder, CO: Westview Press.

Cullen, F. T. (1994) Social support as an organizing concept for criminology: Residential address to the Academy of Criminal Justice Sciences, *Justice Quarterly*, 11: 527–559.

Eck, J. E. and Spellman, W. (1987) *Problem-solving: Problem-oriented policing in Newport News*, Washington, D.C.: Police Executive Research Forum.

Friel, C. M. (2000) A century of changing boundaries, in *Boundary changes in criminal justice organizations: Criminal justice 2000*, Vol. 2, Washington, D.C.: U.S. Department of Justice.

Goldstein, H. (1990) *Problem-oriented policing*, New York: McGraw-Hill.

Griffiths, C. T., Parent, R., and Whitelaw, B. (1999) *Community policing in Canada*, Toronto: Nelson.

Hines, D. and Bazemore, G. (2003) Restorative policing, conferencing and community, *Police Practice and Research*, 4 (4): 411–427.

Hunter, A. J. (1985) Private, parochial and public social orders: The problem of crime and incivility in urban communities, in Suttles, G. D. and Zald, M. N. (Eds.) *The challenge of social control: Citizenship and institution building in modern society*, Norwood, NJ: Aldex.

Kelling, G. and Moore, M. (1988) *The evolving strategies of policing*, Washington, D.C.: National Institute of Justice.

Maguire, E. R. and Katz, C. M. (2002) Community policing, loose coupling and sensemaking in American police agencies, *Justice Quarterly*, 9 (3): 503–536.

Maloney, D., Bazemore, G., and Hudson, J. (2001) The end of probation and the beginning of community justice, *Perspectives*, Summer: 23–30.

Mastrofski, S. and Ritti, R. (2000) Making sense of community policing: A theory-based analysis, *Police Practice and Research*, 1 (2): 183–210.

McCold, P. (2003) An experiment in police-based restorative justice: The Bethlehem (PA) Project, *Police Practice and Research*, 4 (4): 379–390.

McCold, P. and Wachtel, B. (1998) *Restorative policing experiment: The Bethlehem Pennsylvania Police Family Group Conferencing Project*, Pipersville, PA: Community Service Foundation.

McLeod, C. (2003) Toward a restorative organization: Transforming police bureaucracies, *Police Practice and Research*, 4 (4): 361–377.

Moore, D. B. and O'Connell, T. (1994) Family group conferencing in a communitarian model of justice, in Alder, C. and Wundersitz, J. (Eds.), *Family conferencing and juvenile justice*, Canberra: Australian Studies in Law, Crime and Justice, Australian Institute of Criminology.

Morris, A. and Maxwell, G. (2001) Restoring conferencing, in Bazemore, G. and Schiff, M. (Eds.), *Restorative community justice: Repairing harm and transforming communities*, Cincinnati, OH: Anderson.

Nicholls, C. G. (1998) *Community policing, community justice, and restorative justice: Exploring the links for the delivery of a balanced approach to public safety*, U.S. Department of Justice.

Nielsen M. and Gould L. (2003) Developing the interface between the Navajo Nation Police and Navajo Nation Peacemaking, *Police Practice and Research*, 4 (4): 429–443.

O'Brien, S. (1999) *Restorative justice in the States: A national survey of policy and practices.* Paper presented at annual conference of Academy for Criminal Justice Sciences, Orlando, FL.

Pranis, K. (2001) Restorative justice, social justice, and the empowerment of marginalized populations, in Bazemore, G. and Schiff, M. (Eds.), *Restorative community justice: Repairing harm and transforming communities*, Cincinnati, OH: Anderson.

Pranis, K. and Bazemore, G. (2001) *Engaging community in the response to youth crime: A restorative justice approach*, Monograph prepared for the Office of Juvenile Justice and Delinquency Prevention, U.S. Department of Justice, Washington, D.C.

Pressman, J. L. and Wildavsky, A. (1973) *Implementation*, Berkeley: University of California Press.

Putnam, R. (2000) *Bowling alone: The collapse and revival of American community*, New York: Simon & Schuster.

Rosenbaum, D. P. (Ed.) (1994) *The challenge of community policing: Testing the promises*, Thousand Oaks, CA: Sage.

Sampson, R., Raudenbush, S., and Earls, F. (1997) Neighborhoods and violent crime: A multi-level study of collective efficacy, *Science*, 277 (4): 918–924.

Schwartz, S., Hennessey, M., and Lavitas, L. (2003) Restorative justice and the transformation of jails: An urban sheriff's case study in reducing violence, *Police Practice and Research*, 4 (4): 399–410.

Skogan, W. (1990) *Disorder and decline: Crime and the spiral of decay in American neighborhood*, New York: Free Press.

Skolnick, J. and Bayley, D. (1986) *The new blue line: Police innovation in six American cities*, New York: Free Press.

Sparrow, M., Moore, M., and Kennedy, D. (1990) *Beyond 911*, New York: Basic Books.

Stuart, B. (1996) Circle sentencing: turning swords into ploughshares, in Galaway, B. and Hudson, J. (Eds.) *Restorative justice: International perspectives*, Monsey, NY: Criminal Justice Press.

Taylor, R., Fritsch, E., and Caeti, T. (1998) Core challenges facing community policing: The emperor *still* has no clothes, *ACJS Today*, 17 (1): 1–5.

Umbreit, M. and Stacey, S. (1996) Family group conferencing comes to the U.S.: A comparison with victim offender mediation, *Juvenile and Family Court Journal*, 47: 29–38.

van Ness, D. and Strong, K. H. (1997) *Restoring justice*, Cincinnati, OH: Anderson.

van Ness, D. and Strong, K. H. (2001) *Restoring justice* (2nd ed.), Cincinnati, OH: Anderson.

Weick, K. E. (1976) Educational organizations as loosely coupled systems, *Administrative Science Quarterly*, 21: 1–19.

White, R. (1992) *Young people, community space and social control*, Paper presented at Australian Institute of Criminology Conference on Juvenile Justice, Adelaide.

Young, R. (2001) Just cops doing shameful business? Police-led restorative justice and the lessons of research, in Morris, A. and Maxwell, G. (Eds.) *Restorative justice for juveniles: Conferencing, mediation and circles* (pp. 195–226), Portland, OR: Hart.

Conclusions

11

ANDREW MILLIE
DILIP K. DAS

It would be too tempting to claim that law enforcement is at a crossroads. This statement would have been true for most periods in the history of policing since Robert Peel. However, it is clear that the profession faces sizable challenges in this early part of the new century. The five themes explored in this book included some of the more significant. In this concluding chapter, we consider some of the pragmatic aspects and challenges posed by these five themes. The discussion is set within the context of the roles and responsibilities of contemporary policing.

In most countries, law enforcement and policing are subjected to intense scrutiny and myriad expectations. Additional pressures exist in the form of organizational changes and a decreasing monopoly of police in enforcing the law. O'Malley (1997) and Waters (2007) see these pressures as functions of a post-modern world. For example, the idea that a single entity known as a police force is responsible for regulation and surveillance, with the state having central control and monopoly of legitimate force (Reiner, 1992), is a modernist paradigm. However, greater involvement of non-state actors in law enforcement has accompanied the emergence of what has become known as plural policing (Crawford et al., 2005; Jones and Newburn, 2006). Such changes represent a shift toward a post-modern paradigm. Similar post-modern processes are apparent in the move from central state control to a police service that is increasingly expected to respond to localities, communities, and neighborhoods. However, the evidence presented in this volume demonstrates the absence of a definitive change from centralized (modern) to decentralized or plural (post-modern) forms of policing and reveals pulls in both directions especially since September 11, 2001. Policing is now required to be centralized and decentralized—a situation typical of late rather than post-modernity (Johnston, 1998; Newburn, 2001).

Of course, such paradigmatic discussions may not be seem too relevant to a police manager or an officer on the street who must deal with these shifting processes. However, such issues have been presented throughout this volume, particularly in the chapters by Leman-Langlois and Brodeur and Murray that explain the policing of terror and similarly in the chapters by Chatterjee and Elliott and Bazemore and Griffiths covering restorative approaches to policing. The inherent tension of concomitant calls for tougher and softer policing are factors influencing day-to-day policing (as explored by Stinchcomb and Garcia) and police ethics and corruption considered by Skolnick and Prenzler and Ronken; they similarly impact on the development of strategies and investigative techniques, especially with regard to the prioritization and availability of resources (Ratcliffe and Stangeland).

In Chapter 6 John Murray, a former chief police officer for the Australian Capital Territory, observed a noticeable increase in paramilitarism post-9/11 that he considered at odds with the previously promoted community-oriented approaches to policing. Similarly, in Chapter 10, Bazemore and Griffiths call for "a holistic, systemic vision that seeks to incorporate restorative justice principles in all aspects of the profession." This clearly is not possible if paramilitarism remains a dominant feature of law enforcement.

The challenge for today's police forces is to tackle national and international priorities, such as terrorist threats, and at the same time engage with the communities they serve. According to Murray, the two principles are not mutually exclusive. Closer ties to the community represent essential elements in the fight against terrorism. In this way community trust and police legitimacy—based on police responses to the demands of the people—are maintained and local intelligence (including information about terror threats) can be gathered. As Murray concluded: "The road ahead will be demanding for police leaders, but they must resist the temptation to fall back to the methods of policing that ignore the profound and ethically-based principles of community policing."

In terms of wider police work to prevent terrorism, the cost of failure can, of course, be enormous. In this regard, in Chapter 5, Leman-Langlois and Brodeur made an important observation: "It is probable that blame for failure will always be greater than praise for success. This should be remembered when the performance of security services, police organizations, and their individual members is assessed."

According to Stinchcomb (Chapter 1), the day-to-day pressures of policing constitute chronic organizational stressors that cause more stress and burnout within policing than one-off incidents. It is highly plausible that the sustained prioritization of tackling terrorism—and knowledge of the cost of failure—will also contribute to this organizational stress. According to Stinchcomb, organizational stress can be minimized if officers have, for instance, genuinely greater involvement in decision-making processes, receive feedback on decisions made, and have adequate guidance and support from administrators. These factors can be easily overlooked when priorities such as dealing with terrorism are centrally decided.

Of course, the choice between centrally and locally decided priorities is not new. A similar debate that continues to emerge concerns police corruption and ethics (Goldstein, 1975; Sherman, 1978; Punch, 2000). One would have hoped that corruption was a thing of the past in many police departments after major investigations including the Wood Commission in Australia (1997) and the Mollen Commission in the United States (1994). However, the daily temptations are still available and, as Skolnick observed in Chapter 3, officers can still maintain a code of silence, making investigations of malpractice all the more difficult.

According to Prenzler and Ronken (Chapter 4), despite such high-profile investigations in Australia, few jurisdictions could claim to follow advanced models for anti-misconduct strategies. Skolnick emphasized that police departments have to want to change before corruption can be effectively tackled. He claimed, "There are no easy solutions to combating a pattern of police corruption and brutality in departments that seem resistant to positive change." Where problems persist, independent monitors may be necessary so that public confidence in the integrity of policing can be restored. Prenzler and Ronken noted that some advances were made in the provision of civilian oversight in Australia but significant challenges remain.

Other contemporary issues for law enforcement concern developments in police strategy and investigations, as covered in the chapters by Ratcliffe and Stangeland. In Chapter 7, Ratcliffe explains his development of a hotspot matrix that incorporates spatial and temporal information to determine crime problem areas. Ratcliffe noted the fairly obvious fact that resources are required to combat crimes and resources incur costs. This statement will ring alarm bells for any law enforcement practitioner who must allocate scarce policing resources within highly demanding environments. Current emphases on terrorism mean a great proportion of many police budgets is ringfenced. Some departments have additional targets and priorities that allow less scope for developing community policing objectives and crime prevention strategies. Any methodology that produces a more targeted approach to crime prevention will therefore be welcomed. Ratcliffe's hotspot matrix looks promising as a wholly pragmatic solution to allocating crime prevention resources. His model allows the most appropriate prevention and detection techniques to be implemented for each spatio-temporal situation so that resources are not wasted on inappropriate methodologies.

In the introduction to this volume we stated that fundamental changes have occurred in law enforcement and policing across the world since the start of the 21st century. This book has considered some of the more significant challenges, namely, the day-to-day pressures of policing; ethics and corruption, terror, innovations in strategy and investigations, and developments in restorative policing. Running through the book is the tension between calls for tougher and softer policing as well as pulls toward centralization (especially in response to terrorist threats), and decentralized models such as community-oriented policing. Every police agency must make very difficult decisions against a backdrop of very strong political and operational pressures. However, of central importance to these decisions is the maintenance or restoration of the legitimacy of policing decisions—the community must have "confidence in the integrity of policing" (Skolnick, Chapter 3).

This book has not covered all contemporary issues for law enforcement and policing; instead we have focused on those determined to be currently important through online searches of the *Police Practice and Research* journal. A number of other contemporary law enforcement and policing issues are not covered in this volume, for example, police management and intelligence systems such as COMPSTAT in the United States or the National Intelligence Model in the United Kingdom. Other contemporary issues concern education and training, race relations, and transnational crimes such as trafficking and smuggling. If this book is successful, we will hope to cover some of these other concerns in a future volume.

What we hope to have highlighted with this volume is that the law enforcement and policing fields have experienced sizable shifts and challenges to date in the new century. While advances have most definitely been made, significant issues remain, particularly concerning the policing of terror and the impact of terrorism on other law enforcement priorities. This is a problem that is clearly not going to disappear in the short term.

References

Crawford, A., Lister, S., Blackmore, S., and Burnett, J. (2005) *Plural policing: The mixed economy of visible patrols in England and Wales.* Bristol: Policy Press.

Goldstein, H. (1975) *Police corruption: A perspective on its nature and control*, Washington, D.C.: Police Foundation.

Jones, T. and Newburn, T. (eds.) (2006) *Plural policing: A comparative perspective.* London: Routledge.

Mollen Commission. (1994) *Report of the commission to investigate allegations of police corruption and the anti-corruption procedures of the police department*, City of New York.

O'Malley, P. (1992) Politics and Postmodernity. *Social and Legal Studies*, 6(3): 363–381.

Punch, M. (2000) Police corruption and its prevention, *European Journal on Criminal Policy and Research*, 8 (3): 301–324.

Reiner, R. (1992) Policing a Postmodern Society. *Modern Law Review, SS*(6): 761–781.

Sherman, L. (1978) *Scandal and reform: Controlling police corruption*, Berkeley CA: University of California Press.

Waters, I. (2007) Policing, modernity and postmodernity. *Policing and Society, 17*(3): 257–278.

Wood, J. (1997) *Royal commission into the New South Wales police service: Final report*, Sydney: Government of the State of New South Wales.

International Police Executive Symposium (IPES)

The International Police Executive Symposium was founded in 1994. The aims and objectives of the IPES are to provide a forum to foster closer relationships among police researchers and practitioners globally; to facilitate cross-cultural, international, and interdisciplinary exchanges for the enrichment of the law enforcement profession; and to encourage discussion and published research on challenging and contemporary topics related to the profession.

One of the most important activities of the IPES is the organization of an annual meeting under the auspices of a police or educational institution. To date, meetings have been hosted by the Canton Police of Geneva, Switzerland (Police Challenges and Strategies, 1994), the International Institute of the Sociology of Law in Onati, Spain (Challenges of Policing Democracies, 1995), Kanagawa University in Yokohama, Japan (Organized Crime, 1996), the Federal Police in Vienna, Austria (International Police Cooperation, 1997), the Dutch Police and Europol in The Hague, The Netherlands (Crime Prevention, 1998), the Andhra Pradesh Police in Hyderabad, India (Policing of Public Order, 1999), and the Center for Public Safety, Northwestern University, Evanston Illinois, USA, (Traffic Policing, 2000). A special meeting was co-hosted by the Bavarian Police Academy of Continuing Education in Ainring, Germany, University of Passau, Germany, and State University of New York, Plattsburgh, USA, to discuss the issues endorsed by the IPES in April 2000. The Police in Poland hosted the next meeting in May, 2001 (Corruption: A threat to World Order), and the last annual meeting was hosted by the Police of Turkey in May, 2002 (Police Education and Training). The Kingdom of Bahrain hosted the annual meeting in October, 2003 (Police and the Community).

The 2004 meeting in May of that year (Criminal Exploitation of Women and Children) took place in British Columbia, Canada, and it was co-hosted by the University College of the Fraser Valley, Abbotsford Police Department, Royal Canadian Mounted Police, the Vancouver Police Department, the Justice Institute of British Columbia, Canadian Police College, and the International Centre for Criminal Law Reform and Criminal Justice Policy.

The last meeting (Challenges of Policing in the 21st Century) took place in September, 2005 in Prague, The Czech Republic. The Turkish National Police hosted the meeting in 2006 (Local Linkages to Global Security and Crime). We have just concluded Fourteenth Annual Meeting in Dubai on April 8-12, 2007 (Urbanization and Security).

The majority of the participants of the annual meetings are usually directly involved in the police profession. In addition, scholars and researchers in the field also participate. The meetings comprise both structured and informal sessions to maximize dialogue and exchange of views and information. The executive summary of each meeting is distributed to participants as well as to a wide range of other interested police professionals and scholars. In addition, a book of selected papers from each annual meeting is published through Prentice Hall, Lexington Books, Taylor and Francis Group and other reputed publishers.

Closely associated with the IPES is the *Police Practice and Research: An International Journal (PPR)*. The journal is committed to highlighting current, innovative police practices from all over the world; providing opportunities for exchanges between police practitioners and researchers; reporting the state of public safety internationally; focusing on successful practices that build partnerships between police practitioners and communities, as well as highlighting other successful police practices in relation to maintaining order, enforcing laws, and serving the community. For more information, visit our website, www.ipes.info.

The IPES is directed by a board of directors representing various countries of the world (listed below). The registered business office is located at 402 East Jackson, Macomb, IL 61455,USA; Registered Agent Douglas J. March; Tel: 309-837-2904; Fax: 309-836-2736; E-mail: mmdlaw@macomb.com.

IPES Board of Directors

President Dilip Das, 6030 Nott Road, Guilderland, NY 12084, USA, Tel: 318 274 2520, Fax: 318 274 3101, E-mail: dilipkd@aol.com

Vice President Tariq Hassan Al Hassan, P.O. Box 13, Manama, KINGDOM OF BAHRAIN; Tel: (973) 17 756777, Fax: (973) 17 754302, E-mail: Ropac@batelco. com.bh

Treasurer/Director Jim Lewis, 406 Quail Lane, Ruston, Louisiana 71720, USA; Tel: 318 413-0551

Directors

Rick Sarre, GPO Box 2471, Adelaide, 5001, South AUSTRALIA; Tel: 61 8 84314879 (h), 61 8 83020889, Fax: 61 8 83020512, E-mail: rick.sarre@ unisa.edu.au

Tonita Murray, 73 Murphy Street, Carleton Place, Ontario K7C 2B7 CANADA; Tel: 613 998 0883 (w) E-mail: tmurray@ca.inter.net

Mark Chen, Professor, Central Police University, Taiwan; E-mail: mark@mail.cpu.edu.tw

Snezana (Ana) Mijovic-Das, 6030 Nott Road, Guilderland, NY 12084, USA; Tel: 518 452 7845, Fax: 518 456 6790, E-mail: anamijovic@yahoo.com

Horace Judson, PO Drawer 607, Grambling, LA 71245; Tel: 318 274 6117, Fax: 318 274 6172, E-mail, judsonha@gram.edu

Paulo R. Lino, 111 Das Garcas St., Canoas, RS, 92320-830, Brazil; Tel: 55 51 8111 1357, Fax: 55 51 466 2425, E-mail: paulino2@terra.com.br

Rune Glomseth, Police Superintendent, Norway Police University, Slemdalsveien 5, Oslo, 0369, Norway, E-mail: Rune.Glomseth@phs.no

Mustafa Ozguler, Chief of Police, Ankara, Turkey; E-mail: Mustafaozg@hotmail. com

Maximillian Edelbacher, Riemersgasse 16/E/3, A-1190 Vienna, AUSTRIA; Tel: 43-1601 74/5710, Fax: 43-1-601 74/5727, E-mail: edelmax@magnet.at

IPES operates through active support, cooperation and subscriptions of the Institutional Supporters. Our present Institutional Supporters are:

IPES Institutional Supporters

Dubai Police Department, (Dr. Mohammed Murad Abdulla, Director), Decision-Making Support Center, P.O. Box 1493, Dubai, United Arab Emirates; Tel: 971 4 269 3790, Fax: 971 4 262 3233, E-mail: dxbpolrs@emirates.net.ae

Bahrain Police, (Lt. General Shaikh Rashed Bin Abdulla Al Khalifa, Minister of the Interior), Manama, P.O. Box 13, Bahrain, The Arabian Gulf; Tel: 973 17 270800, Fax: 973 17 253 266, E-mail: Colonel Tariq Hassan AL Hassan, Ropac@batelco.com.bh

Fayetteville State University, (Dr. David E. Barlow, Professor and Interim Dean), College of Basic and Applied Sciences, 1200 Murchison Road, North Carolina, USA; Tel: 910-672-1659, Fax: 910-672-1103, E-mail: dbarlow@unfscu. edu

Athabasca University, (Dr. Curtis Clarke, Coordinator, Criminal Justice Program), 10-26312 TWP. RD 514 Spruce Grove, Alberta, Canada T7Y 1C8; Tel: 780-470-4270 , Fax: 780-497-3411, E-mail: curtisc@athabascau.ca

University of Hull, (Dr Bankole Cole, Director of Undergraduate Programmes, Department of Criminology and Sociological Studies), Cottingham Road, Hull HU6 7RX, UK; E-mail: B.Cole@hull.ac.uk

National Institute of Criminology and Forensic Science, (Director, Sharda Prasad, Inspector General of Police) MHA, Outer Ring Road, Sector 3,

Rohini, Delhi 110085, India; Tel: 91 11 275 25095, Fax: 91 11 275 10586, E-mail: prasadsharda@ediffmail.com

Grambling State University, (President Horace Judson), PO Drawer 607, Grambling, LA 71245, USA; Tel: 318-274-6117, Fax: 318-274-6172, E-mail: judsonha@gram.edu

University of Central England, (Mike King) Center for Criminal Justice Policy and Research, Birmingham, W. Midlands B42 2SU, UK; Tel: 0121 3315163, Fax: 0121 3316938, E-mail: Mike.King@ucc.ac.uk

Association of Defendologist of Republika Srpska, (Valibor Lalic), Srpska Street 63, 78000 Banja Luka, Bosnia and Herzegovina, Tel and Fax: 387 51 308 914, E-mail: lalicv@teol.net

University of Maribor, (Dr. Gorazd Mesko), The Faculty of Criminal Justice and Security, University of Maribor, Kotnikova 8, 1000 Ljubljana, Slovenia; Tel: 386 1 300 83 39, Fax: 386 1 2302 687, E-mail: mesko.gorazd@siol.net

Florida Gulf Coast University, (Charlie Mesloh, Ph.D., Director), Weapons and equipment Research Institute, 10501 FGCU Blvd S., Fort Myers, Fl 33965, USA; Tel: 239-590-7761 (office), Fax: 239-229-3462 (cellular), E-mail: cmesloh@ fgcu.edu, fthompso@fgcu.edu

Ohio Association of Chiefs of Police (Todd Wurschmidt), 6277 Riverside Drive, #2N, Dublin, Ohio 43017, USA; Tel: 614-761-0330, Fax: 614 718 3216. E-mail todd. wurschmidt@oacp.org

Kent State Univ. Police Services (John A. Peach, Chief of Police), P. O. Box 5190, Stockdale Safety Building, Kent, Ohio 44242-0001, USA; Tel: 330-672-3111, E-mail jpeach@kent.edu

Justice Institute of British Columbia Law Enforcement & Regulatory Training Program, (Mark LaLonde, Program Director), 715 McBride Boulevard New Westminster, British Columbia V3 L5 T4, Canada; Tel: 604-528-5768, Fax: 604528-5754, E-mail: mlalonde@jibc.bc.ca

Abbotsford Police Department, (Ian Mackenzie, Chief Constable), 2838 Justice Way, Abbotsford, British Columbia V2 T3 P5, Canada; Tel: 604-864-4809, Fax: 604-864-4725, E-mail: imackenzie@abbypd.ca

Royal Swaziland Police, (Isaac Mmemo Magagula), PO Box 49, Mbabane, Swaziland; Tel: 268-606-2312, Fax: 268-404-4545

University College of the Fraser Valley, (Dr. Darryl Plecas), Department of Criminology & Criminal Justice, 33844 King Road, Abbotsford, British Columbia V2 S7 M9, Canada; Tel: 604-853-7441, Fax: 604-853-9990, E-mail: Darryl.plecas@ucfv.ca

National Police Academy, Japan, Koichi Kurokawa, Assistant Director, Police Policy Research Center, Zip 183-8558: 3-12-1 Asahi-cho Fuchu-city, Tokyo; E-mail: Tcr01@anpac.jp

Canterbury Christ Church University (Claire Shrubsall), Department of Crime and Policing Studies, Northwood Road, Broadstairs, Kent CT10

2WA, UK; Tel: 44 (0)1843 609115, Fax: 44 (0) 1843 280700, E-mail claire. shrubsall@canterbury. ac.uk

Police Standards Unit, (Stephen Cahill), Home Office, 2 Marsham Street, London, SW1P 4DF, UK; Tel: 44 207 035 0922, Fax: 44 870 336 9015, E-mail Stephen. Cahill@homeoffice.gsi.gov.uk

Deputy Commissioner Pacific Region & Commanding Officer "E", RCMP (Gary Bass), 657 West 37th Avenue Vancouver BC V5Z 1K6, Canada; 604-2642003, Fax: 604 264 3547, E-mail gary.bass@rcmp-grc.gc.ca

Index

D

Q

R

S

T